BIBLICAL PREACHING ON
THE DEATH OF JESUS

BIBLICAL PREACHING
ON THE
DEATH OF JESUS

WILLIAM A. BEARDSLEE
Emeritus Professor of Religion, Emory University
Director, Center for Process Studies

JOHN B. COBB, JR.
Professor of Theology
School of Theology at Claremont
and Claremont Graduate School

DAVID J. LULL
Executive Director, Society of Biblical Literature

RUSSELL PREGEANT
Professor of Religion and Philosophy, Curry College

THEODORE J. WEEDEN, SR.
New Testament Scholar and Pastor
Asbury First United Methodist Church, Rochester, N.Y.

BARRY A. WOODBRIDGE
Instructor of Philosophy and Religious Studies
Riverside City College

ABINGDON PRESS
Nashville

BIBLICAL PREACHING ON THE DEATH OF JESUS

Copyright © 1989 by the Center for Process Studies

This book is printed on acid-free paper.

Library of Congress Cataloging-in-Publication Data

Biblical preaching on the death of Jesus / David J. Lull and William A. Beardslee, editors; authors, William A. Beardslee . . . [et al.].
   p. cm.
  Bibliography: p.
  Includes indexes.
  ISBN 0-687-03446-9
   1. Jesus Christ—Crucifixion. 2. Preaching. 3. Jesus Christ-Crucifixion—Sermons. 4. Sermons, American. I. Lull, David John. II. Beardslee, William A.
  BT453.B53   1989
  232.96'3—dc20

                                               89-35388
                                                 CIP

Scripture quotations, unless otherwise noted, are the authors' own translations.

Those noted GNB are from the *Good News Bible*—Old Testament: Copyright © American Bible Society 1976; New Testament: Copyright © American Bible Society 1966, 1971, 1976. Used by permission.

Those noted ILL are from *An Inclusive Language Lectionary.* Copyright © 1986 Division of Education and Ministry, National Council of Churches of Christ in the USA.

Those noted JB are from the The Jerusalem Bible, copyright © 1966 by Darton, Longman & Todd, Ltd. and Doubleday & Company, Inc. Used by permission.

Those noted NEB are from *The New English Bible.* © The Delegates of the Oxford University Press and The Syndics of the Cambridge University Press 1961, 1970. Reprinted by permission.

Those noted RSV are from the Revised Standard Version of the Bible, copyright 1946, 1952, 1971 by the Division of Christian Education of the National Council of Churches of Christ in the USA. Used by permission.

Excerpts from "Divine Persuasion and Divine Judgement" by John C. Bennett copyright © 1985, Christian Century Foundation. Reprinted by permission from the May 19, 1985 edition of *The Christian Century.*

MANUFACTURED BY THE PARTHENON PRESS AT
NASHVILLE, TENNESSEE, UNITED STATES OF AMERICA

CONTENTS

PART II—PREACHING ON THE DEATH OF JESUS

ACKNOWLEDGMENTS

This book is written from the perspective of "process theology." "Process theology" could not have become a significant expression of Christian thought unless there were deep affinities between its vision of reality and the Bible. Many such affinities will appear in the course of this book. However, we have put our stress on a different aspect of "process" thought. In a "process" style of interpretation—or hermeneutics—the goal is to hold contrasting insights in tension so that each may be creatively transformed. We find this mode of hermeneutics to be significant for biblical interpretation because too often we have been called upon to choose between the vision of the Bible and the vision of our contemporary world. Although this hermeneutics of choice has made a contribution to biblical interpretation, all too often it results in a narrow and impoverished faith. We have tried to show the way to a richer, more adequate style of interpretation that can respect the differences between the Bible and our world and use these differences to open new horizons.

A commitment to this "process" style of interpretation led us to set as our ambitious goal that all of us would jointly take responsibility for the whole book. We did not simply farm out each chapter to a separate author. We each have reviewed and contributed to the whole work. Of course, a first draft of each chapter was drawn up by one of us, but each chapter was thoroughly altered, edited, and amended by the contributions of others. The sermons in chapters 6 and 9—which are authored by John B. Cobb, Jr., and David J. Lull respectively—are the only exceptions to this procedure. The result is a truly joint project, a testimony to that interrelatedness that is central to the "process" vision of reality. At the same time, the other members of the group want to recognize that without the leadership of William A. Beardslee and David J. Lull the joint work would not have been possible.

We are indebted to a Charles and Mary Ewing Award and to the Board for Theological Education of the Episcopal Church for a grant from the Conant Fund, which made possible the travel by which we were enabled to confer during various stages of the project.

For help in the preparation of the manuscript, we are grateful to Jeffrey D. Groves, Sandra A. Surette MacNevin, and Carol Johnston—students at Claremont Graduate School—to Linda Mattox of Woodbridge Microcomputers and, Glenn Schwerdtfeger and Carolyn Wahlmark at Emory University, who prepared the indexes. We owe special thanks to Rex Matthews, Davis Perkins (now at The Westminster/John Knox Press), Ulrike Guthrie, and Linda Allen at Abingdon Press for their editorial services.

Our book has been enriched by discussions of early versions of chapters 4–7 in the 1984 Society of Biblical Literature "Process Hermeneutics and Biblical Exegesis" Group, the 1985 SBL "Early Christian Apocalypticism" Seminar, and the 1987–88 New Testament Seminar at Emory University. To the participants in these discussions, but especially to J. Christiaan Beker and Adela Yarbro Collins, for their thoughtful responses, we wish to express our appreciation.

Finally, we wish to thank Professors Fred B. Craddock, Richard B. Hays, Gail O'Day, and Clark M. Williamson, who read our manuscript and made many valuable comments on it. We are also grateful to Professor Craddock for his foreword and for providing us with guidance in the final stage of the preparation of this book.

FOREWORD

Timing is not everything, but it is close. "Too soon" and "too late" can be equally fatal for political campaigns, prophetic insights, great sermons, generous gifts, and all manner of worthy endeavors. And conversely, when the time is right, when the soil is ready, when the season has come, the act, the gift, the word fit, they are "meet and right," and the influence of them is beyond everyone's prediction. So it is with the publication of books.

In my judgment, the time is right for the appearance of this volume. For the last ten years, preaching has been on the rise as a concern of the church, as a priority of ministers, and as an academic discipline. Homiletics classes are full; preaching workshops abound; and the flow of literature has been full and of good quality. Rich contributions to preaching have come from theology, biblical studies, and literature. Biblical commentaries with the preacher in mind have appeared. However, the increase of advanced-level courses in preaching in the seminaries and the introduction of graduate work in homiletics into curricula where previously none existed have revealed a lacuna in homiletics literature: a serious and thorough approach to preaching from a clearly articulated theological position. What I have in mind is not a theology of preaching, not a theological defense of preaching, and not a methodology for preaching theology. Rather, the need is for a work that has in mind preachers, teachers of preaching, and seminarians and that openly and honestly speaks from a single and consistent perspective on the way of God in the world, which has a vision of what God is seeking to achieve in and for the world, in part through the proclamation of the gospel. Then from that perspective and with that vision, the whole enterprise of preaching needs to be engaged: its aims, its methods, and its resources, especially the biblical texts.

This book meets that need. There is nothing imperialistic in the content and posture of this volume; the authors do not claim that theirs is the only conversation in town. What is offered is a proposal that takes seriously both biblical texts and modern experiences of reality. Careful listening to biblical texts and honest acknowledgment of the way life is for us sometimes present readers with not one but two or more ways to conduct themselves in the world. Nothing is gained by denying either one's own life story or the truth offered in scripture. The alternatives, often in tension, provide occasions for growth and for discerning the work of God's Spirit in the world. No tough issue or troublesome text is avoided; in fact, the authors have determined to focus on the difficult, but central, issue for us all: suffering and death. They do so by examining biblical texts that treat the suffering and death of Jesus.

Time and again, reading this volume reminded me that one can have strong faith and deep conviction in areas where certainty is unavailable. This benefit alone made the reading much like hearing good preaching; it provided an experience of freedom.

Fred B. Craddock
Candler School of Theology
Emory University

PART I

PREACHING IN THE SERVICE OF THE SPIRIT

INTRODUCTION

Preachers today are facing increasing pressures from parishioners and ecclesiastical judicatories to preach "biblically." In one sense, that is how it should be. However preaching is understood, it should at least be oriented to some biblical text. It is just as true, however, to say that preaching is oriented to the present world of the preacher's hearers and of the church. That dual orientation—to the ancient world of the biblical text and to the present world of the preacher's hearers and of the church—makes the question of "biblical" preaching more complex than it might appear.

Texts whose content appears contrary to modern thought easily press preachers toward one or the other of two equally objectionable options: to ask their hearers to sacrifice either the modern vision of the world or the biblical vision. The latter option is not always expressed quite so bluntly, but it is implied when the preacher reduces the message of biblical texts to psychological and/or moral lessons. Neither form of intellectual sacrifice will lead to the strengthening of faith or to the renewal of the mission of the church.

In this book, we explore a third possibility: an engagement with biblical texts for preaching that does not involve sacrificing either the biblical or the present world of the preacher's hearers and of the church. It is an engagement that leads to a form of preaching that not only concerns freedom, but also serves the expansion of freedom. It is important, therefore, to explore this more freeing way of engaging biblical texts in the context of our understanding of the nature and task of preaching (Part I) before we turn directly to our exposition of "the passion of Jesus" and "the passion of God" in the Gospel of Mark and in the letters of Paul (Part II). At the end of the sections on Mark and Paul, two sermons illustrate this approach to biblical preaching on Jesus' death in Mark's Gospel (chapter 6, by John B. Cobb, Jr.) and in Paul's letters (chapter 9, by David J. Lull).

CHAPTER ONE

THE AIM OF PREACHING

1. Contemporary Reflection on Preaching

Within the past two decades, Protestant churches in North America have experienced a resurgence of interest in preaching. The recent homiletical literature born of this resurgent interest reveals the time and energy that have been devoted to defining and clarifying the task of preaching.[1] Preaching has all too often become no more than "talk about" biblical texts—or worse yet, mere talk with no biblical text at all. Such preaching has rendered the pulpit boring and irrelevant and is disastrous for the church, especially in an age of high-tech electronic communication, when the parish preacher must compete with popular television and radio preachers. One common element in the attempts to renew preaching, therefore, is the awareness that preaching is and must be more than mere talk about biblical texts. A second common element is the search for theological foundations for a style of preaching more oriented toward story, parabolic form, and the performative use of symbol and myth.

These two emphases have grown out of the desire of many preachers to speak in ways more faithful to the biblical message and, at the same time, in ways that arrest attention and move the will to act and to change. Preachers ask, "What guides my selection of the content of my message if I am not simply to repeat the biblical message?" Many have answered this question with the lectionary, only to find the question re-posing itself as they ponder, "What portion of which lection is the most preachable this week?"

The desire to speak more effectively focuses on the use and style of language in Christian communication. Questions about message and text depend on a prior theological determination of the goal or goals of preaching. Although much attention has been given to issues of sermon composition and style, the latter question—What, fundamentally, is to be accomplished through preaching?—has largely been neglected in American literature on preaching and in the works of American theologians. It has been dealt with more thematically, however, in the writings of German theologians, among whom a main theme of theology is its service to preaching—that is, that its purpose is to guide the preacher in the interpretation of scripture and in making its message come alive appropriately in the congregation.

In this tradition, preaching is generally correlated with faith. One preaches so that the hearer may have faith. Consequently, the understanding of faith and of how faith comes to be governs the understanding of preaching. Since faith and how it comes into being are understood differently by major theologians, each also sees preaching in a different light. To state schematically what some of these alternatives are, we have selected five theologians: Karl Barth, Rudolf Bultmann, Gerhard Ebeling, Wolfhart Pannenberg, and Dorothee Sölle.

In Barth's view God has already reconciled the world to God in Jesus Christ.[2] God's Yes to the world is fully manifest in Jesus' resurrection, but that Yes has the fullness of its meaning only in connection with God's No to the nothingness that threatens all creation, an enmity to God that came to its fullest expression in the cross. This event has occurred objectively to us and to our opinions about it. Also, God has achieved what God intended to achieve. The reconciliation of the world does not depend on our response. Nevertheless, it makes a difference whether one knows about this event or not.

Barth's point can be illustrated with a story. During the

return of Halley's Comet in 1910, many people believed the earth would be burned and that this would be by divine judgment. The situation appeared frightening, as though the tail of the comet, with all its fiery noxious gases, would engulf the earth. Suppose, as was the case, these gases were, contrary to appearance, far beyond the earth's atmosphere. Despite all appearance, the earth and its inhabitants are safe and require no further rescue. A few astronomers and physicists know this, whereas most people do not. The ones who know could decide to do nothing, since whatever they say cannot possibly affect the outcome. Still, the quality of life here and now *is* affected. Some of the ignorant may take drastic and inappropriate actions—abandoning housing and goods, possibly even taking their own lives to avoid the anticipated catastrophe. Those who know the truth of the situation can return their attention to other matters, whereas those who think the earth is likely to burn will be preoccupied and paralyzed by their sense of danger. The appropriate action of those who know is to inform those who do not know. They cannot prove what they know is true, but they can announce it with all sincerity just the same. Those who hear and believe will be able to proceed, with them, to the practical actions that will make life better for all.

According to Barth, the announcement that we are safe or saved is preaching. This preaching should be as convincing as possible, but, for the truth of what is announced, no argument can be given. Whether the hearer believes cannot be controlled by the one who announces, since that is God's affair. Only the Holy Spirit can ultimately bring the word home to the hearer. The preacher proclaims the word of salvation, whose effects are as God will have them. God has chosen the occasion of the preaching of the word for the working of faith. Hence, the preacher's responsibility is a heavy one. But only God determines who will believe.

Bultmann understood the situation differently.[3] For him the central event is the cross. The resurrection is the realization of the paradoxical meaning of the cross. It is

God's act in the cross of Christ that awakens faith in the hearts of believers. As in Barth, God's act in Jesus Christ has occurred once for all. Nevertheless, as it is proclaimed, God continues to awaken faith today. This faith is not the knowledge of an objective saving fact; it is the saved condition here and now.

This saved condition is understood by Bultmann as analogous to what Heidegger meant by "authentic existence." It is a way of being in which we assume responsibility for what we are. Its opposite, "inauthentic existence," is living in terms of what others expect of us or out of habit and the desire to be approved. It is being bound by the past. Faith as "authentic existence" is, therefore, freedom from the past and from the law. It is life lived in openness to the future as God gives us that future. The New Testament proclamation of the cross, especially that of the Fourth Gospel and Paul, opens up this new possibility of existence.

The preacher's task, then, is not to announce facts about the past—or about the present for that matter. The task is to elicit faith as an "understanding of existence." The preacher can do that by challenging the hearer to decide, not about something objective to the hearer's existence, but about oneself, about accepting the call to responsibility and openness to the future. As in Barth's case, the outcome of preaching is not ultimately in the hands of the preacher. The preacher can confront the hearer with the call to decision, but whether the hearer decides is a matter for the hearer.

Ebeling developed his understanding of faith in discussion with both Barth and Bultmann.[4] The result was a doctrine of faith as assurance. The sermon is a "word-event," an occurrence of language that, when it is effective, produces assurance. This is a quite different understanding of the relation of faith to preaching from that of either Barth or Bultmann.

Both Barth and Bultmann understood the sermon as one thing and the response as another. The sermon was the occasion for the response. For Barth, the connection of sermon and response expresses a free choice of God rather than anything humanly inherent in the sermon or in the hearing of it. For Bultmann, the point is that human freedom has the last word. The sermon may skillfully bring the hearer to the recognition of responsibility, but the hearer will decide whether to assume that responsibility or to reject it. For Ebeling, however, the "word-event" includes the effect, which takes place only in its being heard and being effective in being heard. The preaching is not a proclamation that may or may not be believed, neither is it a challenge to which the hearer may or may not respond. The preaching as "word-event" is the occurrence of grace.

A father soothing his child is just such a "word-event": the saying of the words is the soothing of the child. A woman telling a man of her love for him is also a "word-event": the telling communicates his being loved. Jesus' telling a parable is a "word-event": the hearer is caught up in the meaning of the parable. The preacher's task, similarly, is not to announce that we are saved but, through words—whatever they may be—to mediate actual assurance of salvation.

This view of salvation is connected with a shift of focus from the death/resurrection event to the ministry of Jesus. The cross is the completion of Jesus' ministry, rather than the one, utterly unique, act of God. It expressed Jesus' certainty or assurance even in his full identity with us in our suffering.

In distinction from all three of these views, Pannenberg understands faith as trusting God.[5] The preacher's task is to encourage such trust. But trust is wrongly directed unless one has real reason to trust. We should not trust just because there are subjective rewards for trusting. We should trust only when there is reason to believe that the object of our trust is trustworthy.

Too much preaching, in Pannenberg's view, tries to evoke or elicit trust or other feelings by manipulating the emotions. In the long run this is disillusioning. People can only really trust when they are shown the evidence for trustworthiness. The task of preaching is to point the hearer to those features of reality that give evidence that God is worthy of our trust. They should believe only as the evidence objectively warrants belief. Hence, hearers are encouraged to listen critically and to evaluate what is said in relation to everything else they know.

For Pannenberg, therefore, preaching involves instruction, argument, and information. Certainly, not all information is pertinent. Preachers select those facts that justify trust in God. They inform their people about the events to which the Bible witnesses. Contemporary accounts of those events should be based on critical historical study. Above all, preachers share with the New Testament writers in announcing the resurrection of the crucified Jesus as the supreme event in history that decisively justifies our trust in God.

Since the mid 1960s, several German theologians have pointed out that all these views of theology and preaching, in their focus on faith and justification, have been personal rather than social in their understanding of salvation and of the central function of preaching. They are persuaded that this individualism contrasts with the dominant biblical message of promise for all humanity in its concrete socio-historical situation. As a corrective, Johannes Baptist Metz, Jürgen Moltmann,[6] and Dorothee Sölle have called for a political hermeneutic. Their movement is in alliance with Latin-American liberation theology and with black theology as well. We will take Sölle as representative of this group of "political theologians."[7]

Sölle notes that the historical-critical method employed by Bultmann and other modern scholars already involves a study of the socio-historical context (the *Sitz im Leben)* of the biblical texts that are interpreted. But the socio-historical context of the preacher and hearer today tends to be neglected. This leads to abstracting the personal or existential meaning from the full political meaning of the texts, and to failure to bring out their implications for the social, economic, and political situation in which preaching takes place.

In this way the true purpose of preaching is missed. This purpose is to draw us, as Jesus' friends, into his work of salvation for the whole world. It requires a political self-understanding more concrete than what is usually called "existential self-understanding." And the movements of liberation for which it calls are movements for overcoming the oppression, exploitation, and mutual destruction of people, who are always also individuals. But individual persons are to be understood in their social, communal reality, so that their individual salvation cannot be separated from that of the whole.

For Sölle, Jesus functions as the representative of us all. In his death, Jesus identifies with us all in our condemnation. In so doing he enables us to accept our guilt without being destroyed by it. He shows us that God is to be found in the victim, not the victor, in the tortured, not the torturer.

Here, then, are five important views of the goal of preaching in recent German theology. Before proceeding, we should note a certain gulf between this sustained theological reflection on the task of preaching by German theologians and the recent American literature on preaching noted earlier. A sad commentary on the pervasive specializing, or compartmentalizing, mentality is the fact that the American discussion has paid little attention to the German treatments, and vice versa. There have been important exceptions,[8] but the gaps are more noticeable than the contacts. Part of the task, as yet incomplete, is the linking of new and creative contributions by American homileticians on preaching style with the insights of German theologians who have been reflecting on what preaching is to accomplish.

There is a strong tendency in the German discussion to set such views of the function of preaching as the five summarized above over against one another as mutually exclusive. To some extent this is inevitable, for there are elements in the theological positions of the five theologians that are strictly contradictory. But there is no inherent reason why all preaching should have exactly the same goal. Reinhold Niebuhr proposed that we should comfort the afflicted and afflict the comfortable. That might mean that there are times and places in which effecting assurance (with Ebeling) should be our goal and others in which calling to decision (with Bultmann) is fundamental. There certainly seems to be no reason to exclude the communication of information as one function of preaching, especially when that information is selected for the purpose of grounding trust in God (as with Pannenberg). Even if we do not view the saving effect of God's act in Jesus Christ as objectively as Barth does, there are times when simply announcing what we believe God has done is also appropriate. And Sölle is correct, too, in pointing out that the neglect of the full political meaning of the text for our time must be overcome if we are to be responsible to the gospel.

This pluralistic approach to preaching does not entail the view that anything goes—far from it. To preach even a good sermon at the wrong time and place would be a perversion of the preacher's task, to cite only one of many ways in which preaching may fail. What we need is an overarching statement of the purpose of preaching that will allow reflection, in each time and place, about what more specific goal is appropriate. We suggest that the task of preaching is to be a means of grace, to mediate and realize God's redemptive and liberating love—in other words, to serve the Spirit. It is the task of preachers to discern *how* preaching is to serve the Spirit in each particular context in which the world of a biblical text intersects with the world of the preachers' hearers.

2. The Spirit Preaching Serves

The Reformers taught that when the Word is proclaimed, the Spirit works within the hearer to effect belief. Even apart from the work of the Spirit, the hearer may give cognitive credence to what is said. One might accept on the authority of the church all the statements of the Apostles' Creed. But such believing, if it is disconnected from the total person, does not save; neither can we turn doctrines into saving faith by an act of will. New ways of perceiving reality and understanding ourselves are always the work of the Spirit.

We affirm this doctrine, but we would not focus as specifically as the Reformers did on the correlation of Spirit and biblical word. The Spirit works in all life and especially throughout human life. John Wesley taught that the Spirit works as much in bringing people to the point of hearing the word as in confirming its truth to them and that it continues equally to work in them in the process of sanctification. Indeed, there is for Wesley no such thing as a human being apart from this working of God's Spirit. There is, in addition to the working of the Spirit, the working of fallen human nature. Actual thoughts, feelings, and actions reflect this double process within. Human nature, corrupted by the fall, resists the work of the Spirit; even after faith has been granted, sinful nature can lead to the rejection of God again. But even that does not put an end to the Spirit's work.

Wesley tried to identify accurately what the Spirit is doing at each stage of life and to distinguish that from what fallen human nature is doing. When he attributes the increase of love to the Spirit, that is not a rhetorical device; it is his strong conviction. Our approach is similar. We do not believe that there are any human beings in whom the Spirit is not effectively at work. Apart from that work, human beings would be nothing more than the outcome of the past processes of the world. They would be in slavery to their established habits of mind and thought. Horizons of interest would be limited to themselves. There are times when people approximate this condition—times, that is, when it is difficult to discern the work of God freeing them to love and to break away from bondage to habit and to the world. But we do not believe that God ever leaves anyone alone. The Spirit is never wholly absent.

In the New Testament, Paul reserves the Spirit for those who live "in Christ," and the Gospel of John gives an impression that the "Spirit of Truth" dwells only within the Christian community. These biblical views appear on one level to contradict our more inclusive perspective. Although there are real differences, on another level, when both John and Paul are seen within a larger horizon of meaning, their views can be seen to be compatible with ours.

As a Pharisee, Paul surely knew and accepted the view in Jewish scriptures that the Spirit of God infused all living things with life in creation and so was not limited to making the new life "in Christ" possible. Such a view is reflected in the "doxologies" found in Paul's letters (for example, Rom. 11:36; I Cor. 8:6; 11:12) and in the reference to the law of God written on the hearts of Gentiles (Rom. 2:15). That Paul reserves the Spirit for the emergence of Christian existence, and uses the language of "ensoulment" for the original act of creating life, derives from his central concern to draw attention to the origin of the gift of Christian existence in God *through Christ* and to emphasize the *newness* of this act of creation.[9] In other words, Paul's view is ultimately compatible with our contention that the source of the possibility of new life "in Christ" is the same Spirit who gives life to every living thing.[10]

The Gospel of John includes both a sectarian emphasis on the presence of the "Spirit of Truth" exclusively in the Christian community and a more universal perspective. The prominence of the latter is evident in the Gospel's "prologue," which contains a hymn to the everlasting, omnipresent Word (or Logos) of God (1:1-18). This hymn sets the tone for the Gospel and provides the interpretive key to John's christology. The "Spirit of Truth," who addresses the Christian community as its Comforter or Counselor *(Paraclete)* and who is sent by the exalted Jesus, not only represents the now absent historical Jesus (16:7-11) but just in that capacity also the Logos of God, which from the beginning is the source of life and enlightenment for everyone. The Fourth Gospel itself says that this Spirit has no independent authority, but can only say "what it hears," which links the "Spirit of Truth" to Jesus and to the Logos of God incarnate in Jesus (see 16:12-15). The larger horizon of meaning suggested by John's Logos christology, therefore, draws the view of the Spirit in the Fourth Gospel closer to our own view, that the Spirit within the church represents

God's presence as the universal source of life and of the enlightenment of all human beings. We believe that this view is faithful to both Testaments and to the creedal affirmation of the Spirit as the Lord and giver of life.

In traditional terms, we can distinguish within the activity of the Spirit the bringing of the unbeliever to faith (justification) and the deepening of faith (sanctification). Most of the German theologies of preaching have focused on justification and have understood the hearers in terms of their unbelief. These theologians know that congregations are usually composed chiefly of believers, but they understand even believers to be also unbelievers. This view reflects profound insights in the Reformation tradition that continue to be valid today, and it identifies justification as the central work of the Spirit served by preaching.

Much of the preaching in American churches, on the other hand, is directed to believers as believers. It too often is not sensitive to the unbelief of believers, but it rightly recognizes that there is a need to deepen faith as well as to awaken it. Consequently, its focus is on sanctification. The emphasis on sanctification apart from justification has often led to the perversion of Christianity into a religion of works that identifies some pattern of conduct with Christian faith. But preaching for the deepening of faith or for growth in faith is not to be excluded.

The distinction between the justifying and sanctifying work of the Spirit, although sometimes useful, is often overdrawn. The work of the Spirit, as the giver of all life, involves both justification and sanctification inextricably. But traditional discussions focusing on those two terms still lack the breadth and depth of the biblical and creedal vision of the creative and redemptive work of the Spirit as the giver of life. People serve the Spirit whenever and however they enhance life, and they can enhance life only as they serve the Spirit. It is equally true to say that they serve the Spirit only as the Spirit enlivens them and directs and empowers them in her service.

The effectiveness of the Spirit depends on many things. Ministers can realistically examine the kind of environment in which people are most likely to come alive, to break with constraining habits and limiting horizons, to overcome guilt and depression, to achieve the integration that releases energy for work in the world. Sometimes this will be in the context of pastoral counseling, sometimes in a church school class, sometimes in a prayer meeting, sometimes on a picket line. If ministers work to produce those environments, they will increase the scope and likelihood of the Spirit's effectiveness. But the preaching of the word is the single most important of all the ways in which ministers can serve the Spirit.

In this book, our attention is on preaching, understood as serving the Spirit. Preachers can serve the Spirit only as they are enlivened, directed, and empowered by the Spirit. But this does not mean that preachers are mere passive and mechanical instruments through which the Spirit speaks. On the contrary, the giver of life is the giver of responsibility. Preachers are called to reflect about their preaching and, by the power of the Spirit, to direct their finest efforts to serve the Spirit through that means of grace.

Such reflection involves the role of the preachers' personalities in their preaching. "Preaching is the bringing of truth through personality," Phillips Brooks once observed.[11] The paradox is that the more attention preachers pay to their personality and the way it affects their preaching, the more self-conscious and less genuine their preaching becomes. It is precisely in the act of self-forgetfulness for the sake of the good news that the preacher becomes the Hermes, the messenger who is the intermediary between humans and the divine. The preachers' vulnerability and passionate involvement in the preaching event contribute to its success just when they are transparent to the word, not when they are cultivating and projecting their personalities. What Paul wrote of himself applies to all preachers: "What we preach is not ourselves, but Jesus Christ as Lord, with ourselves as your servants for Jesus' sake" (II Cor. 4:5 RSV).[12]

The preacher's task is to discern what the Spirit is seeking to do and to provide words that will serve the Spirit in that work. Sometimes the preacher may conclude that the Spirit wants to judge, sometimes to comfort, sometimes to inspire, sometimes to assure, sometimes to challenge, sometimes to draw people into wider movements, sometimes to lead them into psychic depths, sometimes to send them apart into the desert, sometimes to join them into intimate communities, sometimes to prophesy against the society, sometimes to support traditional norms. Good preachers are those who know their people well and discern what will truly enliven and inspire them here and now. It is the timeliness of the word that counts.

There is no way to describe exhaustively the ends of preaching in the service of the Spirit. Life is infinitely complex, and the new life in Christ is infinitely rich. We have already listed with approval the aims of preaching proposed by some important German theologians. If each is conceived as one of the ends of preaching, rather than as its exclusive aim, we would affirm them all as important ways of serving the Spirit. In chapters 2 and 3, we propose to supplement their contributions by accenting certain features of the work of the Spirit stressed in the New Testament and drawing out some implications that we find insufficiently emphasized in current writing on preaching.

CHAPTER TWO

PREACHING AND FREEDOM

1. Expanding the Hearers' World

Paul frequently emphasizes the work of the Spirit as the gift of freedom.[1] This suggests that, if we are to serve the Spirit, our sermons should be occasions for the increase of the hearers' freedom. Barth, Bultmann, Ebeling, Pannenberg, and Sölle all aim at a faith that liberates from fear, from efforts at self-salvation, from destructive guilt, and from hopelessness. Further, and more directly, proclamation leaves it to the hearer to believe or not believe; as such, it encourages choice. This is true even when, as with Barth, the choice of faith is fully the work of the Spirit. Bultmann's call to decision stresses the freedom of the hearer to respond. Ebeling's "word-event" sermon liberates the hearers from anxiety and enables them to act more freely in the world. Pannenberg's encouragement of critical listening places responsibility on the hearer for the free use of the intellect. And Sölle's proclamation seeks to liberate the hearers from bondage to bourgeois ideology and to draw them into the work of freeing themselves and others politically.

We reiterate our affirmation of all these ways in which preaching serves the Spirit by enhancing freedom. Freedom, we must be clear, means something different from what our culture often takes it to be. When Paul speaks of freedom, he means it as freedom to be more related, both to the Spirit and to one another; freedom from the compulsive weight of the past; and freedom to enter more fully and spontaneously into the life of faith and love. This freedom is very different from the freedom to "do your own thing," which is what many have taken freedom to mean, both in Paul's day and in ours.

In spite of the strong emphasis on freedom in the work of the theologians we have just mentioned, the types of sermons they have in mind do not directly function to enhance the freedom of the believer as fully as we think is possible and desirable. The reason is that in each case the kind of freedom envisioned is specified or controlled by the sermon. Proclamation calls for response whether it is given by the Spirit or is the free decision of the hearer. This is true whether the decision is in response to existential or to political preaching. But the terms of the decision are narrowly set by the preacher. The hearers may feel that whatever does not fit with the decision they have made is forever closed to them. Similarly, information elicits critical thinking, but the purpose is still to convince the hearer of that truth, which the preacher already believes. The "word-event" sermon undertakes actually to bring about the assurance that is needed and thereby directly sets people free from anxiety, so that they are enabled to act responsibly and appropriately. But the "word-event" sermon does not set the hearer free in relation to the sermon itself.

We believe that the freedom the Spirit would work in all of us is not simply the ability to say yes or no to what another human being proposes to us. Certainly it includes that ability, so that being put into the position of making a decision can help; if the decision is truly for faith, that faith will continue to work freedom. We are also often blocked by anxiety from exercising our freedom, so that assurance can set us free. But the growth of freedom within us, its spontaneity and creativity, can be accounted for entirely neither in terms of our ability to respond yes or no nor in terms of the strength of our assurance. Focusing on these alone can block the freeing work of the Spirit as often as it serves it. Let us consider how the sermon itself can do more to foster freedom directly, as well as indirectly, through its eliciting of faith.

In ordinary conversation one usually feels oppressed by those who force an argument or a position upon one on their terms, allowing space only to agree or disagree. One feels liberated by those who offer new ideas for reflection or open new angles of vision on familiar things. The word *preaching* has come to have negative connotations because so much of it, following many theories of preaching, has the former character. That is true especially, but not only, for much of what passes as *"biblical preaching."*

We believe, granting all sorts of exceptions, that preaching, normally and normatively, should serve directly in the liberation of the hearer. We believe that the Spirit works for the liberation of all people, and these include the hearers of sermons. Hence, normally and normatively, preachers who seek to serve the Spirit ask what they can say directly to expand and enhance the freedom of their hearers.

Language and freedom are closely related. If someone grew up without hearing any language, that person would have little freedom. Those whose environment has provided them with limited language, or with language that fails to make fine discriminations, are, other things being equal, less free than those with richer language. A sermon that expands the vocabulary and imagery of a hearer has to that extent enhanced the hearer's freedom. But, of course, that is not the primary function of the sermon.

Any given linguistic system also binds those who live in and with it. Every language orders the world in a particular way and conceals the aspects of the world that do not fit that order. Learning a second language can liberate us by making relative the perceptions built into the first. More radical liberation from language is the aim of much of Buddhist teaching, which would have us experience the world directly, not mediated through any conceptuality. J. Dominic Crossan has interpreted the parables of Jesus as ways in which the system of meanings built into language is broken down so that, for a moment, one may encounter the reality that is obscured by it.[2] Preaching can serve in this way, using language against language to liberate from the restriction of language. But this, too, is an extreme function of preaching, sometimes appropriate and even necessary, but not normal and normative for preaching as a whole.

The usual way language liberates is by offering fresh ways of perceiving and thinking. In the sermon, this may be through images and stories as well as in straight exposition, when what is proposed is something that previously has not been part of the hearers' world. Hence, it has the possibility of expanding their world. But it is a suggestion, not a demand. Hearers are free, therefore, not simply to reject or accept but also to adapt, change, and expand. Indeed, they are encouraged to do so. This is precisely what homileticians have been suggesting with their emphasis on non-discursive language. Witness Elizabeth Achtemeier's discussion of the way poetic language functions:

> Finally, artists, of whatever medium, rarely confront us directly with the demand that we accept their words or adopt their views and perceptions. The poet does not say, "This is truth; believe it." The dramatist does not insist, "This is the only way human life is." The painter does not imply, "This is the one shape of reality." Instead, these artists present to us that which they see, in words so evocative and expressions so suggestive that we are enabled to enter into their experiences and to see the world as they see it. They prompt us, by their imagery, their imagination, their nuance of expression, to live through what they have lived and to know what they have known. Thus they enlarge our vision and give us new possibilities for seeing and doing.[3]

A suggestion is often made through language, whether poetic or discursive, but it is not identical with the words uttered. For example: "I have been crucified with Christ. No longer do I live, but Christ lives in me; but the life I now live in the flesh, I live by faith in the Child of God, who loved me and gave himself for me" (Gal. 2:20). Those words will not mean exactly the same thing to all the hearers. What they mean will be something about some aspect of the world of each hearer. It will be that aspect of that hearer's world that will be evoked into attention. If it does not seem important, it will be dismissed from further consideration. That is acceptable. But if it appears important it will elicit response—emotional, thoughtful, or imaginative, as the case may be. The words of the speaker do not control what is noticed in the world, nor do they govern the response. But if they succeed in directing attention to some important feature of that world, then they serve also to help expand that world and, therefore, to increase the freedom of the hearer.

In speaking of aspects of the world, we do not mean simply objects in the world. A suggestion is not a thing. It is a way of perceiving, imaging, or thinking about something— a way that something is, might be, or should be.

To return to the passage of scripture cited above (Gal. 2:20), for one hearer it might bring relief from guilt for past sins through the knowledge that the penalty for those sins has been paid by the substitutionary death of Jesus. For another hearer, it might bring assurance of one's personal worth through identification of Jesus' sacrificial love with God's. And for another, it might bring a strengthened sense of solidarity with all who struggle for justice and freedom, whom the self-sacrificing Jesus represents, and a strengthened sense of that struggle as God's own cause, embodied in the life and death of Jesus.

The book you are reading is an example of an extended suggestion. We are suggesting that preaching should serve the enhancement of freedom. We hope that this idea will expand the freedom of readers. Readers may, of course, find it uninteresting or trivial. In that case, the proposal fails. But if some initial interest is aroused, it will be because readers think about what they know as preaching in a new way—now in a certain relation to the freedom of the hearer. Different readers will not have exactly the same thing in mind when they think of preaching or of freedom, and they will not all respond to the suggestion in the same way. Some may find it false or pernicious; others may find it accurate but rather banal; and still others may find it false with respect to most of the preaching they have heard but attractive as an idea of what preaching ought to be. Different emotions will accompany such evaluations. Sometimes preachers will be stimulated to develop different proposals. If these are new for them, then the freedom already expanded in the first stage of response will grow larger. Previously undeveloped ways of thinking about preaching will become a part of the reader's world through creative, free thinking.

Alfred North Whitehead made the point about suggestions or proposals such as these—he called them propositions—that it is more important that they be interesting than that they be true.[4] This applies in the example considered above. We might have succeeded in formulating a merely factual statement about preaching. It might have elicited immediate assent from readers—but then, probably nothing more would happen. It would correspond with what they already knew, adding nothing to their world, and it would evoke no creative or imaginative response. If, however, we succeeded in juxtaposing preaching to freedom in an unfamiliar way, even if we are not quite right, our proposal might have some importance.

That the primary concern, with respect to imaginative proposals, is interest rather than accuracy does not imply that approximation to truth is unimportant. We believe that our proposal has importance largely because it does correspond to much that goes on in preaching. Proposals that are radically disconnected from reality may attract attention momentarily, but they cannot evoke sustained interest. For example, the proposal that preaching is the direct speaking of God through mediums might attract momentary attention by its oddity, but nothing more. Unless what is said has some positive relation to reality, unless the proposal is at least somewhat plausible, it cannot serve the freedom of the reader. Truth adds to interest.

Preaching in the context of worship requires far more care than writing a book, if it is to serve freedom rather than restrict it. Readers of a book know that they are free to respond as they will to what a book offers. But a long tradition and ecclesiastical structure invest the preacher's words with near sanctity. There is a tendency to hear them as dogmatic announcement rather than as suggestion or proposal. Because they are associated with a sacred book and its message for our time, they tend to take on the absoluteness of the sacred. If preaching is to serve the cause of freedom, preachers will need to work against some of the habits of mind traditionally associated with their role.

This emphasis on the freedom of the hearers from the sermon and from the preacher does not take away from the power and authority of the preaching office; it only shifts its understanding. Too often we have thought of power as the ability to compel others to do our will or to accept our thoughts. Divine power has also been thought of in terms of compulsion and control. But the power of God as seen in Christ, especially in the *crucified* Christ, is the power to make alive and to set free. The power to kill and restrict is one that humans come by all too easily. What makes alive and sets free is often disturbing, disruptive, and destructive of established order. It puts to death much that we have been, and, in this way, it resembles the human power to kill. But this painful and threatening work of the Spirit is for the sake of life and freedom. The preacher who serves the Spirit's exercise of this power indeed has power and authority! But this power and this authority do not bind the people; instead, they empower the people. Christ and the Spirit whom preaching serves set people free for freedom (compare II Cor. 3:17 and Gal. 5:1).

Since the Enlightenment, when Westerners have thought of the extension of freedom, they have thought chiefly of the freedom of individuals. This Enlightenment individualism has roots in the gospel and has a truth that we appreciate and affirm. We have already noted that each hearer of the sermon will in fact bring to it a different world, and the expansion of that world will have its distinctive character. In chapter 3, we will discuss at some length the diversity of individual experience within the congregation and the danger that ideas that are liberating for some may be oppressive to others.

Nevertheless preaching is not primarily directed to an audience composed of individuals in chance association. It is addressed to a congregation, a Christian, community. The proposals that are made are offered to the congregation for its collective response. The congregation as a whole is freed from oppressive and limiting ways of thinking and feeling. Ideally, the sermon, with its proposals, becomes an event in the shared history of the people. As that history grows through such events, the congregation would develop new sensitivities and new ways of interpreting other events and, therefore, of responding to them. The imaginative world created by and embodied in the congregation is thereby expanded.

The preacher's role is not to express personal opinions at random. As a human being and a Christian, nothing is outside the scope, but as a preacher one assumes responsibility and authority to make a particular type of proposal—namely, that which is suggested by scripture as being relevant for the freeing of people. It is the preacher's chief responsibility to remove obstacles so that the congregation may hear what the Spirit is trying to say to each member. The church is the community that lives by the history centering in Jesus Christ, to which the Bible witnesses. Preachers are set apart because they are judged to have some knowledge of that history and witness and to have some ability to relate it to the current needs of the community. Because the biblical witness teaches that the Spirit sets us free, we have dared to say that the service of the Spirit in the community is the service of freedom. Because of the great diversity of ways in which the scriptures attest to the Spirit's liberating work, and because of the great diversity of ways in which the scriptures have served to facilitate that work in the community, we have proposed a pluralistic understanding of the preacher's task within the overarching concern to serve the Spirit.

The service of freedom is certainly not limited to proposals about the meaning of scripture for today. Freedom may be served at the ballot box or even on the firing line. But it is important for this service that there be one place reserved for explicit and consistent attention to the scriptural witness. That place is the preaching office of the church.

The emphasis on freedom may appear to be in opposition to an emphasis on righteousness. But preaching for the enhancement of freedom is at the same time a call to conform to the purpose of God, which is always righteous freedom. That call involves openness to the working of the Spirit and readiness to act and live as the new horizons of understanding and sensitivity require. Resistance to new proposals and insights often arises from unwillingness to live in ways appropriate to them. Faithful response to the Spirit is costly, but because it is the acceptance of the Spirit's gift through responsiveness to her call, it is also perfect freedom.

2. Freedom Through the Conflict of Proposals

So far we have spoken of a style of preaching that helps the Spirit free the hearers by offering biblical proposals for imaginative reflection, thereby expanding the hearers' world. We believe that it is an appropriate type of preaching. But this formulation exaggerates the continuity of the world of the biblical witness with the existing world of the hearers, even when the hearers are Christians. There is some continuity, and it is possible to grow through imaginative appropriation of proposals suggested to us by the scriptures. But there are times, many times, when the scriptural word stands in sharp opposition to our world of thought and feeling.

Much of the German reflection on preaching discussed above presupposes a gulf between the thought world of scripture and our own. This is a problem of such magnitude that it requires attention here. A review of the theologians noted above will help clarify the issue.

Barth does not deny the problem, but of all these theologians he goes farthest in minimizing it.[5] He holds that we can share with the biblical authors their witness to Christ without much concern for those features of their world view that conflict with ours. Indeed, we can make our own much of their language and imagery. To a large extent, therefore, the difference between our age and the biblical one can be bridged by assimilating ourselves into the thought forms of the Bible. There is, at any rate, no need to emphasize the conflict.

Bultmann agrees with some of Barth's theological points, but he adopts an opposite position on this issue.[6] He emphasizes the gulf between our world view and that of the biblical authors, and he stresses how deeply all their formulations are shaped by their alien world view. To find the gospel in the context of these unacceptable ideas and myths requires a sharp distinction between the existential meaning of what is said and the mythological conceptuality within which it is said. The preacher's task is to disclose the existential significance of the biblical message while freeing believers from any commitment to the mythology. Bultmann, therefore, does not do away with the tension between the scriptural message and our contemporary habits of mind, but his view of preaching focuses attention on what is the real—that is, existential—issue. For Bultmann, the thought world generated by modern science is as normative for the Christian as it is for anyone else; the gospel's claim and challenge must be formulated within that thought world.

Ebeling follows Bultmann in this analysis, but he goes further than Bultmann to remove the intellectual conflict between Christian affirmation and the modern thought world.[7] Bultmann's language suggests a transcendent personal God; Ebeling's does not. Bultmann focuses on the death and resurrection of Jesus as the decisive act of this God; Ebeling refers to the ministry of Jesus as it can be known through the historical-critical method. The word-event that brings assurance is not derived from the modern thought world, but it is not in conflict with it. It can be recognized and appreciated by those who live fully within the modern world. Ebeling, therefore, more completely than Bultmann, accepts the modern point of view, seeks to understand what happened in Jesus from that point of view, and then, through preaching, tries to enable that type of event to continue in the church.

Pannenberg's approach is also unabashedly modern: We should say nothing that we are not justified in saying by criteria that can be defended in the secular context, and we do not try to assimilate our thinking to the thought forms of the Bible.[8] But unlike Bultmann and Ebeling, Pannenberg engages in argument with other moderns about the correct way to study and interpret history and even science. There are features of post-Enlightenment thought, he believes, that unjustifiably predetermine what can be judged true in the beliefs of other ages. There is, for example, a prejudice to the effect that nothing can have happened in the past that is of a type unfamiliar in our own time. This leads to a reductionistic reading of history, especially the history of religions. But a truly historical approach, appropriate to all our modern knowledge, deals with the evidence for the occurrence of unique events on its own terms. It does not prejudge in terms of ordinary modern experience. All this comes to focus on the resurrection of Jesus. Many historians, including New Testament scholars, declare in advance that a resurrection cannot be regarded as a historical event. They, therefore, do not examine the evidence for its occurrence by critical-historical methods. This is wrong, Pannenberg declares. If the evidence that the resurrection occurred is sufficient, and he thinks it is, then we should readjust our views of history, in the same way that sufficient evidence for natural phenomena not predicted by our theories should lead us to revise those theories.

Sölle takes the difference between the biblical world view and ours as seriously as anyone.[9] Apocalyptic ideas, however biblical, are simply incredible to us. We know, Sölle believes, that the course of history depends on human action and is not in the hands of a transcendent God. But the situation of political oppression is as characteristic of our present world as it was of the biblical world. The biblical response to that oppression remains relevant to us. Within that response, Jesus' embodiment of radical and liberating love and his invitation to others to live and act in that love remain the absolute norm that transcends all changes in world view.

Underlying all these treatments of the authority of scripture seems to be an assumption that Christians must find something there that stands beyond all relativity. Whereas the concern for absolutes leads fundamentalists to take every statement in the Bible as indisputable fact, it leads many modern theologians to deny the contemporary relevance of much of the language of scripture, sharply contrasting that with what is really and indisputably authoritative. We believe, on the other hand, that this quest for something of absolute authority is mistaken. Both the fundamentalist and the liberal treatments of the problem lead us astray.

It is our conviction that Christians should take all biblical language seriously, but that they should treat it as offering imaginative *proposals*. The response to these biblical proposals is in fact, at least in contemporary North American society, quite individual. It depends on the life experience of the person, and we are a highly diverse people. The danger, therefore, is of continuing fragmentation of the community of faith into a multiplicity of Christians with conflicting convictions.

The effort to oppose this fragmentation by defining a "canon within the canon" or by insisting on the sacrifice of the intellect before biblical authority does not work. It alienates and fragments in its own way—or, worse still, it enslaves the hearer to falsely absolutized principles or ideas. A healthier community results from open discussion of varied ideas, all emerging from serious appropriation of scripture. The problem remains, however, and we will return to it in chapter 3.

To treat biblical texts as proposals of imaginative possibilities is not to deny them authority. Far from it. Every suggestion coming from scripture has authority—namely, the authority of proposals that have been influential in shaping the life and community of those who have listened to scripture in the past. That what they suggest differs from the edicts attributed to modern science is certainly highly relevant to how people will respond to them, but there might yet be something worthwhile in them. By their very nature, the hypotheses of the sciences also are nothing but proposals. When they have led to making particular world views absolute, the Newtonian one for example, the consequences have been just as bad as when biblical proposals have led to making the biblical world view absolute. Both world views are important suggestions, inviting critical and imaginative response. Each has enough truth to be taken seriously, and each has enough error that any claims to absoluteness should be rejected.

In the Bible, it is not only the world view that should be treated as an imaginative proposal. The same holds for the ethical teachings of Jesus or the theology of Paul. Here, too, there are suggestions, this time of still greater importance, because they are suggestions that have elicited enormous response through Christian history, much of it, though certainly not all, quite admirable.

Whereas Bultmann, Ebeling, Pannenberg, and Sölle, in different ways, believe that the role of the theologian is to extract from this mass of biblical suggestions certain conclusions that can be presented as unqualifiedly norma-tive and absolute, we disagree. The role of the theologian is, instead, to clarify the present situation in relation to scripture. This task cannot be done once and for all. The church in every generation needs to confront all the scriptural proposals again. To do so will be disastrous, however, if the proposals of scripture are understood as absolutes before which believers must sacrifice their minds. Such absolutization turns the Bible into the enemy of the Spirit. But the Bible will serve the Spirit if Christians seek to understand the suggestions that biblical texts make.

Christians should allow themselves to be confronted by these biblical suggestions in their full strangeness. It is not always the task of the preacher to extract the acceptable kernel and discard the husk. The hearer of the sermon should not be protected from the offense of strange, and sometimes false, ideas in the Bible. If treated as proposals, even they can be liberating. Sometimes it will be in the strangest and most disturbing of proposals that the Spirit will find the greatest opportunity.

The general point we are making here is that modern forms of thought should not be established as absolutes any more than should the teachings of scripture. Yet both should be taken with great seriousness. Their clash leads to the next step in our understanding of preaching for the enhancement of freedom: the contrast, within the sermon, of biblical and contemporary ideas and images.

In section 1 of this chapter, we spoke of making proposals suggested to the preacher by scripture. Those suggestions can bypass the least palatable aspects of the scriptural language and offer proposals that invite serious attention as possible expansions of the hearers' world. But we believe that it is even more important to deal with the challenge posed by the many conflicts between the Bible and the hearers' world. If that is to happen, it is important that the scriptural proposals themselves be heard.

Let us consider this possibility in relation to questions of world view, which most of the Germans have largely excluded from theology and preaching. Many biblical passages speak in terms of a world view of earth with a heaven above and a nether world below, with considerable commerce between them. The dominant modern world view has abolished heaven and the nether world and has no place for God in the explanation of natural phenomena.

Although we assume that the biblical picture is false to reality, we believe that the dominant modern world view is also false. Yet, most of those to whom readers of this book will preach have allowed their thought world to be shaped almost exclusively by that modern world view. The task of preachers, in this connection, is not to present their personal world views as the only correct way to view reality, although they are certainly free to offer their insights as suggestions. Their primary task is to make the biblical proposals as convincing as is practically possible in their real challenge to the world view actually functioning in most hearers.

There is a risk in doing this. The hearers might simply be

confused. They might think that as Christians they *should* accept the biblical world view and feel guilty for not doing so. Worse yet, they might accept it! Or they might rigidify their commitment to the dominant modern world view in defense against what they feel is an unwarranted assault. But if the biblical world view is presented as an imaginative proposal, one that the preacher encourages hearers to take seriously, responses of this kind are less likely to occur. Instead, the biblical proposal might be considered in its strangeness, and elements in it might appear to have some convincing power, however different they are from the modern world view out of which one has lived. When brought to full consciousness, some elements of that customary world view might appear less evident than had been supposed, whereas others might seem simply incontrovertible.

Now a new possibility arises. The sermon has led to critical reflection on two proposals. It might even have assisted in the critical evaluation of both. Although both have persuasive power, they do not cohere. The hearers are helped to understand the relation between the proposals. But the remaining tension is not to be relieved immediately by compromises. It calls for something more: a leap of thought in which elements that are incompatible within the existing horizon of meanings become compatible at another level. One's thought world is not merely expanded; it is transformed.

An example would be the contrast between the modern understanding of astronomy and the biblical view that the heavenly bodies obey the will of God (see Matt. 5:45). Since the sun rises and sets according to regular rules, it has been common since the eighteenth century to say that God's hand can be seen in the power that started the sun and moon in motion, but that nowadays we see God's presence only in the inner lives of persons.[10] Of course, people in Jesus' day and long before also knew well that the sun moved in a regular pattern. But then it was also believed that the earth was stationary and that it was the sun that moved. Since Copernicus revolutionized the paradigm of our universe, however, we have known that it is the other way around. "The rising and setting sun" rings true today as a description of what appears to our eyes but not as a description of what we know to be the case—namely, that sunrises and sunsets are the effects of our planet's spinning on an axis in an orbit around the sun. Matthew 5:45, however, implies something that was taken for granted in biblical times—namely, that God's presence and power are seen not only in our inner lives, but also in the whole range of actions and events within which we live. We can be reminded of that by these biblical writers in spite of, or precisely because of, their archaic astronomy.

What this illustrates is that we can encounter the biblical proposal that God is immanently and inwardly active in all events as a challenge to the mechanical understanding of events on which the dominant modern paradigm of the universe is based, and in terms of which most theologians think about the world. More important than striving for coherence or conformity between these two views—for example, by pointing to elements of indeterminacy and openness in small-scale events in modern physics, though this is certainly to the point—is the biblical conviction that all such events have value and carry value, since they too embody the divine presence. This contribution from the biblical side can become a challenge to rethink the dualism, determinism, and mechanism that run so deeply through our modern thinking about the world, and that make belief in God increasingly problematic. In this illustration, the hearers' world is transformed toward an openness to God's presence in events that, before the encounter with the biblical text and its strange world view, had seemed to be merely products of mechanical laws.

Another example of contrasting proposals can be found in the biblical hope for the end of the world, which was closely related to cosmology, for it involved both cosmology and history. The *parousia*, or return of Christ, is described in the Synoptic Gospels as an event in which Christ will appear "coming on the clouds of heaven" (Matt. 24:30 par. RSV). From the modern perspective, it is difficult to imagine Jesus' suddenly materializing and descending on an escalator of clouds to meet the faithful. But that imagery should not be dismissed out of hand just because we no longer live in a three-story universe. That strange apocalyptic way of describing the experience of the real presence of Christ in some future, triumphal, culminating event needs to be taken seriously and allowed to serve as a challenge to the closed and despairing view of history that so many hold today. The faith that a new beginning can be made could emerge from this conflict of imaginative proposals.[11]

These examples of the clash of world views have been taken from that aspect of the scriptures that has been most consistently neglected in modern theology. We have selected them to show that something can be gained from listening even to the strangest feature of the biblical proposals. We do not propose that cosmology become the main topic of preaching.

To illustrate our point in a more typical manner, consider Jesus' teaching on possessions. Actually this is in at least as great opposition to what Christians believe today as is the biblical cosmology. What are they to make of teachings that, if followed straightforwardly, as Jesus no doubt intended, would strip them of most of their possessions and economic security?

Again, it is not always the role of the preacher to solve this problem for the congregation by explaining that Jesus' teaching applies only in the context of apocalyptic expectations, or that what is important is poverty of spirit rather than economic poverty, or that Jesus meant these extreme teachings only for those who were too attached to property and that those who are committed instead to the realm of God[12] can enjoy their wealth with impunity. These are all interesting proposals and can be presented as such. But if they inhibit attention to the radical demand of Jesus, they become impediments to freedom.

The deep-seated conviction, as common in antiquity as in the modern period, is that the truly fortunate are the rich—that is, those who own some property and have security for the future (which includes most readers of this book). This conviction should be confronted sharply by the teaching that the rich cannot enter the realm of God.[13] This is not to say that Jesus is right and that modern Christians are wrong. Jesus' proposal is serious and important; however, at the same time, it is not absolute. There is serious and important truth to the view that moderate wealth is desirable. But, as Albert Schweitzer saw, if Christians today are to hold on to world affirmation responsibly, they must wrestle with the world negation of Jesus.[14] That wrestling will not leave them unaffected.

Two proposals confront each other. Neither readily gives way before the other. Jesus' proposal cannot simply be added as an extension of the existing world of thought and sensibility, because it does not fit. A few Christians find that they must choose between these two worlds and decide for Jesus. That is certainly admirable. But most find that they cannot. To abandon all property and to give up all insurance and retirement programs would pose grave burdens on persons they care about, even if they were willing individually to make considerable sacrifices. Are Christians then condemned to live in a way that they recognize as biblically unfaithful, or will they defend it as faithful despite its apparent divergence from Jesus' teaching?

There is only one way out of this impasse, and that is the leap of thought to a new level, in which the truth of both proposals can be held together without softening the differences. One hearer might decide to organize his or her life around a cause to which he or she felt called by Christ, subordinating thereto all decisions about possessions and economic security. Another might see how the whole economic system is based on an understanding of the goodness of possession and consumption that cannot be sustained when confronted with Jesus' teaching and might be moved to fresh thought and courageous action about the great public issues of the day. Such responses to preaching involve an expansion of freedom and are possible only as the work of the Spirit.

Even themes, images, and ideas from the Bible that have

come to be deeply ingrained in the language of Christian worship and devotion, and are more central for theology than either cosmology or poverty, are subject to the same clash between biblical and modern presuppositions. These fundamental Christian images and ideas also need to be presented in preaching as proposals, just as is the case with the two previous illustrations. It is for this reason that we have chosen biblical presentations of the death of Jesus as the principal scriptural proposals to be interpreted in this book.

The image of a life given for others, by its very nature a basic challenge to human tendencies toward self-preservation, has its own recurrent power as a proposal that calls for a deep reexamination and redirection of the energies of life. More than that, the particular ways in which the death of Christ is given concrete meaning in the New Testament— such as cultic sacrifice, the death of the righteous person, and the suffering that precedes and accompanies the end of the world—are not part of the contemporary, immediate world of experience. How they might speak to that world is the focus of Part II.

Our argument, therefore, is that scripture is foundational and constitutive for preaching, but that it is not an absolute authority. There can be no such absolute authority for preaching, for the pattern of Christian faith and life cannot be established on the basis of any absolute authority. Rather, this pattern arises in the exercise of freedom in the interplay between the history and tradition that are met in the Bible and flow from it, and the claims of the present. This freedom is the work of the Spirit. To recognize the foundational, but not absolute, role of the scripture in preaching can free us to confront the barriers that spring up in its use and also to listen creatively to, and be transformed by, those aspects of the Bible that are not immediately congenial or acceptable. It can also make possible a more explicit place for the Spirit in the understanding of preaching.

The notion that the Spirit's work involves transcending biblical proposals, even those of Jesus himself, might appear to some to reduce the sense of scriptural authority too much and to misconstrue the proper role of the Spirit in "inspiration."[15] And yet, that is precisely what early Christian evangelists themselves did. Jesus' "hard" word about the exclusion of the rich from God's realm[16] was "softened" by early Christian evangelists, who thought it better to say that it is difficult, but not impossible, for the rich to enter God's realm.[17] Jesus' own authority to radicalize the law of Moses (see Matt. 5:21-48), which also demonstrates the work of the Spirit, is, by the same work of the Spirit, reversed, as in the case of Jesus' teaching on divorce.[18]

In short, as these examples show, holding scripture to be inspired by the Spirit did not lead to absolutizing what the scriptures said. On the contrary, the same Spirit that animated the original scripture opened the way to transforming what it said into a new word germane to new times and circumstances. What Paul says of the law—"the letter kills but the Spirit makes alive" (II Cor. 3:6)—is true of any authority, whether it is scripture, tradition, or modern ideas.

Freedom to reinterpret the biblical text is nothing new, although often in the past the freedom that was actually exercised was not fully conscious. What we have been saying is that, though there is no predetermined limit to the direction freedom of interpretation will take, there are two basic constraints. One of these is that the sermon be a serious engagement with the biblical text. The other is that it be sensitive to the leading of the Spirit. Here the advice of Paul—not to "quench the Spirit" but to "test everything" (I Thess. 5:19-21)—and of the author of I John—to "test the spirits, to see whether they are from God" (I John 4:1 NEB)—provides some help by pointing to the things that are characteristic of the work of the Spirit: mutual love, trust in God, and devotion to God's purposes through faith in Jesus Christ.[19] In other words, preaching must be judged by the aims that it serves—those of the Spirit or those of some other source. Difficult as this criterion is to specify, nothing less will do.

CHAPTER THREE

THE ENDS OF PREACHING

1. Building the Church

The previous chapter emphasized the enhancement of the freedom of the hearers of the sermon collectively, but also in their personal individuality. The meaning of what is said will not be identical in any two hearers if the Spirit creatively relates it to their personal experience. The integrity and identity of each person are respected and strengthened in the world of the Spirit served by preaching.

One can find in the Christian faith real encouragement for individuality, but individuality must not lead to individualism. Freedom becomes abstract and empty except as it relates us concretely and effectively to others. Christian freedom is relational freedom. The expansion of understanding extends the network of relations and bonds people more richly to one another. As Paul Tillich said so well, individuality and participation mutually require each other.[1]

The participation that is emphasized in the New Testament is in the community of Christians, the church. As we noted in the second section of chapter 1 (see pp. 25-26), Paul so stresses the work of the Spirit in the church that he obscures the point that the giver of new life through Christ is also the one who gives life to all. We stress the universal work of the Spirit, but not to the exclusion of its particular presence in the church.

Paul describes Christianity in Thessalonica and Galatia as beginning with experiences of the Spirit following his preaching of the crucified Messiah (see I Thess. 1:2-10 and Gal. 3:1-5). It is this same Spirit that bonds the many members of the church into one body, the "body of Christ" (I Cor. 12:12-13). According to Luke-Acts, the Spirit empowers the church's witness to Jesus as the Messiah.[2] And in the Gospel of John, the Spirit guides the church into all Truth.[3] The work of the Spirit, therefore, includes the witness within the church to the presence of God—a witness that brings freedom and truth. It is important to reflect on how preaching serves this work of the Spirit in the church.

The church is a community whose identity consists in the way it lives out of its own past. Central to that past is Jesus Christ and, above all, Christ crucified. The church lives in the memory of Jesus, retelling the story and repeatedly reenacting his death and resurrection in hope of the fulfillment of his promises. Sharing the story as our collective story constitutes us as a community of Christians. Where that story is not known, or where there is indifference toward it, there is no church. According to the Reformers, the church exists wherever the Word is rightly proclaimed and the sacraments rightly administered. Through Word and sacrament, the Spirit unites us in the body of Christ.

It is right and necessary to focus on Jesus Christ as the center of the history that gives identity to the church. Through this center, all that preceded Jesus and all that has followed him are understood and appropriated as ours. But this does not relegate the Hebrew scriptures, which we call the Old Testament, to secondary status. It is through Jesus Christ that we are grafted onto the history of Israel. Apart from that grafting, we cannot know Jesus as the center of the history that gives identity to the church. Similarly, the story does not end with Jesus. Within the established canon, the Acts of the Apostles carries it on. It has proceeded another nineteen centuries, and we are now writing new chapters.

The church can survive from generation to generation

only as this story is passed on from generation to generation as its story, the story that gives Christians their deepest identity, the story for whose present continuation they are responsible. This transmission of the Christian story can be done, should be done, in many ways. The story can be told by parents to children, by teachers to their pupils, by artists to those who see and hear their work, by evangelists to those who have not heard or have forgotten, but also and especially by preachers to their congregations. It is told by reading the scriptures, but it can best be brought alive as the community's story in preaching. People become Christians as the Christian story is appropriated as their shared identity.

Too often the story has been sanitized and sentimentalized. This is especially likely to happen when it is viewed as a source of moral lessons or good examples, as in much church school literature. Or it is told as the story of victories to encourage the Christian troops to keep trying. But the Bible itself stands foursquare against such distortions. There the sins of the ancestors in the faith are recited as clearly as their virtues, and defeats play a role as great as victories. To be grafted onto that history is to become part of a community that has at once testified to the creative-redemptive work of the Spirit, both within the community and in the whole world, and has also acknowledged the community's own lack of faith and repeated idolatry.[4] The heroes of the faith are also sinners, and they make mistakes. But it is not necessary for Christians to agree with all the ideas of priests, prophets, or apostles to acknowledge the history they created as the one that gives Christians their identity.

Earlier, we noted that preachers need not present the biblical text as the one final authority, but that they do need to present to their congregations the meaning and claim precisely of the biblical text. This requirement is not posed arbitrarily by the congregation. It is inherent in the identity of the church as the community that lives centrally from that history. The church must come to terms ever more fully and ever more accurately with that past. Since this past constitutes what the church is, to know it as its past is to know itself.

To clarify the option for the poor, so characteristic of the Bible, is to understand why Christians today stand with the oppressed rather than with the oppressor even when their own economic or political interests, narrowly defined, are those of the oppressor. When Christians understand who they are through the centrality of Jesus Christ in the history that gives them their identity, such clarification strengthens their commitment to liberation. To clarify the negative relation to Judaism, which subtly (and not always so subtly) pervades the New Testament, is to come to understand the unconscious (and sometimes conscious) anti-Judaism that pervades Christian culture to this day. In the light of Jesus Christ, such clarification calls for the repentance—the *metanoia*—through which alone the Spirit of holiness can purify us.

This need to serve the Spirit as it unites us with the church is a major reason for the use of story in preaching. The primary story that is to be told is the story of those who have gone before us and have shaped our heritage. This includes the familiar stories of the Bible, the early martyrs, the church fathers, the medieval saints and mystics, the Reformers, the missionaries, and our denominational leaders. But it also includes the less familiar stories of ordinary Christians, of those who were rejected as heretics and, above all, of the costly leadership and generous service of exploited Christian women, which have been so minimized in our collective memory. Without a truer and more inclusive history, the church cannot overcome its distorted, patriarchal self-understanding and practice.

But even this is not enough. We live in a religiously pluralistic world. Our grafting onto the ongoing Christian story can lead us to understand ourselves as being over against Jews, Moslems, and people of other religions. It can make us desire our success at their expense. This "triumphalism" is a large part of our collective story. It is only in recent times that, in the light of Jesus Christ, it has been named and confessed as sin and has been partly overcome. But it remains a powerful temptation as long as the story that constitutes Christian identity excludes the stories that provide identity for others.

H. Richard Niebuhr knew that the schism produced by the Reformation would not be healed until Protestants had appropriated Roman Catholic history of the past five hundred years and Roman Catholics had appropriated that of Protestants.[5] To a remarkable extent, Roman Catholics have come to be able to tell the story of Luther as part of their own story. Protestants have been slower to exchange their sectarian stories for an inclusive one.

We will not overcome the alienation of Christian from Jew until, in a similar way, we learn the story of Judaism from the time of Jesus to the present and finally come to understand ourselves as heirs of that story, too. The story at whose center Jesus stands is not simply the Christian story, narrowly understood, but the total history of the Spirit who is present in all God's creative-redemptive work in the world. That means that Christians in India, for example, must come to accept the story of Hinduism as their story appropriated in the light of Jesus Christ, and that someday all Christians will accept the whole history of life on this planet as essential to their identity. But this is all to be attained by broadening our centrally determinative story, the biblical one, not by weakening its particularity.

Since Christians have at times defined themselves over against followers of other religious paths in imperialistic and triumphalistic terms, we wish to affirm the efforts of those who follow different religious paths to preserve the particularity of their own visions precisely as they interact with the Christian one, if they choose to do so. Jews, in particular, have been offended, often rightly so, by Christian evangelistic efforts among their people. Their foundational visions, like those of the other religions, will continue to have their own validity for those who live from them. We believe that it will be possible to discover many points at which the several visions converge. But, precisely because we believe that through Jesus we have access to the Spirit of the God of all, we fervently hope that other historical routes in which the divine purpose has been active may continue to grow. And we recognize that each might be transformed in ways that will prevent the fusion of the different visions.

Further, there is a danger today in stressing the need to broaden our story. For many people, even in the church, their identity has been shaped more by other stories than by the Christian one. Through our public schools, they have found their identity in the story of the United States, or through immersion in particular causes they have found identity through the stories of those movements.

Nevertheless we must renew the power of the particular Christian story with a new awareness of other important stories. We must tell our own story in such a way as to enhance openness to the stories of others and to encourage the widening of Christian identity. Since Jesus is the center, no circle that excludes any part of the story of the world so loved by God is large enough.

We noted earlier that preaching in the service of the Spirit is usually for both the believer and the unbeliever, recognizing that even the staunchest believer is also in some measure an unbeliever. In the light of what we have said in this section, that means that the task of preaching is both to invite persons to become a part of the community that lives from and in the Christian story and to help those whose identity is already so constituted to understand better that story and its meaning for the present. The former task requires that the story be presented as an inviting one, the latter, that the sins and failures it includes be fully recognized.

These two tasks are not, as it might appear, in conflict. What is truly inviting about the Christian story is that it enables us with total honesty to recognize who we are in the context of the costly forgiveness symbolized and enacted in the cross of Christ. That invitation is communicated best by the honesty with which we appropriate and tell our story, which at the same time serves the broadening and cleansing of Christian identity.

2. Realization of the Truth

Preaching in the service of the Spirit has as its goal increasing the freedom of the hearers as well as bringing them together as the church. In the New Testament, however, the Spirit is also the bearer of Truth. Preaching, therefore, is also directed to bringing the hearer to the Truth. This end of preaching is not separable from that of grafting hearers to the foundational story of the church, of increasing freedom, and of expanding the world of understanding. It, too, can best be accomplished through offering imaginative proposals. It will repay us, therefore, to reflect on Truth as that to which we are led by the Spirit and that which is promoted by the Spirit.

The context of the aphorism "the truth will set you free" in the Fourth Gospel (John 8:32) makes it clear that the reference is to the liberating knowledge of who Jesus really is and who his followers truly are: Jesus is God's representative and his followers belong ultimately to God.[6] The difficulty with this original context is that it makes it easy for the reader to limit its horizon of meaning, with the result that the Truth that Jesus and the Spirit bear does not open up to the enlightenment bestowed on everyone from the beginning of creation to the present and into the future (John 1:9). Without that inclusiveness, the Word of Truth brought by the Spirit becomes narrow in two ways: It is reduced to the ethical, religious, and existential—that is, it reduces the Truth about human existence in the world and before God in a way that excludes so much of God, the world, and human existence. And it is tied to the socio-historical context of the Johannine community, a context that is difficult to enter, and even offensive to many, because of its blatant enmity toward "the Jews." But the prologue to the Gospel of John shows us that the Truth, to which the Spirit bears testimony, is the Logos through whom everything was made and which enlightens all people. It is this Truth that was enfleshed in Jesus. Any truth is too small that cannot include the Truth that was coming into the world from the beginning. This Truth surely does not exclude information, but just as surely it is not primarily a matter of information. The deepest faith does not coincide with the largest amount of information. The Truth in question is the Truth that heals our brokenness and overcomes the distorted visions of the world by which we live.

The Truth into which we are led is already realized in God. Indeed, the Truth is nothing else than God's knowledge, for God knows all things as they truly are. Our thought becomes more true as it becomes more like God's.

This approximation cannot be quantitative, since our approximation to infinity is trivial. The likeness of which we speak must be one of kind or character. We can look at the few things of which we can have knowledge in a way that approximates God's perspective on them. Even that can only be approached in a fragmentary way. But that approach, however remote, is both painful and transformative.

Let us consider this more concretely. I experience my own interests and concerns from within and those of others from without. My tendency is to view my neighbors in the light of what they can do for me or the ways in which they threaten me. This distorts my perception, since God looks upon the hearts of all—that is, God knows all of us in the mode in which we know ourselves, but fully and accurately. Now, I cannot experience my neighbors from within, as God does. In that sense, Truth is closed to me. But I can realize that my neighbors have interests and concerns just as deeply felt as mine and, in Truth—that is, for God—just as important as mine. I can also, to some extent, imagine how they feel. In short, I can approximate the Truth about my neighbors and myself, while recognizing that the approximation falls short of the Truth. To whatever extent I do this, my own interests and concerns are changed. I see the desirability of acting in a way that considers all the interests involved. I might actually reflect on the situation with these other interests positively in view. My behavior might be affected.

Preaching can serve the Spirit of Truth as the preaching relates to ourselves and to our neighbors in two main ways. First, it can undertake to make real to the hearers the actuality of Truth—that is, of the divine perspective on the world. It can point out how differently things appear from that perspective when compared with our finite and sinful ones. It can illustrate that difference in innumerable ways.

Second, preaching can help hearers to think and feel differently toward their neighbors. By illustration and example, it can help the hearers to break out of their imprisonment within themselves and appreciate the situations and feelings of others. It can point to spiritual disciplines that can cultivate the habit of provisionally adopting the perspectives of others, to avoid the hasty judgment that so easily comes when others are viewed only in relation to ourselves. Knowing that in Truth we are loved together with others, we are freed to love others as well.

No less important than viewing our neighbors as God views them is experiencing ourselves as God experiences us. This is the basis of confession. We come before God to acknowledge what we are in Truth. The recognition that we have concealed much of this Truth from ourselves leads to self-examination and to a new level of acceptance of responsibility for ourselves. The struggle to see ourselves as God sees us is painful, but its expansion of self-knowledge is healing.

Furthermore, to see ourselves as God sees us is not finally to condemn ourselves. It is to know ourselves as sinners, to be sure, but as *forgiven* sinners. Since we know that the One who forgives us is the One who knows us completely, we are freed from any need to be defensive and condemning. Because in Truth we are forgiven, we can forgive ourselves. Having forgiven ourselves, we are enabled to forgive others. Because in Truth we are loved, we can love ourselves. Loving ourselves, we are freed to love others as well. This knowledge of the Truth can enable us, therefore, more nearly to approximate the Truth about our neighbors.

Much of the preaching advocated by the German theologians discussed above is appropriate here in the service of the Spirit. Indeed, preaching for justification has concentrated on this dialectic of sinfulness and forgiveness before God. But it is an understanding into which we can enter more and more deeply in the process of sanctification as well.

The Truth that is God goes far beyond ourselves and our immediate neighbors, important as these are. It is Truth about nation states as well. Reinhold Niebuhr taught us that our very capacity to transcend ourselves for the sake of a larger community, our capacity to give ourselves sacrificially for its sake, leads to investing excessive finality in that community.[7] In the modern world, this community has usually been the nation state for whose defense or glory millions have given their lives. The Truth, however, is that our nation is of no more value or ultimacy than any other. Our tendency to see international issues in the light of our own nation's narrow interests is a revolt against the Truth, just as surely as is our tendency to view our neighbors in terms of how they affect us.

It must be the preacher's task to confront these idolatrous habits of mind. This confrontation can be partly direct, pointing out that the Truth is all-inclusive and impartial and not shaped to national partisanship. The preacher might also be able to offer opportunities for understanding the point of view of other nations and especially of those regarded as enemies. To offer the opportunity to look at the global scene through Soviet eyes, even briefly and fragmentarily, would do much to serve the Truth. The task of preaching, therefore, includes helping congregations themselves to look at public affairs in the light of the Truth.

These are long-familiar requirements of preaching, and the distortion of our vision by personal and group self-interest has long been recognized as a threat to perception of the Truth. But in recent years many other distortions that characterize our perceptions and govern our actions have forced themselves on our awareness. We of the middle class view the world through glasses that filter out much of the Truth experienced and known by the poor. We who are white are blind to the experience of those who are black or Hispanic. We who are male have not understood the world of female experience.

The Truth that confronts us here is far more difficult to appropriate than the Truth of the existence of neighbors much like ourselves. For the male, to become aware of female experience is to become aware that male experience is not only limited but also distorted, that even the finest ideals it has generated are frequently oppressive to women. This realization of Truth does not immediately suggest solutions, but it does demand the risk of untried alternatives.

It is difficult and costly to help people to realize imaginatively what it is like to live in a way very different from their own accustomed way, so that the reality of the other way becomes part of the Truth by which we live. Yet, it is more important with every year that passes. Preaching cannot bear the whole burden, but unless the expansion of sensitivity and understanding is initiated and stimulated through preaching, it is unlikely to become foundational to other aspects of the church's life.

Preaching in the service of the Spirit of Truth is preaching that offers the opportunity to widen the horizons in which life is understood. It calls on hearers to look at the world as God sees it—that is, as it is in Truth. It calls on them to look at themselves as God sees them—that is, as fragmentary and sinful parts of the vast whole, who are nevertheless loved as being of unique importance. This double Truth sets us free. In the New Testament stories of Jesus' death, scripture decisively witnesses to this double Truth and to the freedom for which this Truth sets us free. We turn in Part II to those stories—especially in Mark's Gospel and in Paul's letters—and their witness to the Truth about God, the world, and ourselves.

3. Evocation of Feeling

In our exposition so far, we have dealt with ideas, images, identity, and Truth. None of these can be abstracted from feeling. Ideas and images that are not felt do not exist in the real world. The uniting of people in the fellowship of the church and the establishment of their identity as Christians is as much a matter of feeling as of understanding. The Truth that challenges our limited perspectives is effective only as its challenge is felt. Preaching in the service of the Spirit must be preaching intended to evoke those feelings desired by the Spirit. On the whole, this can be done better by offering suggestions based on the Bible than by manipulation of the hearers. The feeling of being free is one of the most important feelings to be evoked.

The feelings of which we speak are emotional. The feeling of the idea or image is not as such an emotion, but it is always clothed with emotion. If that emotion is boredom, the feeling will have little intensity. We have stressed the importance of interest. But interest is not the only important emotion. Ideas and images arouse joy and sorrow, hope and despair, guilt and purgation, attraction and revulsion, love and hostility. When the whole range of emotion remains unawakened, the effectiveness of preaching is truncated.

This attention to emotion has been inhibited in Protestant discussion of preaching by focus on the word. The preacher strives to be faithful to what is objectively given. Good preachers are also aware of the all-too-common corruption of preaching when the preacher adapts the message for the sake of arousing emotion, usually catering to the unregenerate fears and prejudices of the hearer. The reaction against this emotionalistic distortion of preaching is too often a one-sided emphasis on the objective nature of the message. This emphasis on the objective is in danger of leaving the world of emotions to irresponsible manipulators. The results are disastrous. Humans are emotional beings more fundamentally than they are thinking beings. The great forces that shape history have depended as much on tribal and national feelings as on the ideas and images that express and arouse them. Indeed, action never follows from ideas and images alone. It is always motivated in part by emotions that attach to these. Preaching that does not move its hearers is a failure.

The point here is emphatically not that moving the hearers as such is the proper purpose of preaching. The primary consideration remains that of the end to which they are moved and whether the pattern of emotions aroused is appropriate to the gospel. The truth of the message remains uppermost. But the truth of the message is meaningless if it is simply a matter of accuracy appreciated only by the preacher. The reality of preaching is its impact, that which is actually felt by the hearers, and that is as much a matter of the emotions elicited as of the objective pattern of ideas and images they are led to entertain. One reason for emphasizing the free response of the hearers as being central to the concern of preaching is that such free response is most likely to be accompanied by healthy and appropriate emotion.

Gerhard Ebeling is the one among the German theologians discussed above who is most sensitive to the importance of emotion. The assurance that the successful sermon effects is certainly emotional in character, and this emotion is certainly appropriate to the gospel. We differ from Ebeling only in that we believe preaching can appropriately serve the Spirit's arousal of other emotions as well. It is more important that hearers are renewed in their love for one another, that they forgive their enemies from their hearts, that they feel themselves freed from the burden of guilt, and that they care more about the poor than that what is said on each point measures up to high standards of objective accuracy. Of course, accurate statements are far more likely to evoke appropriate responses than are vague and sloppy ones, so long as the quest for accuracy is not for the sake of the preacher's self-image but rather for the sake of responsibly guiding the hearers. The finest preaching is that in which the message is spoken with utmost objective faithfulness in the rhetoric that is most likely to elicit the appropriate emotional response.

Up to this point, we have reflected on the feeling of the ideas and images offered by the preacher. But what is felt is not limited to these. One feels the events within one's body, one's neighbors, one's world, one's past. Preaching might bring these feelings into prominence. Indeed, if ideas and images do not arouse and deal with these feelings of the actual world of the hearers, they are unlikely to be effective.

This raises another question. In addition to feelings of the ordinary world, the sermon also arouses feelings of the divine presence. This is a subtle and complex topic. In a book dealing with the significance of Jesus' death, it will be easy to give the impression that preaching in the service of the Spirit focuses on the historical figure, Jesus of Nazareth, rather than on the present working of the Spirit. This impression is partly correct, since Paul speaks of the Spirit as a gift that comes from preaching centered on Jesus as the crucified Messiah, Luke connects the power of the Spirit in the church with the ascension of Jesus as the crucified and risen Messiah, and John similarly relates the Spirit of Truth, the Paraclete, to the absence of Jesus from the earthly community of faith.[8]

It would be a distortion of these early Christian theologians, however, to limit the Spirit's work to witnessing to the historical Jesus alone. For Paul it is precisely the preaching of the gospel of the crucified Messiah that opens the way to a life of faith and service to "a living and true God";[9] it is God who supplies the Spirit;[10] and it is this Spirit who bears witness to believers that they are God's children.[11] According to Acts, the Spirit inspires preaching "the mighty works of God."[12] And in the Gospel of John, the Spirit of Truth is sent from God and bears witness to the Truth in God—that is, it is one with the Logos of God, which was incarnate in literally everything that was created, then particularly in Jesus of Nazareth, and then in the church. Indeed, especially in the Fourth Gospel but also in the other Gospels, the mission of Jesus is to bear witness to God as the source of all Truth. Preaching in the service of the Spirit seeks, therefore, through the preaching of the word of the Cross, to open our hearts and minds to the reality of God.

Because preaching belongs to worship, it partakes in worship's character of taking place before God. Worship is at once the enacting and the articulating of the appropriate human response. In both ways, it is a particular and focused realization of God's universal presence. That presence of God is the Spirit. The Spirit makes us free, unites us with the church, and leads us into Truth. The ultimate gift of that same Spirit is the Spirit herself as the fulfillment of life, and that gift includes the recognition and realization of the Spirit's presence.

The creative and redemptive activity of the Spirit, however, does not depend on the felt experience of the Spirit's presence. Many Christians know that they are enlivened, justified, and sanctified by the Spirit, and they celebrate that truth without thinking of themselves as immediately aware of the Spirit's work. The divine presence is a part of all human experience, and in worship this aspect of experience is lifted into focused attention. God's presence need not be merely believed—it can be felt as well.

The church knows, however, the great possibilities of self-deception and the danger that those who do not attain to numinous feelings will feel cheated or guilty. Preaching, therefore, must communicate that the Word of God includes the good news that we are accepted, forgiven, and loved quite apart from our religious feelings, and that its call to us is not primarily to cultivate the conscious awareness of the Spirit but, rather, to receive the Spirit's gifts and respond in appropriate service to the Spirit. But all this can be fulfilled and become more joyous as believers, in worship, become more aware of the present work of the Spirit.

4. The Diversity of Hearers

We have spoken of preaching the Truth as opening ourselves and our hearers to the divergent reality of life for those whose placement or situation in life is very different from our own. We have spoken of preaching to evoke feeling as, among other things, evoking the feeling of the divine presence. And we have set both Truth and feeling in the context of enlarging the freedom of those who hear the gospel—in the sense of freedom to be aware of their interrelatedness and responsibility—and to be open to the new vision that they do not yet see, or see only dimly. We believe that all of this is a primarily corporate event for the congregation as a whole. Yet, in contrast to many ways of understanding preaching, we assume that it is good for a sermon to call forth differing responses in different listeners. Indeed, this will inevitably happen, for it is the nature of language to evoke a range of imaginative possibilities or proposals. What each listener will hear in any given sermon will depend in part on her or his situation and level of maturity.[13]

When we think of preaching as offering proposals and as a stimulus to the integration of contrasts, we can see the diversity in a less threatening way than would be the case if we were to think of preaching as the presentation of a point of view that is to be shared by all. Knowing that our listeners will always hear differently can be liberating for the preacher. It can also be a reminder to trust the Spirit. We do not expect the same depth of response from everyone.

One way to view the diversity of hearers, therefore, is to see it in relation to the ongoing process of growth in attitude or character, a growth that will give stability to the quest for truth and for feeling or emotion, which we have mentioned above. The whole question of "faith development" has begun to receive attention, especially in the work of James W. Fowler.[14] Fowler has proposed a six-stage sequence of faith development, from the undeveloped faith of the infant through steps in which one depends on the authority of others and of the group within which one lives, to the rare transcendent, total, and selfless commitment of "universalizing faith," in which one goes as far as is humanly possible beyond the concrete historical forms that shaped one's faith to share in the reality in all forms of faith.

An analysis of Fowler's work would take us too far afield. We can only suggest here our preference for a less sequentially oriented, more situational approach to different kinds of faith. The least that needs to be said is that preachers should be aware that their sermons will be heard by persons who have different levels of maturity or stages of faith. The kind of self-transcendence that different hearers are able to derive from preaching will vary enormously. Further, we do not always live at the highest levels of maturity that we have attained. We often surprise ourselves and others by responding with less maturity than we might have. And, even more important, more complex levels of maturity carry with them more complex possibilities of destructiveness and sin. The intransigence and intolerance of "saintly" people are all too well known. Preachers, therefore, are called upon both to recognize what is genuine in an immature response and to help the hearer set this response in a trajectory of growth that will keep open the possibility of further transformation.

So far we have been thinking of the response of the individual hearer. From this point of view we may say that the Spirit continually and persuasively lures both preachers and hearers to entertain the highest possibilities for their life situations—those possibilities most consonant with the "mind of Christ." We are aware that each person will generally tend to be attentive to proposals that appear to reinforce previously held orientations. It is the desire of the Spirit, however, to stretch our thinking and expand our horizons to entertain new possibilities of transforming our attitudes. This understanding of preaching as being directed toward "faith development" will remain central as long as we are thinking of the growth in faith of the individual.

But there is another point of view from which to approach the diversity of hearers. That is the diversity of situation. "Situation" can mean the particular social setting within which a person lives, with its potentialities and its supporting aspects as well as its pressures, its brokenness, and its limitations, all of which are factors that support development or hinder it.

"Situation," however, has still another aspect. A person may be in a situation that demands that, to be responsible, she turn away from her own development and make an outright commitment to a cause that needs to be served.

This devotion to a cause corresponds to the second stage in Fowler's model of "faith development," sketched above. But "situation" can relativize development even more sharply. Movements of liberation, for instance, often grow by eliciting unswerving loyalty to a leader—a kind of loyalty to an authority outside oneself that seems to work against the maturity in faith that appears normative according to Fowler's model of "faith development." But within the situation of struggle, such leader-loyalty seems appropriate to many. This kind of loyalty has its drawbacks—and they are real—but many of those who live in struggles for liberation believe that the kind of self-integration that we associate with growth in faith is a luxury of the secure. Against our vision of faith as the ability to entertain, and be freed by, appropriate and heightened alternatives or proposals (a view that is similar in many ways to Fowler's next-to-the-highest stage of faith), many persons—including many Christians—regard the freedom that can emerge from a struggle to change the system as the most important kind of freedom. Faith, they believe, can be important only as it reinforces their loyalty to their group and, often, to its leader(s). There may indeed be situations where such faith is actually the most liberating kind.

A related issue arises when we listen to the responses of women to images that have often simply been assumed as correct in our preaching. Preaching on Mark's story of the death of Jesus, for example, has often emphasized the call to self-sacrifice and giving up one's own aims. Many women in the church, however, find this emphasis oppressive. Strength and dignity are what faith must give them if they are to remain in the orbit of the Christian faith.[15]

Consequently, we are led to the question of whether the degree of sophistication in conceptual and experiential awareness that we have articulated is the normative standard by which preaching in the service of the Spirit must be guided. Fowler is aware of this issue also: "The real issue is whether the faith development of average people in other cultural areas can fruitfully be understood and characterized by the stage constructs we are working out."[16]

67

As we consider the matter further, these two perspectives—that of "faith development" and the one from "situation"—interpenetrate each other. As we noted in our discussion of preaching and Truth (see page 58-60), a prime consideration in preaching is precisely the realization of the differences of "situation." It has been noted, for example, that strange things happen to the gospel of the oppressed when now the oppressor—and here we include the middle-class, institutionalized individual—takes it and proclaims it to other oppressors. Preaching to the affluent must communicate an awareness of the difference of their situation from that of the poor, so that they may come alive to the predicament of those who have less. It is also true, however, that the harsh, judgmental preaching of the opponent of oppression needs to be seen as being in tension with the preaching toward growth and toward the convergence of opposing positions.

We can illustrate the interplay between these two aspects of the diversity of hearers by thinking about proposals that could be entertained in preaching on two closely related texts.

> And Jesus began to teach them that the Human One must suffer many things, and be rejected by the elders and the chief priests and the scribes, and be killed, and after three days rise again. (Mark 8:31 ILL)[17]

> And Jesus summoned the multitude with his disciples, and said to them, "If any will come after me, let them deny themselves, and take up their crosses, and follow me. For those who would save their lives will lose them, and those who lose their lives for my sake and the gospel's will save them." (Mark 8:34-35)

One person might be led to the following conclusions: Since nothing happens except as God wills it, Jesus' announcement that he must suffer and die is a public acknowledgment of his divinely appointed fate. God has willed it and, because of Jesus' faithfulness, God vindicated and rewarded him by raising him from the dead. If we follow Christ and take up our crosses, then God will save and reward us, as God did Jesus. We are like Jesus in that God gives us our crosses, our personal afflictions and tragedies of life. It is God's will that we face them, and if we bear these crosses faithfully, God will reward us. Such a "faith of resignation" embodies trust in God, but it can discourage responsible human engagement in the struggles of the world as a response of faith. Because of this weakness, this kind of faith may be viewed as less than fully responsive to the call of the Spirit.

Another set of proposals might be as follows: God does not will such things as Jesus' suffering and death; God really desired that Jesus be successful in his mission. But in the concrete circumstances in which his mission developed, Jesus himself recognized that his impending death was an inevitable result of his commitment to the cause to which he had devoted his life. If Jesus had not been willing to suffer and die, he would have compromised his commitment and would have been unworthy of himself. Yet, through the resurrection, God vindicated the cause for which Jesus gave his life.

When the Gospels tell us that Jesus called us to deny ourselves, to take up our crosses, and to lose our lives for Christ's sake and the gospel's, what this means is that we are called to the cause of Jesus as it can best be served in our time. That may mean joining movements to liberate the oppressed against the establishments that are oppressing them—and, if need be, to take up arms and risk our own lives in the cause of human liberation, love, and reconciliation. Such a faith draws us out of ourselves into a cause that becomes the center of commitment. With this kind of faith, there is always the danger that the believer may think that the cause justifies ruthless and destructive actions for its sake. We can offer no foolproof way of avoiding this danger, but the general direction of a safeguard is clear: We must be aware that the cause itself is part of a larger picture.

The limitations of faith as devotion to a cause demand that we reflect upon another kind of faith. We can never achieve a fully universal point of view, but we can come to see our own project as an expression of a Spirit who is also at work, in other forms, everywhere and at all times. From this larger perspective, the proposals heard in the sayings quoted above would shift the emphasis away from the cause toward the self-giving, cruciform life-style itself as the center of what Jesus' death means to us and of which Jesus is an embodiment. The commitment to this life-style would then rank higher than the specific cause to which a person was dedicated. And much of the destructiveness of "the end justifies the means" would be avoided to the extent that we were grasped by the authenticity, truthfulness, and persuasiveness of the style of life seen in the stories of Jesus in the Gospels.

In affirming one's faith in the resurrection, one is saying that the "parable" offered by the life and death of Jesus is a revelation and particularization of the universal, divine call and hope for all life. In this perspective, the sayings from Mark that call us to lose ourselves and take up our crosses are heard as the urging of the Spirit for us to emulate the life of Jesus pictured in this Jesus-tradition and to discover that life is lived authentically, fully, and abundantly as we live the life of servanthood that these sayings express. This faith knows that the life of commitment is not a life in isolation, but is related to and taken up into the power of life itself. It is also free to maintain a critical stance toward any particular agenda, even as it also knows the importance of commitment and courageous action.

Following the faith-development model, these three interpretations of the Markan sayings have been arranged in ascending degrees of self-transcendence, of freedom from preoccupation with oneself. However, this model cannot be the sole norm for the response to preaching, as we saw in the discussion of "situation." As we said, there will be times when a strong assertion of one's own self, and of one's group's status and claims, may be the appropriate response to the Spirit. On any given occasion, the response to the Spirit will embody both the freedom from preoccupation with oneself and the freedom to become engaged in the actual situation, as well as one can perceive it.

Behind the complexity of the normative issue lies the

issue of whether there is a common "we" with whom preaching is shared. Are we in any appropriate way able to suggest that all preaching should heighten contrasts of various proposals to open up new, though paradoxical, alternatives? Are there some people who would be better off without this opportunity? In the short run, this question must indeed be answered yes, as we have suggested above. Some situations call for a simple and direct response.

But a more comprehensive view will not stop there. What all humans have in common, which makes communication possible, is that all human experience is enhanced—made more intense and (as has been shown above) more truthful—by the work of the Spirit in offering new possibilities. All have "fallen short" of the mark, and all alike stand to gain by responding affirmatively to the Spirit's lure or possibilities. That common need validates the inclusiveness and appropriateness of our understanding of preaching in the service of the Spirit. The larger question is: Which possibilities are the most relevant ones in any given situation and at any given level of "faith development"?

To some extent, preachers answer this question every time they suggest ways of applying a text's proposals. Good preachers assist the Spirit in eliciting highly relevant proposals; inept ones elicit proposals that are received as too incongruent, or just boring. It would appear that there is an optimal constellation of proposals for persons at various stages of "faith development" and in different situations. Discernment, judgment, and balance are required because preachers will almost always be speaking to persons at different stages of "faith development" as well as in very different situations.

Everyone might be freed to some extent by entertaining the proposal, for instance, that "even citizens in the Soviet Union are our neighbors." But that proposal will have more relevance for persons who have reflected on their own selfhood as individuals, as well as for those who have reflected on our interdependent human social situation. As we noted above, these two aspects of our existence interpenetrate. The proposal still has influential power for everyone, but it has even more influence for those who are experiencing the divisiveness of extreme individualism and nationalism.

What about those persons who still find the biblical world view quite acceptable and have not noticed its incongruities with some of their working assumptions about reality? Should preaching in the service of the Spirit mean freeing them from what at present is not perceived as limiting? Yes, to be truthful, preaching needs to create an environment in which one may eventually come to recognize and embrace a larger vision of reality. But no, that is not the immediate goal. The immediate goal is to set persons free within the world view and biblical understanding they have. Serving that goal first may, as a consequence, lead to a transition from one stage of reflection on faith to another.

Our conclusion must be that no one sermon can elicit feelings appropriate to each stage of faith development or to each situation. We must look for the extended opportunities in the year's preaching schedule that allow not only for broadening exposure to different and contrasting texts through the use of a lectionary, but also for developmental and situational considerations with respect to which texts and themes are selected. For instance, some texts and the feelings that are elicited by them may be helpful to men, but may not really be appropriate for women, and vice versa. And the message of empowerment and self-determination that is appropriate to black communities and to Native Americans might tend to reinforce tendencies toward oppression and bondage when heard by white communities. Similarly, a message appropriate for middle-class whites could be quite inappropriate for Hispanics or blacks.[18] Preaching that has this awareness can embrace both its pastoral-supportive and its prophetic-confronting responsibilities. Preaching in the service of the Spirit is both, and it is enhanced by both.

PART II

PREACHING ON THE
DEATH OF JESUS

INTRODUCTION

The Truth into which the Spirit leads us often seems totally disconnected from the truth that biblical scholarship tries to establish. Scholarship has, indeed, often become detached and specialized. Nevertheless, we believe that both the traditional historical scholarship about the Bible and the newer literary and sociological approaches must be central to our use of scripture. "Biblical" preaching cannot bypass them. If it does, such preaching will either ignore central aspects of the biblical world and life or fail to face realities with which we have to deal in our present world.

Building up the church requires preaching to offer imaginative proposals suggested by the Bible that will challenge the vision of the world in which we and our hearers live, and that open the way to its transformation. The most profound encounter with the biblical world takes place when we confront it in its strangeness and take account of its differences from our world.

In the chapters that follow, we turn from a discussion of the aims of preaching to consider this kind of wrestling with the Bible, which we believe is essential for sustained and deep interaction between the biblical world and our own. Here we deal in some detail with the creative tensions introduced into our world by encountering presentations of Jesus' death in the New Testament. The "passion" of Jesus is not the only theme of Christian preaching, but it is a central one. We have chosen this theme partly because of its intrinsic importance in the New Testament and in the contemporary church, but also partly because it compels us to think about the contrast of the biblical and modern worlds.

From the various treatments of Jesus' death in the New Testament, we have selected two of the most important for extended discussion: Mark's Gospel and Paul's letters. Our discussion moves in three steps: first, a look at how these writers present Jesus' death to the Christians of New Testament times (chapters 4 and 7); then, theological reflection on their presentations in preparation for preaching today (chapters 5 and 8); finally, two sermons that illustrate how we might preach on selected texts about Jesus' death in the Gospel of Mark (chapter 6, by John B. Cobb, Jr.) and in the letters of Paul (chapter 9, by David J. Lull). We believe that this approach to "biblical" preaching will open us both to the strangeness of the biblical texts and to their potential for transforming our visions of the world.

A.
Mark

CHAPTER FOUR

MARK'S STORY OF JESUS' DEATH

1. Narrative Ambiguity and Unfinished Readings

How can one person's death help another? Or even, can one person's death help another? The Gospel of Mark does not reflect or theorize about these questions. In one sense, these questions do not really fit this Gospel, because in the Gospel drama it is presupposed that the event of Jesus' death serves the purposes of *God,* which raises an additional range of questions. But a central mystery of our human existence and of our faith, the strange way in which one person's suffering and death may and do help others, is sharply in focus as the story is told. Everyone who reads Mark as a whole will quickly see that the death of Jesus is at the center of the story and how starkly it is set forth. But this Gospel does not present a Jesus who is carefully explained or easy to understand. By drawing the reader into a story that is complex and filled with ambiguity, the Gospel involves us in the mystery of life and death, and it compellingly invites us to follow the same path Jesus followed.

The clues Mark offers to the meaning of the cross can be read in such different ways that, even after thorough study, one is left wrestling with an ambiguity, which is not completely resolved, about the meaning Mark gives to the death of Jesus. Frank Kermode's brilliant book on the ambiguity of narrative makes this point in a telling way by using Mark as the central case for its thesis.[1] As we shall see, the various ways of taking the story remain a puzzle to scholars, who often disagree about how that puzzle is to be solved.

At first sight, it may be frustrating to face the fact that at certain central points this Gospel can be taken in more than one way. Readers may be frustrated, in part, because we are so uncomfortable with ambiguity. We prefer to grasp and know things with definite clarity and certainty—a clarity and certainty achieved through making distinctions, refining the contrasts, and choosing among them. But when preaching (or for that matter, reading) is thought of as encountering imaginative proposals, the experience of ambiguity looks different.[2] Because of its unsettling and unstable character, generated by contrasts and tensions— often even extremely severe contrasts and stressful tensions—ambiguity can evoke in us an openness to considering new possibilities. Such a response takes place in much the same way as an impressionistic stained-glass window, created out of glass of diverse shapes and contrasting colors, can evoke in us ever-anew openness to fresh appreciation for novel symbolic meanings.

We do not believe that the ambiguity of Mark's text will lead us into a morass of uncertainty. Much in Mark is very clear, and even when there is more than one way of seeing the point, the two or three options are related to one another. (Illustrations are given in the exposition that follows.) But we take the ambiguity seriously. We do not expect to find in a text, even a biblical text, an explanatory key that will resolve all our questions. We take the Gospel of Mark as offering us imaginative proposals that engage us seriously. Precisely by their contrast with what we expect, or what we usually experience, the proposals of the Gospel of Mark offer the promise of a new and deeper vision of the world. At the same time, our encounter with Mark will always be an unfinished one, and the contrasts and tensions within it will always be able to challenge us anew.

2. Jesus' Death as a Violent Story

The death of Jesus has been so thoroughly incorporated into Christian piety, and is so deeply penetrated with religious meaning, that it is hard for us who are familiar with it to realize how harsh a story it is. To the first-century reader and hearer, the violence would have been all too apparent, and the specific mode of the violence would have caused offense to many. In the hellenistic world, crucifixion was a cruel and humiliating death. We really have very few detailed descriptions of the actual act of crucifixion in Roman times. "The passion narratives in the Gospels are in fact the most detailed of all. No ancient writer wanted to dwell too long on this cruel procedure."[3] Even the word *cross* was treated with distaste among the Roman citizenry.[4]

No positive references to crucifixion, even as a metaphor, appear to exist in the literature of the time. Probably the nearest thing to an exception to this statement is the famous passage in Plato's *Republic*, in which Glaucon pictures the degrading suffering of the innocent just person.[5] Christian writers, so far as we know, were the first to draw from this passage the theme of the *crucified* just person; other ancient writers who referred to Plato's text eliminated this aspect of the passage.[6] In the ancient popular romances, when heroes or heroines are condemned to death by crucifixion, they are either spared at the last minute or taken down from the cross before they die—crucifixion in its final sense is reserved for the wicked.[7] Plenty of violence can be found in the ancient stories of heroes, as in the *Iliad* or in the dramas about Agamemnon or Oedipus. But such an ignominious death as crucifixion was never thought appropriate for heroic figures. Reserved largely for the lower classes and slaves, crucifixion was considered too inhumane a punishment for Roman citizens, regardless of the crime.

Understandably, early Christians showed a certain

defensiveness about the way in which Jesus met his death. This defensiveness is evident in the apologetic schema Mark used in depicting the trial of Jesus. Pilate is portrayed as doubting the truth of the charges against Jesus (15:5). Aware that "it was out of envy that the chief priests had delivered him up" (15:10 RSV), Pilate was prepared to release Jesus. He found nothing for which Jesus should be condemned (15:12-14). This apologetic motif, which tends to shift the blame for Jesus' death away from the Roman ruler, establishes a strongly anti-Jewish tone in the story of Jesus' death in Mark (a bias present also in the other Gospels), with which the modern interpreter must wrestle much more seriously than Christians usually have through the ages.[8]

To many educated Gentiles, therefore, the proclamation of the crucified Jesus would have been offensive because it was in sharp conflict with the way they imaged heroic people. For them the issue was not whether a heroic person could become a victim of violence (as noted above); rather, the issue was that the Christian story describes an appalling kind of violence. The stories told among educated Gentiles assumed a clear separation between what could happen to people who were carriers of destiny and what could happen to "common" people.[9] Most Gentile readers would intuitively have placed Jesus among the insignificant people because of the manner of his death. It should be added, however, that others—so-called marginal people, those without power in the social structure—would not necessarily have reacted in this way.

Many of the Jewish people were marginal in this sense in Roman days. But within their tradition was a quite different problem in the story Christians were telling about Jesus. What was offensive to Jewish hearers was not so much the ordinary or even degrading manner of Jesus' death, nor that Jesus died as a political criminal. Judaism had long been accustomed to the brutality of oppressive overlords, and many Jewish heroes had died as "outlaws" at their hands. For Jews, the difficulty in the Christian proclamation was the identification of a crucified person specifically as the

Messiah. The Messiah was by definition thought to be victorious over the enemies of the people, not humiliated and defeated. From the Jewish point of view, to say that a messianic claimant had been crucified was to say that this person was not in fact God's chosen agent, since the world had not changed. This contradiction in the Christian claim seems to have led some Jews to argue that Jesus' death on the cross branded him as cursed and condemned him as a criminal (Gal. 3:13). A similar conclusion was drawn later by Celsus, who was a second-century c.e. pagan critic of Christianity.[10]

Among the Gospels, Mark tells the story of Jesus' death most starkly and with the least effort to make it palatable. Not only so, but more than in any other account, this Gospel weaves the climax of the story into the whole fabric of the narrative. It is to Mark that Martin Kähler's famous description of the Gospels as "passion narratives with extended introductions" most properly belongs.[11]

It is worth noting how frequent are the passages that refer to the climax of the story, and how thoroughly integrated they are into the whole narrative. Even before the turning point of 8:27-33, the death of Jesus is clearly predicted, both in the words of Jesus himself (2:20) and in a narrative comment (3:6). From Mark 8 on there are almost two dozen references to Jesus' death, or to the similar fate of followers, before the crucifixion story.[12] Then, in the crucifixion story itself (15:20b-39), the offensive words *cross* and *crucify* occur seven times.[13] Even in the story of the empty tomb, where Jesus is now proclaimed as resurrected, Mark speaks of him as "Jesus of Nazareth, who was crucified" (16:6 RSV). It is obvious, therefore, that the passion and death of Jesus is the dominant theme that reverberates through the whole Gospel.[14] From 8:27 to the end, the way of the cross is the driving force propelling the drama to its conclusion.

Within the final climactic part of the story, Mark dramatizes in detail how Jesus Christ, the Child of God, was betrayed, abandoned, and denied by Jesus' chosen disciples;[15] how Jesus was ridiculed and condemned to death by the religious authorities for claiming to be the Christ—that is, the Messiah;[16] and even how Jesus felt himself to have been abandoned by God (15:34).[17]

It is also in the crucifixion scene that the contrast between Mark's presentation of Jesus and the traditional expectation of a victorious Messiah are most strongly stressed. The inscription on the cross, "the Ruler of the Jews" (15:26), and the taunt of the chief priests, "Let the Christ, the Ruler of Israel, come down from the cross" (15:32), bring into vivid focus the paradox of Mark's claim: The crucified one is the one proclaimed Messiah.

3. Interpretive Framework: Blood Covenant and Ransom

The question of how Mark interpreted Jesus' death is a many-sided one. It is also a question that provokes more than one answer. Here we can explore only certain lines that appear to be the most important as a preparation for our interpretive task, which will come in the next chapter.

First, it is important to be clear that, despite the unrelenting soberness of Mark's presentation, this author understood Jesus' death as a way to vindication. Further, though the motif of following Jesus' way receives much more extensive attention than does the question of what Jesus as the Christ has done for us, this latter theme is at the foundation of the story and of the faith that it reflects. As John Knox said, speaking of the early Christian faith generally, unless something had been done "for us" in the death of Christ, it could not have been important as a disclosure of God's love, which could then become a model for our way of life.[18]

Still, there are few explicit references to Jesus' death as an act that was done "for others." The narrative of Jesus' death refers to the cross as an act of faithfulness to God's mission in the world, but only indirectly, by the way scripture is used to shape and interpret the story. Psalms 22 and 69, especially, have been drawn upon to cast meaning on this event. The explicit rendering of Jesus' death as atonement or as vindication against the forces of evil does, however, appear earlier at key points to provide for the reader a framework within which to interpret Jesus' death.

There are not many references to what later came to be called atonement theology in this Gospel. But this motif is present, very clearly, in the important passage about the Last Supper, especially in the statement, "This is my blood of the covenant, which is poured out for many" (14:24 RSV). These solemn words speak of Jesus' death as a sacrifice that inaugurates a new covenant, just as sacrifice had been associated with earlier covenant ceremonies. The reader might hear in this passage an echo of Exodus 24:8, where Moses throws blood on the people at the conclusion of a covenant ceremony. Though the parallel is not a close one, in this period some Jewish readers of the Exodus passage connected it with the atoning and reconciling functions of sacrifice, and Christian readers of the Hebrew scriptures may well have made a similar connection.[19] For centuries, readers of Mark have also seen an allusion to Isaiah 53:12: "one bore the sins of many." This connection may also have been made by Mark and the first readers of the Gospel.[20]

Mark 14:24 is the only passage in the Gospel where the term *covenant* is used, but in Mark's usage the phrase "realm of God" fills much of its function.[21] God was understood to accept the blood or life of the sacrifice as a gift that inaugurated the new covenant-community relationship with God. Recent studies have made clear how this theological view of sacrifice interpenetrates with a sociological one, in which the death of the victim absorbs and deflects the violent and destructive urges of the community that offers the sacrifice.[22] Though the function of satisfying or serving as a catharsis for the inner destructive urges of the Christian community cannot be ruled out in Mark, the pattern of the narrative shapes a different emphasis. The shortcomings of the church are strongly emphasized, but violence as such is ascribed principally to outsiders or opponents (an exception is 14:47).

This fact leads us to the second image this Gospel uses to interpret the death of Jesus: the ransom motif. The saying in Mark 10:45 ("For even the Human One came not to be served but to serve, and to give his life as a ransom for many") comes at the culminating point of the teaching about discipleship that follows the third passion prediction. It is the final word about Jesus' death, which has been the focus of the long passage from 8:27 to 10:45.

A "ransom" is familiar to us as a payment to kidnappers. This use was also familiar in the ancient world. Julius Caesar, for example, was kidnapped and held for ransom early in his career. But the more common usages were for the setting free of either captives or slaves. The immediate force of this metaphor, when it is turned to religious usage, therefore, is that of freedom, of being set free from bondage.[23] The ransom language of Mark has parallels in the literature of the struggles of the Jews in Maccabean times. These parallels are especially close in IV Maccabees, a hellenistic Jewish writing probably from the same general time as Mark. For instance, in IV Maccabees 6:29 we read: "Let my blood serve for their purification, and accept my life as a ransom for them."[24]

It would be a mistake to distinguish too sharply between the images of sacrifice and ransom. Both express the conviction that the costly gift of a life may be liberating for those who come within its field of force. Though such images are not frequent in Hebrew scriptures, perhaps because of their strong opposition to human sacrifice, they were widespread in the world in which the author of Mark lived.

Scholars have differed and do differ sharply on the extent to which the language of sacrifice and ransom can be ascribed to Jesus himself.[25] We cannot go into this question, except to say that it is not at all surprising that Christians, in the light of their understanding of the cross and resurrection, said many things about Jesus that he would not have said about himself. As for the Gospel of Mark, clearly the author presupposes these meanings of sacrifice and ransom without having to reflect about them.

Of course, the context in which Mark uses these motifs has a bearing on their meanings. The overall framework of the Gospel is one of conflict. It is not unreasonable to see the conflict image as the dominant one for Mark's interpretation of Jesus' death, as it is for the encounter with demonic opposition earlier in the Gospel. Elisabeth Schüssler Fiorenza, for example, comments on 10:45 that it "does not speak of a liberation from sin but of making free citizens of many."[26] That is, for Mark the emphasis was not on atonement for sin as a way to meet the demands of divine justice so much as on liberation from oppressive forces.

Mark is not concerned to sort out these different emphases. No thought is given, for instance, to the question concerning to whom the ransom was paid. But the small amount of space given to these images of sacrifice and ransom is not a sign that they are unimportant as the story unfolds. On the contrary, they are powerful images that provide much of the energy of the narrative. They are not examined because they are largely taken for granted. As images, they invite the hearer to come into a field of force in which God's loving concern works to set people free and to reconcile them to God's own self and to one another. How these images of sacrifice and ransom, so strange to our world, can expand our hearers' worlds as they grapple with the meaning of suffering is a question taken up in our next chapter.

4. Tensions in Mark's Story

Lest we "spiritualize" this ancient hope for freedom, we would do well to remember that many early Christians saw their situation and their Christ in terms of a struggle between the weak and the strong in a socio-political sense. They believed in the reversal of these power roles through the intervention of God, an intervention now promised, or even begun, they believed, in the action of Jesus before his death, in God's action in the resurrection of Jesus, and in the destruction of the Temple. This expectation, that God would rescue the weak from the power of their strong opponents, is a principal theme of apocalyptic literature (such as Daniel and Revelation). The use of apocalyptic terms like *realm of God, resurrection,* and *the Human One* shows how fundamental the language of apocalypticism was for early Christianity, and also for the Gospel of Mark, which includes the "little apocalypse" (Mark 13).

Placing the paradoxical event of the cross in the center of Mark's story indicates that apocalyptic language has been shifted from its original locus—namely, the final triumph of God in the resurrection of the dead, to a new location in the cross—without, however, abandoning the resurrection.[27] In Mark's Gospel, however, it is Jesus' death that is understood as the eschatological event, signifying God's defeat of the powers of evil. This paradoxical location of the divine victory in the cross is at the heart of Mark's way of telling the story of Jesus. In a different tradition from that of Mark, we see this development already in Paul.

Tension in this apocalyptic vision is strong in Mark. Mark 13, for example, is directed in part against wrong apocalyptic hopes. But Mark 13, including its warnings against false expectations, is a proclamation of hope. As James M. Robinson says, "In the resurrection the force of evil is conclusively broken and the power of God's reign is established in history."[28] At the same time, "the struggle between the Spirit and Satan continues in the history of the church."[29] For the present, the way of suffering and the cross is the only true path for those who follow Jesus, but a decisive victory for God lies in the near future. As Eduard Schweizer puts it, "Thus keen anticipation and glad hope characterize the attitude of the Church toward history despite all the suffering. . . . The goal is the power and glory of God and the return of his chosen people."[30] When we allow the note of final victory to sound in this way in our interpretation, Mark's Gospel encourages the reader to be more conscious of hope and victory than it seems to when read only as a critical rejection of an apocalyptic vision.[31]

There is a similar tension in the interpretation of the portrayal of the disciples—particularly the twelve[32]—in Mark, which is pretty much a story of their inability to understand Jesus.[33] This negative portrait of the twelve serves to highlight the true path that is shown by Jesus, both in his deeds and in his words about following him. On Donahue's reading, discipleship in Mark is not exclusively linked to following Jesus. Ultimately it is a matter of "doing the will of God."[34] That is to say, the immediate existential traits of suffering as Jesus suffered are, to put it strongly, incidental. The heart of the matter is not "suffering" but "doing God's will." Mark's story of Jesus, however, shows that "doing God's will" can lead to "suffering." The costliness of discipleship, the way of the cross, and the inevitability of suffering, therefore, are at the heart of Mark's teaching about being a follower of Jesus. This story is full of the tension between conventional strength and the giving up of oneself that is called for by God's mission in the world. In contrast to Jesus, the disciples serve as a clear reminder of how easy it is even for those close to Jesus to miss the point of Jesus' teaching and example and to choose instead the way of conventional strength.

In such a polarized portrayal of discipleship, the "disciples" (or "the twelve") represent the undesirable and failing characteristics of discipleship, in contrast to the more authentic form of discipleship represented by other "followers."[35] The Gospel narrative offers to the reader of its own time, and of any time, a sobering and uncompromising challenge and reminder of the threat against Jesus and his way that can and does emerge from within the inner circle of those who bear Jesus' name.

Yet, that is not the whole story of the disciples in Mark. For one thing, there are suggestions in Mark that what the disciples of Jesus do not understand before his death and resurrection will become clear later. This seems to be assumed in 9:9-13 for Peter, James, and John with their understanding of the Transfiguration. Even clearer is 13:9-13, for it speaks of the disciples, to whom the passage is addressed, as testifying with great courage for their faith. When these suggestions are taken seriously as part of Mark's story, the misunderstanding by the disciples is seen as part of the unfinished nature of the story. The disciples' story appears to continue beyond the end of the Gospel.

To most readers, therefore, the disciples appear in Mark's story as ambiguous figures, rather than clear failures. As Elizabeth Struthers Malbon puts it, the Markan story, by portraying Jesus' followers as *"fallible* followers," presses on the reader the constant risk of failing always to be a loyal follower.[36] From this angle of vision, the disciples lead the reader into the complexity of the life of following Jesus. They cannot understand Jesus before his death, and there is no assurance that they will wholly understand him afterward. They show elements of insight even from the beginning, especially since they do recognize Jesus' greatness (4:41 and 6:51-52), and share in his work (6:7; compare 13:32-37). That is not enough, but it is a beginning. As Vernon K. Robbins has pointed out, the disciples would be seen as generalized figures who represent the difficulty of responding wholeheartedly to the challenge of Jesus.[37] Mark's message is that to follow Jesus is not an easy way, even for those with all the advantages of the original disciples. It is in the light of this story of Jesus' death and of his followers that readers of Mark are called to examine themselves.

5. Mark's Ending

We must now turn to another striking feature of Mark's Gospel—namely, its much-debated ending. In most modern editions of the New Testament, the text of Mark breaks off with the portrayal of the women fleeing in fear after encountering the angel, or young man, at the empty tomb (16:8). Although scholars of the stature of Rudolf Bultmann and Phillip Vielhauer have held that Mark originally had a report of resurrection appearances,[38] most interpreters of Mark today hold that the author intended the story to end with 16:8. What once seemed to modern readers a difficult or impossible ending is now almost universally taken to be the intended conclusion of the work.

What does the ending mean? Our answer depends on how we answer a different kind of question. What kind of story is the Gospel of Mark? How does it speak to the hearer? How does it draw readers into its story line and make its effect? Stories require time, so that they play "anticipation against realization, arousing expectation and providing fulfillment, presenting possibilities and offering resolutions."[39] The movement of anticipation and realization connects the reader's world with that of the story; both are worlds of continuing time. As it may in any story, the time of Mark's story extends beyond the end of the plotted narrative. The anticipated reunion of the disciples with Jesus in Galilee is the "real" end of the story.[40] That does not mean that Mark is a story with a simple "happy ending" or resolution. Though the story points forward to the reunion of the disciples with Jesus, it does not bring the reader into that time. The reader is left in the difficult world in which the disciples are left. The Gospel leaves us with unfulfilled expectations and in an open present.

This openness is created by ending the story with the flight of the women who had visited the tomb and without any narrative of the risen Jesus' appearance to the disciples in Galilee. Does this "silence" mean that the disciples never met or reunited with the risen Jesus?[41] Or is the ending another instance of the effort Mark expects the reader to make to fill in parts of the story that are left unnarrated? The thrust of the total narrative leads the reader to expect that the misunderstandings of the disciples will be overcome.[42] From this point, one may go more than one way. Some conclude that the ending is ironic: It does not mean what it literally says, and we may know that the women, in spite of their initial failure, did communicate their message—of the resurrection and of the forthcoming meeting in Galilee—to the disciples.[43]

Similarly, but even more strongly, Schüssler Fiorenza argues that the women were, rightly, afraid of being found at the tomb, for if they were, they would have been associated with the newly executed criminal. Their silence, however, was a silence about making any *public* report. They are presented as model disciples, and we are to understand that they did report the message of the angel about the resurrected Jesus, but only to the other *disciples*.[44] "Mark 16:7 and 8b, therefore, are not to be related as command and disobedience of the command, but as command and obedience which brings the message to special designated persons but does not inform anyone else."[45] Here, as elsewhere, the women represent true discipleship; it is the men disciples who fail. Schüssler Fiorenza sees the contrast between women and men disciples as confronting the church of the author's time with the challenge of a form of discipleship that rejected hierarchy and domination. The women are properly emphasized because in Mark's view, "Those who are the farthest from the center of religious and political power, the slaves, the children, the gentiles, the women, become the paradigm of true discipleship."[46]

Thomas Boomershine, however, argues that the women are presented to elicit the reader's sympathy but are also portrayed as thoroughly wrong in not risking a proclamation of the resurrection. This view shifts attention away from the consequences of the women's silence within the narrative setting and focuses instead on the faith or weakness of the reader or hearer of the Gospel. Mark's ending calls the reader to *repent* of fearful silence.[47]

For Dan Via, on the other hand, the ambiguity of the ending is of a piece with a paradox of revelation/conceal-ment that pervades the entire Gospel. Before the resurrec-tion, Jesus teaches the disciples plainly, but they consistently misunderstand. The resurrection changes the situation of the disciples, but not absolutely. Christians live in a time before the final consummation, when ambiguity remains. They are still prey to false christs (13:5-6, 21-22) and misunderstanding. The women's silence is a sign that for the time of the Church revelation retains an element of concealment or mystery.[48]

These readings of the end of Mark, despite their differences, all stress the linkage between the story of Jesus' death and the lack of any account of the appearance of the risen Jesus. By ending in this way, Mark releases the reader—who *has heard* the angel's Easter message even if the disciples have *not!*—into a world in which Jesus was put to death. In that world, the reader will face the same forces that Jesus faced. And in that world, Jesus' faithfulness is the model for his followers, who must take the angel's message of Jesus' resurrection and of his promised appearance at its word.

This Gospel offers the reader a strange kind of presence of Jesus, one that does not simply assure the believer that "things are basically all right." Mark does promise the reader an experience of presence, but it leaves the reader anticipating its fulfillment.[49] Mark invites the reader to reach, in the story line, beyond the plotted narrative, beyond the moment of the women's silence, and imaginatively to take part in a reunion of the disciples with the risen Jesus.

That does not require that the disciples become "infallible" followers. The story is an open one at this point, as at so many others.[50] However, the context within which the follower of Jesus lives, as well as his or her view, is altered. As Eduard Schweizer interprets Mark, though Jesus is not present as he was during his ministry (nor as he will be at the end), the time between Easter and *Parousia* is "a period of probation, full of tribulation, yet not of total desolation." Jesus is "in some different way, still present in his word . . . even more, Jesus will still be present to them after Easter in his name. . . . Finally, he promised them that the Spirit will teach those who do not know what to say (13:11)," so that Jesus is "absent yet present."[51] For Schweizer, the disciples are in a changed world. How that change could be interpreted in the modern world is a question to be addressed in our next chapter.

From Mark's Gospel, we understand that the moment of faith belongs to a larger story, which includes promises for the future (Mark 13) as well as recollections of Jesus' words in parables and other sayings (Mark 4) that orient the difficult present and make it part of a larger whole. Nevertheless, this Gospel does not lead a reader into an easy world. Mark's story looks forward to a final resolution, but the Gospel narrative resolutely holds the reader in the difficult present. The present has been transformed by the reader's participation in the story, but the reader is left in the same "in between" position in which the Gospel leaves the disciples.

The tensions in Mark's story are clearly meant to open the listener to a world of faith. The image that dominates the moment of faith in Mark is the story of the death of Jesus. This story allows nothing else to detract from it or to lessen the total commitment called for in faith.

6. Jesus' Death and Our Knowledge of God

The images of sacrifice and ransom, the apocalyptic vision, and the ending of Mark's Gospel are problematic for many modern readers, even those who enter sympathetically into the many hymns based on their themes. Questions about the moral character of a God who requires sacrifice or ransom, especially *human* sacrifice or ransom, are not new or recent. A God who has the power to defeat all evil in the world and usher in a new age free from evil, but has never yet exercised that power, perplexed Christians from the beginning and is either incredible or loathsome to modern and postmodern readers. And who can fathom the story of a God who sends a faithful servant to suffer the cruel death of crucifixion, only to send an angel to tell his followers that he has "risen"? Serious engagement with these images, visions, and narratives, problematic as they are to us, can lead us to expand our understanding of God and of how God is active in the world.

Mark's work is full of irony and paradox, and nowhere is this more profoundly at work than at the central point of the role of God in the narrative, for God is inconceivably great and powerful. This was certainly the conviction of the author, a conviction that the audience was expected to share. Yet, God's presence and power are decisively represented by Jesus' death. As Donahue puts it:

> This Jesus is a figure of power in conflict with the powers
> of the cosmos and of hardness of heart (3:5; 6:52; 8:17). Yet

broken, and abandoned by the source of all power, he dies as one who is radically powerless. During his life his power is manifest yet hidden.[52]

How the climactic moment of Jesus' presence—the moment of his death—relates to our knowledge of God is central to Mark. Like the other questions we have studied, it can be answered with more than one emphasis. If Jesus' message, life, and death are fully summarized in the cross, then the cross becomes the revelation of God's own way and character. The "weakness" of Jesus reflects the reality that God's power faces real resistance, which prevents God from compelling belief and overpowering the oppressive forces. That is why God does not stoop to exercise their style and means of power. As Rhoads and Michie put it, "God also wills, in this first stage, to establish his will over humans, but not by force. God's rule is such that people, including the agents of God's rule, are to use power to serve others, not to force and oppress them."[53] This vision of God's power manifested in the cross stands in tension with the different vision of God's apocalyptic triumph in the future (a tension we discuss in the next chapter).

In Mark, Jesus, who is portrayed as a servant, is the decisive revelation of God. Mark's view of Jesus' relation to God is usually approached through the complex route of the study of the so-called christological titles (such as "Messiah," "Child of God," and "the Human One"), each of which expresses a different aspect of representing God. Our quest, however, lies at a different point—namely, with the question of how to relate a narrative moment to a larger framework. Those who stress the narrative moment of the cross as the decisive revelation tend to relativize what they regard as remnants of another view of power that appear, for instance, in miracle stories or in the apocalyptic judgment anticipated in Mark 13. In this view, the decisive revelation of God in the cross overrides the image of God's power as being coercive.[54]

Those who see the narrative moment of the cross in a larger narrative context see a more complex situation. Jesus is indeed the decisive revelation and is normative for the present task of the church and the believer. The total picture of the Gospel of Mark shows, however, that this "power in weakness" is embedded in a vision that expects God's total and decisive victory, which will completely disarm God's opponents and render them impotent. Then the interpretive issues (which we shall address in the next chapter) are: Can the hope and expectation of faith rely on a final exercise of coercive power, as in traditional apocalyptic literature and in much modern theology? Or can the vision of God's power disclosed in the story of Jesus, and especially in his death, be taken as the decisive clue to the way of working of a God who freely offers nonviolent love to the world?

Interpreters who approach Mark from this point of view may also point out that we may easily misread the "weakness" of Jesus. Reviewing the figure of Jesus as he moves through the narrative, and recollecting the strong but not victorious figures who appear, for instance, in Greek tragedy, one may conclude that Jesus is intended as a figure of strength.[55] Further, such interpreters may note that, though Jesus is at the center of Mark's drama, Jesus himself in this narrative emphasizes that God is sovereign and that even God's Child does not know the secrets of God (13:32).[56] This reading finds Mark more open than he is often taken to be, since Mark leaves the reader with the unfinished task of relating the two visions of divine power that are worked together in the narrative.

7. Conclusion

Mark's Gospel demands much of the reader, not only to fill in parts of the story that extend beyond the plot,[57] but also to establish a perspective from which to read the Gospel. The hearer's or reader's particular situation, interacting with the Gospel, contributes to the way the Gospel is read. Are we going to focus on the elements of paradox and reversal, the unprotectedness of both Jesus and his followers, and the identification of Jesus' way of the cross as the only clue to the divine nature and purpose? Or will we set the elements of paradox and reversal more fully into a narrative time of memory, hope, and decision, giving the precarious present in which the gospel is proclaimed a fuller orientation of explicit and conscious hope?

These two ways of reading Mark are actually very closely related. Each sees what the other sees, but each asks the reader to be grasped by a different combination of elements of the complex story. In chapter 5 we propose ways of preaching that arise out of an encounter with this complex and challenging Gospel.

CHAPTER FIVE

TOWARD A THEOLOGY OF SUFFERING

Interpreting Mark's Story of Jesus' Death

1. Issues in Telling the Story

As we saw in the previous chapter, Mark's story is dense and full of mystery. Whatever light it throws on our own understanding of suffering will not come by way of oversimplification. On the contrary, it can help us to see the oversimplifications that so easily come into our own thinking. In particular, many people today try to deal with suffering in a world that for them is without God. Mark can help us to see that the world is not without God, and yet that the simple versions of how God is related to suffering do not work. We cannot enter directly into Mark's world, but, by holding it in creative contrast with our own, we may be able to see possibilities in our own that have escaped us. It is with this perspective that we turn to the story of Jesus' death as Mark tells it.

The story of the death of a friend is hard enough to tell, but how do you tell the story of the death of one who had divine favor as God's "beloved Child" (Mark 1:11)? And if the way of death is ignominious and repulsive,[1] how could one speak of it at all, let alone give it meaning? As if that were not enough, the story that had to be told was the story of the violent death of the one who was supposed to inaugurate God's final, triumphant rule in the world. But that is precisely what the earliest Gospel attempts to do: to tell the story of Jesus of Nazareth, the Messiah and Child of

God (Mark 1:1), who suffered many things, was rejected, and was condemned to death on a cross.[2] The news that "Jesus of Nazareth, who was crucified," *had been raised* (16:6) gave hope, but Mark's way of telling this part of the story added to the mystery, as we showed in the previous chapter.

This story remains just as much a mystery for us today as for the Christians for whom the Gospel of Mark was written. In some respects, Mark's story of Jesus' death is *more* of a mystery to us. The Markan community drew upon traditions that interpreted Jesus' death in terms of a "ransom" myth (10:45) and a covenant sealed with blood (14:24). Neither of these ways of interpreting the cross can be entered into easily by Christians today—at least not by those who belong to Western cultures. Although the "ransom" myth and the "blood covenant" are not the primary symbols in Mark's interpretation of Jesus' death, they were living traditions available to the Markan community in a way that they are not for many Christians today.

For other reasons, Christians today may be less able to appreciate the depth of the mystery of the cross than were the earliest Christians. The latter knew well the Jewish expectation of the coming of the Messiah, who would defeat God's enemies and the enemies of Israel. Early Christians, therefore, could feel the weight of the story of the cross crushing their hope that Jesus would be this Messiah.[3] Two millennia after Christianity went its own way, separate from and over against Judaism, it is difficult for us to enter into this hope of our Jewish ancestors in the faith and to appreciate their sense of defeat at the crucifixion of Jesus, who they had hoped was the Messiah.

There has been a loss not only of the Jewish roots of messianic expectation, but also of the belief that God's emissaries will be protected by God from defeat. To put it cynically, we have come to expect the good to die young. The story of Jesus' death fits well this expectation. Given the political situation at the time, we are not surprised at the Roman execution of an itinerant Jewish charismatic, whose popularity could be construed as a threat to peace and

97

stability in the Syrian province of the early Roman Empire.[4] That is what one would expect, at any rate, if one lacks confidence in the belief that God protects the "good" and defeats their enemies.

It is precisely this belief that many Christians, as well as Jews, find difficult to accept today, as the popularity of the book by Rabbi Harold S. Kushner, *When Bad Things Happen to Good People,*[5] so dramatically attests. It appears that God allows the innocent to suffer, or fails to prevent their suffering—or perhaps even causes their suffering as part of some grand scheme beyond our comprehension. Moreover, the ending of Mark's Gospel is so troubling because it concludes without telling of the reunion of the disciples with the risen Jesus, leaving the disciples—and Mark's hearers and readers—in the same disordered world that brought Jesus to the cross.[6]

On the other hand, the primary message of Mark's story of Jesus' death, expressed by placing together predictions of the passion-resurrection and discussions of the nature and cost of discipleship (8:27–10:52), seems to hold more promise for the modern reader, for it is relatively easy to understand selfless endurance of suffering and rejection, even to the point of dying, out of a devotion to God's purposes and a desire to see them actualized "on earth as in heaven." We can admire Jesus' resolve not to be turned aside from the path that lay before him; we can also admire his resistance to every effort to rescue him from death on a cross.[7] Precisely in this resolve and resistance we can see a Jesus who practiced what he preached: Those who try to save their lives will lose them, but those who lose their lives for God's sake will save them (see Mark 8:35).[8] This portrait of Jesus can serve as a powerful model for those who need the courage to "make a last stand" in response to what they perceive to be the call of God.

Even here, however, difficulties remain. For one thing, Mark's story of Jesus' death implies that physical force is not to be used in resistance to unjust governing authorities, a policy questioned by Christians of different ideological persuasions (but particularly by some Christian liberationists). In addition, although the teaching that the ideal form of discipleship is self-denial is a needed corrective for those who tend to put themselves before all others, it has also been a less than liberating word among women and nonwhites, for whom it has meant continued oppression. Moreover, the ideal of self-denial offers no word of grace, much less liberation, to men and women who are unable to fulfill the ideal—that is, it is a curse and not a blessing to the majority of Christians.[9] Self-sacrifice and martyrdom as forms of devotion to God's purposes have brought us the inspiring, liberated, and liberating lives of such "saints" as Polycarp and Francis in the ancient church, and Martin Luther King, Jr., and Mother Teresa in our own time, as well as Mahatma Gandhi who, although not a Christian, was deeply influenced by the stories of Jesus in the Gospels. But the glorification of self-sacrifice and the elevation of martyrdom as the purest form of devotion to God's purposes have also led to the justification of the use of violence and terror to further what are perceived to be God's causes, as we have witnessed in times of war—not only in the acts of war by our enemies but also in our own nation's acts of war. Finally, the promise that those who deny themselves and endure to the end will be saved (Mark 13:13b) raises the painful question of why God seemingly allows or actually causes suffering, and makes one ask whether God is unwilling or unable to prevent it in the first place.

2. Approaches to Suffering in Mark's World and Ours

For preaching, the central question Mark's story of the death of Jesus poses is that of God's role in relationship to suffering and victory over it. Christians have traditionally tried to understand suffering in the framework of God's rule or sovereignty. Some believe that God is the all-powerful, holy, and just creator of the world—and that God is totally loving as well! These two beliefs are compatible with each other, and they can account for the experience of suffering, only as long as suffering can be explained as a consequence of human evil or as a helpful aspect of the process of human growth. Then suffering can be understood as divine punishment, testing, or discipline. It can be seen as God's punishment of wrongdoing and viewed in a moral sense as something that we bring on ourselves. Even innocent suffering, which cannot have this kind of meaning, can be seen as a test or discipline in which the innocent sufferer will be vindicated and the suffering compensated for, even rewarded, in the future. One can also acknowledge that some suffering comes from a purpose of God that we cannot understand.

Many people in our own time have simply given up all belief in God because these traditional explanations of suffering do not seem to make sense in the face of the immensity and the meaninglessness of suffering as we see it in our world today. The Bible is often read as if it uniformly supported the belief in a God who is in total control. But this kind of faith, deeply ingrained as it is in the Christian tradition, was questioned long ago, especially as an explanation of undeserved, inordinate, or innocent suffering. The book of Job and the Gospel of Mark are classic challenges to any simple belief that suffering is the will of God. The rediscovery of Job's challenge to traditional religious explanations of suffering is a sure sign of the quest for a fresh understanding of suffering.[10] Job differs from Mark by its strong element of outrage and protest—an element that is not, however, entirely lacking in Mark (see pp. 107-08 and 115-20).

Job's suffering is presented as a matter between Job and God; others enter into the story only to set the frame for this central interaction. Mark, however, tells of Jesus' suffering, not as the fate of a single individual alone, but within the context of the fundamental interrelatedness of all persons, brought out pointedly by the images of ransom and sacrifice.[11] It is no accident that, among the biblical writings, Job and Mark have been the focus of new and deeply probing study,[12] precisely because in our own day, as in the days of Job and Mark, traditional explanations of suffering have been thrown into complete disarray.[13]

Those who have lost confidence in traditional ways of thinking about suffering may find it easy to enter into one of three fairly simple solutions that were already explored in early Christianity. One is that of Stoicism, which influenced ancient Christianity chiefly at a time later than the New Testament period, but can be seen already in the "code of household duties" in I Peter 2:11–3:7 and in some of the military metaphors of the New Testament.[14] The Stoic is convinced that true freedom, and so also true happiness, lies entirely within a person's moral character[15] and in being detached from the causes of suffering—external circumstances and Fate or Fortune (an ancient deity).[16] According to Dorothee Sölle, the Stoic's "instructions on how to overcome suffering present, on the one hand, possibilities for the avoidance of suffering and, on the other, use of unavoidable suffering."[17] The Stoic way of dealing with suffering, as Sölle points out, is to maintain inner "tranquillity" in the face of suffering (one's own as well as that of others) by affirming one's freedom in spite of the circumstance, so that suffering is not allowed to enter one's "soul"—as a result, the Stoic denies the reality of suffering.[18] Though this would be a badly oversimplified way of reading Mark, this "stoic" endurance no doubt has often been preached from texts like 8:34 ("Take up your cross . . .") and 13:13 ("The one who endures to the end will be saved . . .").

As the depth and extent of human uncertainty and insecurity have come home to us in the late twentieth century, with the telling of the full stories of the outrageous cruelty of slavery, the inhumanity of the treatment of Native Americans, the horrors of the holocaust suffered by Jews in Europe, and the nuclear holocaust suffered by Japanese civilians in Hiroshima and Nagasaki, as well as stories of other arbitrary and meaningless destructions of human life,[19] the stoic approach may have commended itself more and more, especially to Christians, for it offers a pattern by which many could live from day to day.[20] Perhaps that accounts in part for the continuing popularity of such comic strip characters as Ziggy and Charlie Brown. Many seem to identify with them and find a measure of hope for their own stoic survival through the lives of these two guileless, indomitable characters who, though constantly and unjustly "put upon in life," still manage in their own indefatigable ways to survive by accepting and enduring through suffering. But the dignity that stoicism gave to ancient Stoics, and that can be seen in Ziggy and Charlie Brown, was denied to black slaves, Jews in the Nazi death camps, and civilians in Hiroshima and Nagasaki, however they bore their suffering. To silence outrage over their suffering with a stoic response would only increase the evil of their suffering.

Another way of dealing with suffering when the traditional ways are shattered has been to turn to some form of apocalyptic hope for a reversal of the human condition, with the faith that soon it will all be different. Freedom from suffering can come, according to this alternative, only when God finally intervenes, destroys the evil world, and creates a new world in which nothing evil occurs.[21]

A related, but different, option is that of a gnostic dualism in which the world is depicted as not simply in the grip of evil but as itself inherently evil. In contrast to apocalypticists, gnostics do not await God's action in bringing history to a close but consider themselves utter "aliens" within the world and seek individual escape from it. As the "elect," whose true home is above but who are temporarily held hostage in the prison of flesh, they seek union with a transcendent "spiritual" reality.[22]

For preaching, the attractiveness of these apocalyptic and gnostic "solutions" to suffering is that they permit one to proclaim a very simple, direct, and uncomplicated message, filled with absolute assurances and unqualified confidence. Although Mark does not offer much of a base for the gnostic type of preaching, the apocalyptic type can be based especially on many sayings in Mark 13, though this is a very one-sided way to take them (as we shall show below). The appeal of such a message is that it is unencumbered by the need for both emotionally and intellectually satisfying answers for the insoluble, enigmatic ambiguities of life in this world and for the haunting questions of Job, which still plague any affirmation of the goodness, justice, and fairness of life lived in fidelity to God within this world. Yet, as appealing as these apocalyptic and gnostic forms of preaching are in offering simple "solutions" and absolute assurances, they raise as many questions as they "solve."

Preaching that promises a future or a transcendent, "spiritual" world free of suffering can easily imply that life in this present world, with all its suffering, is devoid of value and meaning. To the extent that it does imply this, the world is irredeemably evil, and the question of why an all-powerful and perfectly loving God created (or allowed) life in this present world in the first place is posed in the most radical way. One reply, characteristic of gnosticism, is to deny that the supreme, true God is the creator of this present world. Few preachers today go so far in spelling out the implications of this promise, but neither do they give sufficient reasons for why this is not the conclusion to which it inevitably leads. The inconsistency of this kind of preaching—or its "failure of nerve"—is also seen in the way in which Christian gnostics, who since the first century have preached freedom from the clutches of this world and full, transcendent union with a "spiritual" world beyond, have never quite been able to disengage themselves totally from life in this present world and to shake off its vestiges as they put on the "spiritual" garments of life in the so-called world beyond.[23]

Moreover, this kind of preaching has never delivered on its promises, a criticism to which its apocalyptic form is particularly subject. Almost two thousand years have passed since an early Christian apocalyptic preacher first proclaimed the imminent end of this evil-possessed world and the creation of a "new heaven and a new earth." While, in every generation since, an apocalyptic cousin has continued to preach the same message, the world still goes on and no "new heaven and new earth" have appeared on the cosmic horizon. Some modern-day Christian apocalyptic preachers see a sign of the coming of this new creation in the nuclear holocaust that appears to them to be imminent—and, with some hermeneutical effort, they might be able to claim support for their vision in the book of Revelation and in II Peter 3:1-13. But support would be more difficult to secure from Mark (and Paul), whose commitment to a final "apocalypse" is not as strong as that of these modern preachers, and whose vision of the final "apocalypse" is much less negative. A hopeful sign for Christianity is the continued preference in the "mainline" churches for a vision in which this present world, even with all of its undeniable evil, remains a place where the promise of God's realm still has a future.

As we read Mark from the perspective of our own time, it is painfully clear that God's transformation of the world, begun through the life and death of Jesus, has not been completed. Its progress has been slow, and at times negligible. And the present capacity of the nuclear arsenals of the world powers to destroy the whole earth threatens to thwart God's purposes permanently, so far as the course of events on this planet is concerned. Our distance in time and culture from the foundational events of our faith makes it impossible for us to force the exact structure of New Testament faith into life again, much as we might like to. But we can look into its expressions of faith for elements that open a new path of response to our situation. Mark is of great help here. Though this Gospel can be read as affirming an apocalyptic way of dealing with suffering, as well as a stoic way of acceptance, Mark can also, and more profoundly, be read as posing a challenge to the under-standing of God's role in suffering and in victory over it as it is understood in these perspectives.

This Gospel leads its readers into the world of Jesus' suffering and death, and of the disciples' struggle with those events as well as with their own suffering, to show a way of faith in the midst of the searing questions that suffering raises. Mark does not spell out this faith in all its aspects—that was not needed. Our task is not so much to repeat this faith in God and in Jesus as the Christ but, rather, to allow it to enter into creative contrast with other ways of understanding God's role in suffering and in victory over it.

3. Ways of Dealing with Suffering in Mark

As Mark tells the story of Jesus, three ways of dealing with suffering are set out: eliminating suffering; evading suffering; and meeting suffering directly, to the end—death, even death on a cross—and without mitigation. For Mark, Jesus models the way to follow. The disciples, however, serve as a reminder of how hard a way it is and of how easy it is to evade the harshness of life, especially in the name of faith, religion, or God's cause. In Mark, the disciples typify traditional, and quite understandable, ways of responding to suffering: hoping for the elimination of suffering by God's swift and all-powerful intervention and evading suffering. Although Mark's Gospel holds up Jesus' way for emulation, it does not wholly reject the others.

If we follow Mark's own account, we see that Jesus gathered disciples during a period when his power over evil forces was demonstrated by his bringing relief to sufferers through a ministry of miraculous healing (1:16–8:26). One does not find in Mark a stoic willingness to be content with the existence of suffering or a passive acceptance of it. On the contrary, Jesus seeks its elimination by struggling against forces that cause others to suffer and by sending the disciples out to do the same (3:13-19 and 6:6*b*-13). Moreover, Jesus, in apocalyptic fashion, proclaims that the coming sufferings of "the End" will cease when the "Human One" arrives on the clouds "with great power and glory" to gather the "elect" (13:26-27). Jesus also offers the assurance that "the End" is near, even though "the hour" cannot be known (13:28-37). Hoping and working for the removal of suffering, and the correlative belief in God's power of intervention, therefore, cannot in and of themselves be wrong.

The second and sharply contrasting way of dealing with suffering is by evading it. In the Gospel of Mark, this way is often associated exclusively with the disciples, and in one important respect it is the way they exemplify. But it should be noted that Mark's portraits of both Jesus and the disciples show ambiguity toward the evasion of suffering. In itself it is not wrong to avoid suffering. That is a very natural human response and a way of affirming that we are not intended to suffer. What makes it wrong is the denial of human interconnectedness and the lack of trust in a power to see us through suffering.

The disciples are ambiguous figures when it comes to recognizing their interconnectedness. They seem to loathe the thought of *Jesus'* suffering (8:31-33; 9:2-13, 30-32); yet, they are at times ready to suffer with him (10:38-39*a* and 14:31) and to risk taking up arms in Jesus' defense (14:47). But in the end they take to flight (14:50).

Jesus' ambivalence is no less dramatic. To be sure, Jesus rejects Peter's temptation to turn aside from a path that would lead to suffering, rejection, and death (8:31-33); and Jesus rejects the attempts to get him to demonstrate his power by saving himself and coming down from the cross so that mocking onlookers might "see and believe" (15:29-32). But Jesus also struggles with the question of whether to avoid suffering. According to the Gethsemane narrative (14:32-42), Jesus asks God for an alternative to death on a cross before expressing a willingness to do whatever would further the establishment of God's purposes "on earth as in heaven."[24] Mark's Gethsemane story, which illustrates the saying of Jesus in 8:35, implies that Jesus really could have played the coward and escaped crucifixion, leaving the fulfillment of God's purposes in suspension. Although Mark does not say this outright, without that assumption the story is inexplicable.

It would be wrong, however, to interpret Mark's view that the crucifixion accorded with God's "will" (14:32-42) as implying that all suffering is God's "will," much less that everything that happens necessarily accords with God's "omnipotent" will. Even the view that only through Jesus' crucifixion could God's purposes be fulfilled expresses the *hypothetical* necessity of Jesus' death, not that it was ordained from the beginning.[25] Much of Mark's story of Jesus makes little sense unless Jesus' death is to be considered genuinely contingent. The authorities could have accepted Jesus' call to repentance instead of taking action against him (see 11:27-33); or once Jesus was arrested, Pilate could have released him (see 15:6-15). "The betrayer" bears a curse and so, by implication, could also have acted otherwise (see 14:17-21). If Jesus' mission was to be accomplished, it was necessary *(dei)* for him to remain faithful to it throughout any circumstance, even the threat of execution on a cross. But since the governing authorities were determined to make and carry out such a threat, and since one of Jesus' disciples had decided to play "the betrayer," Jesus "must" die on a cross if God's purposes are to be achieved through him. The words of Jesus' prayer in Gethsemane—"All things are possible to [you]; remove this cup from me; yet not what I will, but what [you will]" (14:36 RSV)—suggest other contingencies: God could have prevented the death of Jesus, but could still have accomplished God's purposes through Jesus. If Jesus had not been willing to do whatever would fulfill God's purposes, God could have passed on the mission of accomplishing those purposes to someone else or could have abandoned the mission altogether. In each case, God's own decision, as well as Jesus', would have been involved.

So in Mark, it is not only the disciples who face the temptation to evade suffering, their own and that of others, but Jesus, too—and even God! Even the knowledge that Jesus' suffering accorded with God's "will" does not prevent an outcry of protest against God's abandonment, of which Jesus' death on the cross seemed to be a sign (15:34). That Luke, who portrays Jesus as the preeminent exemplar of the martyr's piety (Luke 23:44-46), did not preserve this outcry (and neither did John) suggests that at least one early Christian interpreter of Mark 15:34 read it, not as the beginning of a psalm of victory, but as a lament. What this protest and the scene in Gethsemane with the disciples make clear is that no one—especially God—ought to abandon people in their hour of suffering. And yet that is precisely what God appears to have done, if it was within God's power to rescue Jesus from death on a cross (see Mark 14:35-36)! Among the Synoptic Gospels, it is Mark who emphasizes the point that such a rescue was within God's power.[26] Of course, the evangelist knows, and the reader will soon learn, that God did effect a rescue of sorts, and a dramatic one at that—God resurrected the crucified Jesus (16:6)!

In Mark's Gospel, it is Jesus who depicts the third way of dealing with suffering—namely, the way of active endurance. Of course, the disciples also claim to be ready to follow Jesus, even to the point of enduring death for his sake,[27] but their deeds never match their expressed intentions.[28] And yet 13:9-13 suggests that the disciples later on come to be able to do so. And Jesus is portrayed as one who struggled with his own suffering, but who was willing to accept it for the sake of proclaiming the gospel of God's liberating rule in the world.[29]

Mark's story of Jesus' death implies that the motivation for choosing this way of dealing with suffering is not a stoic "apathy," which seeks psychic tranquillity under all circumstances—even in the face of great suffering, whether another's or one's own—nor is it a cynic "love of hardship," whose aim is to build character. Although elements of these perspectives cannot be completely excluded,[30] the motivation actively to endure suffering is located in Jesus' devotion to the mission of spreading the gospel of God's liberating rule in the world, which was more important than Jesus' safety. This way of dealing with suffering offers a view of life in which death—even death on a cross—is not the greatest evil that a person could suffer. It would be worse to compromise one's deepest commitments and highest hopes, in short, to turn away from the call and promise of God (8:34–9:1). In this sense, the similarity to cynic or stoic perspectives is closer. Yet the Jesus of Mark's story is constituted by his relatedness to other human beings and to God in a way that contrasts strongly to the self-sufficiency of the stoic or cynic.[31]

Sölle eloquently reminds us that "unconditional submission" fails to consider the duty to abolish suffering and its causes.[32] The way of submissiveness as the traditional Christian response to suffering finds some support in a certain interpretation of the story of Jesus' death (see I Pet. 2:13–3:7). But if we take Jesus in the Gospel of Mark as a model, we can see that enduring suffering need not mean passivity and nonresistance. On the contrary, in Mark, Jesus' voluntary endurance of suffering is an assertive, even aggressive, form of resistance. Jesus struggled against the suffering of others and its physical, personal, social, and "supernatural" causes. He is seen bringing comfort to those who mourn (5:21-43) and is characterized as a healer of those who are oppressed by physical and "supernatural" forces (3:7-12 and 6:53-56). One healing story depicts Jesus as extending this aspect of his ministry to a gentile woman—someone who was considered doubly "marginal" as gentile and as woman—and thereby opening the way to the emancipation of marginal persons from both physical and social oppression by creating liberating social structures, at least within the early church (7:24-30). This identification is emphasized in Jesus' table-fellowship with "tax collectors and sinners" (2:15-17) and again in the story of the woman who anoints Jesus "beforehand for burying," which would be told "wherever the gospel is preached in the whole world . . . in memory of her" (14:3-9 RSV).[33]

In Jesus' own suffering, endurance includes protest to God and defiance of the governing authorities. While accepting the call of God, Jesus expresses outrage at the price of devotion to God's purposes, an outrage that is addressed as much to God, whose call is uncompromising, as to the world, whose evil raises to the ultimate the cost of faithfulness.[34] And while submitting to the authority of Roman and Jewish officials, Jesus defies and resists their authority by being silent and unwilling to compromise his commitment to proclaiming God's sovereign and liberating rule in the world (see 14:60-62 and 15:2-5). So the endurance of suffering can also be a form of active resistance, leading to redemptive transformation.

Finally, it is important to remember that although Jesus entered the city of Jerusalem as one of the "marginal" people (a Galilean), nevertheless he brought with him a following and a reputation as a prophet. Jesus was not powerless, like the legendary Simon of Cyrene, a stranger to the city who had come "from the country," and who was compelled to carry Jesus' cross (15:21). Jesus had the freedom to choose "endurance" as a way of dealing with suffering; it was not forced upon him.

4. Suffering and God's Power

The Gospel of Mark holds these three approaches to suffering in creative contrast: the elimination of suffering through human action and, in the end, by God's swift intervention; the evasion of suffering, even at times seemingly by God; and the voluntary endurance of one's own suffering without mitigation, when needed to further the establishment of God's purposes. The traditional vision of the elimination of suffering by direct divine intervention does justice to only the first of these approaches. It is often overlooked, however, that even where one would most expect this view—namely, in the empty-tomb scene[35]—the element of direct divine intervention is muted by Mark's enigmatic ending, which relativizes this traditional vision of God. By postponing the divine victory to the future, Mark leaves the believer, at least for the present, in an "open," unfinished story. One might expect to find faith in direct divine intervention in the miracle traditions of the period in Mark's story of Jesus *prior* to the arrest, trials, and crucifixion (1:16–8:26).[36] Even here, however, God does not act *directly*, as one agent *alongside* others, but only *in and through* Jesus. Indeed, the only example of direct action by God in this section of Mark would seem to be the heavenly voice at Jesus' baptism (1:11; see also 9:7).

Mark, therefore, does not presuppose an image of God as "omnipotent." In the strict, traditional sense, this doctrine cannot be found anywhere in the Bible. Of course, much of the Bible supports the view that God has all the power needed to accomplish anything God chooses—that is, that no other power can successfully resist God. Typical in the New Testament is the view that "all things are possible" to God.[37] The traditional doctrine of "omnipotence," however, strictly means more than that. It implies that literally *all power is God's,* that in fact there are *no powers other than God.* This doctrine cannot be found in Mark. The whole Bible, for that matter, takes for granted the belief that demons, angels, human beings, and the rest of creation all have power beside God's. Hence God's power is exercised against real resistance, as Mark's story of Jesus' death dramatically illustrates. This story makes no sense unless it is assumed that Jesus' disciples, the governing authorities, and even Jesus himself really had power to *resist* and to *thwart* what God was trying to accomplish in and through Jesus.

When Jesus' proclamation (in deeds as well as in words) of God's liberating rule in the world meets with opposition, an opposition that would lead to Jesus' death, it appears as though God's power will be successfully resisted. When Jesus struggles with the threat to his own life that the continuation of his mission had brought, again it appears that God's efforts will be defeated, or at least that God will have to choose some other way to achieve God's purposes if Jesus does not continue. In the end, though, the death of Jesus is the result of genuine *resistance* to God's power. This resistance does not, however, prevent God from doing what God had decided to do in and through Jesus, even if God achieves it in a far less than ideal way—namely, through Jesus' crucifixion. God's power is supreme in the only truly meaningful sense, since God literally has an infinite number of ways ultimately to accomplish anything God chooses. No greater power than this is coherently conceivable![38]

We began with Mark's story of Jesus' death on the cross and asked what God appears to be like in its light. Approaching the question of God's role in suffering and in victory over it from this angle uncovers a dimension of Mark's passion narrative that is often overlooked. One can see in Mark's story of the cross that God, limited by the contingencies of the created order—the unpredictable actions of men[39] among the friends and foes of Jesus—does not act directly, as one agent alongside others, to bring about faith and victory over evil. When faith comes, it comes by means of a kind of "persuasion," as is illustrated by the centurion, who acknowledges the true identity of the crucified Jesus after seeing how Jesus died (15:39).

A traditional theist might point to the eclipse (15:33) and the rending of the Temple curtain (15:38) as evidence that God's victory over evil is through the exercise of direct divine power. How curious it is, then, that a God who is able to act in such a unilateral fashion did not (would or could not?) use that power to rescue Jesus from the cross! This failure to act is set forth in bold relief by the taunts of the chief priests and others.[40]

At this point, Mark implies that one form of victory over evil has been accomplished. That victory is to be located in Jesus' refusal to reject God's mission, whether at the urging of the disciples or under pressure from the religious and governing authorities, even in the face of the penalty of death. Apparent defeat is seen to be a victory when it is viewed in the light of Jesus' steadfast endurance and acceptance of God's mission. That is God's victory as well as Jesus', since it was God's mission that was at stake.[41]

This is no ordinary victory. For one thing, it comes with no little physical and existential pain. This raises serious questions for the reader. What person would wish another to suffer so in body and spirit? How much less would an all-loving God! Can we really believe that this is how God would have had Jesus' life turn out if God were in total control? Surely God's perfect love would earnestly desire that all sinners repent and accept the liberating word of one who represents God, rather than that Jesus be killed at their hands.[42] God does indeed desire repentance and does not will suffering for the innocent, but God's power could not attain God's purposes apart from Jesus' crucifixion, because God's power is limited by the genuine power of others to resist it. Whether that same divine power could have prevented Jesus' crucifixion, we do not know, since much would depend on the uses of power by others. In any case, Jesus' crucifixion happened; that much we do know.

Mark's passion narrative does not directly address our questions about divine power. The reader's questions raised above presuppose more reflective distance than Mark's story has. It is a story of the opening of possibility where no opening seems possible—an ironic contrast of the seemingly triumphant exercise of violent earthly power and the deeper story of how God's will was achieved in spite of real opposition. As we reflect about Mark's story of divine power with more reflective distance, we rightly infer that God's power is limited by the power of others. What might have happened if human beings had reacted differently to Jesus' words and deeds is not really in view in Mark's story.

The implication of Mark's story is that God accepted what happened as the unsurpassable expression, under the circumstances, of God's struggle with evil on behalf of those who suffer. God's acceptance is expressed through the voice of the centurion in Mark 15:39: "This was a Child of God!" The centurion echoes God's own voice, heard earlier (see 1:11; 9:7; and 12:6), and the voices of the demons and evil spirits (1:24; 3:11; and 5:7), which in turn are echoed by the high priest (14:61). God's identification of Jesus as God's own Child implicitly answers Jesus' lament expressing the sense of being abandoned by God (15:34), suggesting that God takes suffering into the divine self.[43]

According to a more traditional apocalyptic scheme, the figure of Christ, or the "Human One," inherits the features of a God who addresses evil with an arsenal of violent power. Nowhere is this apocalyptic scheme more striking than in Daniel and Revelation. Mark's drama of Jesus' death stands in marked contrast to such a scheme, in which God's exercise of power is affirmed and dramatically demonstrated in classic images of violence and victory. In Mark, the apocalyptic figure, the extramundane "Human One," is cast in the role of a historical and mortal figure, Jesus of Nazareth (2:10 and 28), whose primary identity is found not in violent power but also in suffering and dying for others.[44] This dimension is not entirely lacking in the book of

Revelation, as the image of the "lamb that was slain" shows, but overall the balance is tipped in favor of displays of violent, divine power. In Mark, the suffering and death of Jesus reveal to human beings the divine power of this "Human One" (15:29-32 and 39). The demons and evil spirits, on the other hand, recognize Jesus' true identity only in miraculous displays of power (1:24; 3:11; and 5:7).

5. Evil Forces

By viewing Mark's story of Jesus' death in the light of the problem of suffering, we gain a different angle of vision on God's power. But we also find that evil is seen differently. In the apocalyptic scheme of things, the world is caught in the grips of a battle between good and evil forces.

In Luke (22:3) and in John,[45] "supernatural" forces of evil play a role in Jesus' death. In Mark, on the other hand, violence is unleashed against Jesus, God's representative, not by these forces,[46] but only by other human beings. These include Jesus' own chosen followers[47] and Jewish religious authorities (Pharisees, scribes, elders, and chief priests), who all also represent God.[48] Also included are a Roman official, Pilate (Mark 15), and his collaborators, the Herodians (12:13). While "supernatural" forces of evil— traditional apocalyptic figures—are present in Mark's story of Jesus in the form of demons and unclean spirits, Jesus renders them impotent because they oppress *others*, not because they pose a threat to *Jesus*. Even the governing authorities—other traditional apocalyptic representatives of evil—are not the primary agents of Jesus' death in Mark's story. A centurion at the cross affirms that Jesus is a Child of God (15:39). The Herodians participate in the attempt to entrap Jesus (12:13), but Mark puts the role of Herod in the background (6:14-29), in contrast to Luke, who introduces a "trial" before Herod (23:6-16). And in Mark the soldiers, at the initiative of Pilate after the trial (15:15*b*), abuse Jesus inside the governor's palace (15:16-20), but Pilate tries, unsuccessfully, to press the innocence of Jesus (15:6-15), a motif that receives increased attention in Matthew, Luke-Acts, and John.[49]

The point is that violence against Jesus in Mark is not the work of "supernatural" forces of evil but of "good" people.[50] This ironic twist, known long ago,[51] opens up the possibility of seeing reality from a point of view different from the common religious perspective that neatly separates good and evil into two readily identifiable camps. Violence and suffering, and other forms of evil, are the result of agents within the created order who thwart God's purposes by resisting God's power. The parable of the sower (4:3-9), which plays so important a role in Mark's interpretation of Jesus' parables, makes the point that violence and suffering are part of the divinely created order itself.[52] Indeed, Mark's whole narrative pattern challenges the need to have a God whose power can eliminate all forms of evil "once and for all" as a way of addressing the problem of evil.

6. Faith and Protest

With the recognition of the existence of evil precisely within the created order, and not beyond or outside it, Jesus' outcry of protest on the cross takes on significance in the attempt to understand suffering. In most of the New Testament, protest and outrage are much more muted than in Job, since faith in the God who has come near in Jesus as the Messiah has almost overcome the note of angry protest—almost, but not quite. Even in the relatively late New Testament book of Revelation, which is full of apocalyptic confidence in the victory of God, one hears the outcry of protest on the lips of Christian martyrs: "How long, sovereign Lord, holy and true, until you judge and avenge our blood upon the inhabitants of the earth?" (Rev. 6:10; compare Ps. 90:13*a*).

In Mark, whose way of dealing with suffering is "beyond protest," so to speak, powerful words of protest nevertheless appear in the climactic scene of the crucifixion: "My God, my God, why did you abandon me?" (15:34 GNB). Of course, these words come from the opening of Psalm 22, one of the psalms of lament, which cry out against suffering or persecution but end with a note of faith and trust in God. This was surely known both to the author of Mark and to the first hearers of this Gospel. Nevertheless, Psalm 22 as a whole remains a profound outcry of protest. It is also noteworthy that Mark quotes only the opening words, decrying God's abandonment of the sufferer. Among the other accounts of the crucifixion, only Matthew (27:46) has preserved these stark words, indicating that they were no easier to interpret and to absorb into Christian faith then than they are now (see pp. 107-8). Although the principal way of dealing with suffering in Mark consists of trust and endurance, at this turning point in the story of Jesus' death the element of trust is complicated by an outcry of protest.

This outcry, so familiar to us, is found elsewhere in the Bible. Job, for instance, protests against God for what he has unjustly suffered (see p. 100), cursing the day when he was born (Job 3), as did Jeremiah (Jer. 20:14-18), another great protester. Job's protest also takes aim at those who would comfort him with traditional "theodicies" (6:24-30 and repeatedly), and so Job's outrage is aimed directly at God as well (7:11-21; 31:35-40; and repeatedly). Though Job has been seen as a paragon of traditional piety (see James 5:11), largely on the basis of its ending (chap. 42, esp. vv. 2-6) and because of a long-standing interpretation of Job's words in 19:25a ("I know that my redeemer lives" RSV),[53] the dignity and daring of Job's contest with God are bolder expressions of protest than we find almost anywhere else in the Bible. In large measure it is this bold, powerful protest against unjust and outrageous suffering, and the inability to accept traditional words of comfort, that make Job such an important and difficult book today.

The cry of protest, therefore, is as "traditional" as is faith. These two, faith and protest, are connected in two related, but different, ways. First, the outcry to God is part of the life of *faith*. God accepts the outcry, with its anger and frustration, into God's own experience. The faithful do not have to find a way to "swallow" the anger that unjust and inordinate suffering arouses. Rather, as Mark also knew well, outrage and protest are part of what we bring to God and part of what God accepts and transmutes in the creative divine experience.

That this is the case is at least implicitly confirmed in the classic nature and form of Hebrew laments. These laments begin with the plaintiff's outpouring of hurt and anger over being unjustly victimized by adversaries (or tragic fate), including sometimes being abandoned by God when God ought to have intervened in defense and support of the innocent and faithful. Yet, the laments almost always conclude with joyful thanksgiving and affirmations of faith that God has come (or will come) to the defense of God's faithful servant and that all has been (or will be) rectified.[54] This transformation in attitude—from anger over rejection and victimization to confidence in vindication and rectification—suggests that, in the course of ventilating their anger before God, those who offered their laments felt that anger absorbed by God. Precisely experiencing their anger as mercifully received and absorbed by God, the plaintiffs realized that God had indeed heard them. Thus they gained faith and confidence that God had been (and would continue to be) caringly and supportively present in response to the plight of God's servants. In this way, the laments bear witness that protest in the midst of suffering can be part of a strong and fully faithful relationship to God and may actually strengthen it.

That is also what is implied by Mark's placing of a powerful outcry to God at the center of the story of Jesus, when that outcry is seen in the framework of the whole narrative. The scene in Gethsemane and the outcry on the cross point out God's apparent *inaction*.[55] Jesus prays for God to *do something* to prevent what was about to happen (14:33-36); then Jesus protests when God appears to do nothing (15:34). So God could be blamed, at least indirectly, for the crucifixion of Jesus. Pastors frequently hear a similar protest when people experience tragedy, particularly senseless tragedy. Their pain is undeniable, and it is compounded by a crisis of faith created by a traditional

117

vision of what is possible for God. In such an existential agony, many people lash out at God, blaming God for not intervening—as their faith had promised God would. Mark's Gospel and its readers undoubtedly shared such a vision and crisis of faith, expressed in Jesus' protest.

The element of protest in Mark's story of Jesus' death recognizes that for the sufferer the present is so filled with isolation and alienation that it can appear to be empty of God. As J. Dominic Crossan puts it, Mark created the gospel genre as a "form for absence."[56] But Mark also knew that there is nevertheless more to life than appears in these empty moments! Precisely because today there is a widespread breakdown of faith in God's ongoing purpose and presence, it is of the utmost importance to struggle seriously with this "nevertheless."

One way of affirming this "nevertheless" would be to cling to the confidence that, *in the end,* God's purpose will win out and completely overcome evil. This apocalyptic form of the "nevertheless" can certainly be found in Mark.[57] Many have found solace in this way of faith during the harsh and tragic periods in their lives and in history, which erode away trust in God's goodness or presence, or both.[58] In the end, however, this way of affirming the "nevertheless" is, as Crossan rightly sees, a "form for absence," for it leaves the *present* empty of God—or at least it certainly can appear to be so from the perspective of the sufferer. From the sufferer's point of view, nothing seems really present except suffering and its various known and unknown causes. Authentic faith, however, holds tenaciously to the belief that God is omnipresent, ubiquitous—that God can never be absent from any moment of time or any region of space. To borrow the message of Matthew's birth narrative: God is with us (1:23)! Or, as a contemporary affirmation of faith puts it: "In life, in death, in life beyond death, God is with us. We are not alone. Thanks be to God!"[59]

But what about the cross, or any other moment of human suffering that seems so empty of God? If it feels as if God is so absent from the experience of the sufferer, how or in what way can God actually be present? What comfort can sufferers have? For that matter, what comfort can those who share empathetically with the suffering of others have in the belief that God is concerned or even cares—in the face of God's apparent absence? These questions lead us to another way of affirming this "nevertheless." By placing *suffering within God* and by placing *God within the experience of suffering itself,* not as the cause or origin of suffering but as its final resting place, we can say that God is present to all who suffer as the Companion and Co-sufferer, who embraces all their pain and angry protest. Like the suffering servant of Isaiah 53, God experiences fully the suffering of the sufferer, in all its terrible reality.[60]

If the Gospel of Mark is taken as a whole, from the point of view of the narrator and not only from the point of view of its heroic figure, Jesus, we can see that God is present in Jesus' death as both Victim and Victor. Viewed from the perspective of the person of Jesus himself, much like any sufferer overwhelmed by pain, God does indeed seem absent, as we have suggested. Jesus' cry of abandonment can be viewed in this light as the plaintive cry of one who feels forsaken by God. But from the perspective of the larger world of the Gospel story, others know that God is present. In Mark's Gospel, God's presence is manifest in the rending of the Temple curtain (15:38), in the inspiration of the centurion's confession (15:39), and, most important of all, in the resurrection of Jesus (16:6). So, from one point of view, that of the Markan Jesus, Jesus' life ends on the most negative note of despair—betrayed and abandoned by friends, vilified and humiliated by civic and religious authorities, and seemingly abandoned by God in Jesus' moment of greatest need. But from the point of view of Mark and the Gospel's readers, the crucifixion scene ends on a positive note of hope and prepares for the confidence that hope is not misplaced—as can be seen in the empty tomb scene, which concludes the Gospel.[61]

A different, but related, way in which faith and the outcry of protest are connected can be seen in the religious roots of the struggle against suffering and its many causes. It is often by crying out in indignation that we are put in touch with what God is doing.[62] God is known, however, not in *misery itself* but in *the sufferer* and in *the protest and struggle against suffering*. The God of the Bible accepts and creatively transforms the fear and anger that arise out of suffering. But the biblical God also *does* something about the suffering itself and its causes. The faith that God responds to those who cry out to God, which is a fundamental part of "biblical" faith, is traditionally oriented toward a God imaged as one who can reach out with a mighty arm and defeat the powers of evil (see, for example, Ps. 44 and Luke 1:46-56). What is at stake in this vision of God, however, is something more fundamental than its various symbolic expressions—namely, the faith that God does take suffering seriously and is actively engaged in the struggle against it. From the Hebrew faith in God's active and purposeful presence *in history* (see, for example, Deut. 6:20-25), this conviction passed into a more transcendental, apocalyptic form of faith, which focused on God's presence *at the end of history*.[63]

This form of faith is important to the story of Jesus in Mark.[64] However imperfect, the apocalyptic vision of God's victory over suffering and its causes provided a framework within which faith and the outcry of protest could be held together, for it offered a way of understanding God's *action*. It is in this light that we can understand Mark's strong emphasis on the servant who voluntarily endures suffering: The sufferer can cry out in protest and at the same time trust that God's mighty arm of deliverance will demonstrate its power. In Mark's story of Jesus, this trust is brought into focus in the final scene at the empty tomb, to which we now turn. Difficult as it may be to affirm all that this emphasis entails or implies, the task of biblical preaching is to allow the tension between alternative imaginative proposals to transform creatively the hearer's vision of the world.

7. Suffering and the Resurrection: Mark's Ending to the Story of Jesus' Death

The attention of this chapter has been on a theology of suffering that might be drawn from Mark's story of Jesus. It is striking that Mark's emphasis on suffering, which permeates the Markan narrative of Jesus' life and death, also dominates the resurrection narrative in Mark 16:1-8. When the women are amazed at finding Jesus' tomb empty, an angel responds by announcing: "Do not be amazed; you seek Jesus of Nazareth, who was crucified. He has been raised, he is not here" (16:6). What is surprising is that even here, in the proclamation of the resurrection, our attention is still kept on Jesus' identity as the one "who was crucified"[65]—and the emphasis one might expect to be found on the glory and power of the resurrection, which we find in the other Gospels,[66] is present here much more enigmatically.[67]

Furthermore, the meaning of the angel's instruction to go and tell Jesus' disciples that Jesus is "going before" them to Galilee and that they will see Jesus there (16:7) remains unclear. All agree that this tradition about Galilee has something to do either with an appearance of the risen Jesus or with the Parousia of Jesus as the promised "Human One."[68] In either case, the angel's message is that the disciples will encounter the living Jesus in Galilee after his death in a decisive way. But it clearly identifies the living Jesus whom they will encounter there as the one "who was crucified"—and it suggests that Jesus is not yet reunited with his followers, who await the message that they will meet him in Galilee.

In our previous chapter, we saw that the ending of Mark might be given two different interpretations. In one interpretation, which emphasizes the finality of the narrative ending, the ending suggests that the disciples never grasp the meaning of Jesus' life and death, and what it means to be his "follower." That explains why the time between the crucifixion and the promised encounter with the living Jesus is a time of Jesus' *absence* from the Christian community.[69] The other interpretation, which observes a distinction between plot- and story-time and encourages the reader to project the story beyond the narrative ending, emphasizes the promissory, anticipatory character of the ending and suggests that those who failed within the narrative as told were later able to move beyond their earlier failure.

These two ways of reading Mark's ending, however, are close in their understanding of what it is like to follow Jesus in the time after the Gospel narrative ends. In the first, a life of following Jesus has to contend with Jesus' absence; in the second, Jesus is "absent, yet present"—present in his word and name and indirectly in the Spirit (see pp. 88-92). Both agree that Mark refuses to close the story on a simple note of victory and that Mark anticipates a time when Jesus' followers will be subjected to the same forces that brought about Jesus' death.

What options are open to preachers of this enigmatic message in our own time? Like the early church, which added a traditional ending to Mark,[70] we too know the faith that the living Jesus still leads his followers and can be encountered in Christian communities. This message arises from a certain kind of "canonical" reading of Mark, which has been adopted by Christians from ancient to modern times. On its own terms, it is valid.[71]

For preaching from Mark, however, there is a great advantage in not blurring in this way the distinctiveness of Mark's story of Jesus and its message. The preacher will do better to look to Mark's own story for its imaginative proposals. The first of these creative proposals arises from a reading of Mark's enigmatic ending, with its suggestion of Jesus' absence in the Christian community (see pp. 88-89), as a message of judgment on followers of Jesus who had failed to keep faith in a crucified Messiah. For them, as for many Christians today, the cross symbolizes only the old, hostile world, which they fear because they believe that the coercive power of the world is the only real power. The ending of Mark's Gospel, according to one reading, stands in judgment on Christian communities who follow the path of conventional power. This reading renews in each new circumstance an attack upon complacency and upon the belief that we are securely situated in the world of faith. It breaks up the world of the hearers.

Another proposal about the message of Mark's ending

for today springs from a reading of Mark that recognizes much in what has just been said that rings true to the Markan vision and to our own experience of the church in the world. The cross does symbolize a kind of defeat for God and for God's representatives at the hands of a world in which hostile forces resist, often with deadly violence, those who seek to carry out God's purposes. This harsh reality has been brought home to us by the life and death of such persons as Mahatma Gandhi, Martin Luther King, Jr., and many others who are less famous. These lives, and the way they ended, also demonstrate only a *proximate* victory in this world, which comes from their affirmation of God's purposes in spite of all temptations to ignore or reject them; from their continuing to trust in God, being devoted to God's purposes when failure and the blows that life can deliver come; and refusing to give in to complacency, despair, or desperation out of a false confidence in victory.

But, we would add, the only assurance of *ultimate* victory is that God receives their trust, loyalty, and faithful actions as God's own and absorbs—that is, experiences—and transmutes their lack of trust and loyalty, their failure to act faithfully, their acts that simply failed, and the tragic blows that they suffered, and in all of this remains loyal to them and to those on whose behalf they labor in love. In this way, God's love embraces the whole, indivisible world. Any interpretation of the cross that denies, obscures, or blunts this truth does not measure up to the full reality of the cross and its power as a symbol. What some regard as the weakness of the cross, this proposal takes as its power.

On this interpretation, the Christian community that gathered in Galilee to "see" the risen Jesus, who was *crucified*, can represent every Christian community, which always is a community of those who more or less fail to grasp the full reality of the cross and who wish for a more secure grip on victory than the cross appears to provide. "Galilee" itself can represent for us the real world in which we find ourselves. This is a world in which God needs and calls people to be instruments of God's redemptive and liberating work in the world. It is a world in which engaging in God's causes involves the risk of suffering, perhaps even dying a violent death, because this world includes forces that can and do resist God's purposes and God's representatives. In short, "Galilee" is a world in which ambiguity is the order of the day, in which life is experienced in its tragic consequences, in which evil is often perpetrated as much by "good" people as by the "demonic."

Finally, the ending of Mark's Gospel can also be a symbol of God's own refusal to give up on the work of redemption and liberation in the world. One way of interpreting the story of Jesus' resurrection, which Mark's ending proclaims, is that the death of Jesus did not result in God's giving up on what God had sought to accomplish in and through Jesus.[72] The ending of Mark's Gospel can suggest that God's liberating rule in the world, seen in Jesus, continues in and through the Christian community after the death of Jesus. Then "Galilee" would also represent a world in which God's realm continues to emerge (see Mark 1:15), an arena where God still seeks to achieve God's redemptive purpose through those who strengthen the influence of the greatest (coherently conceivable) power—God's wisdom and love, which alone are the source of all redeeming and liberating possibilities for the world.

8. Conclusion

We have now seen how holding the many elements of Mark's story of Jesus' death in creative contrast results in a vision of God's power and action that differs from the more common ways in which the question of suffering is viewed either in terms of God's unlimited power or in terms of God's inaction. According to Mark, Jesus' death on the cross affects God insofar as God accepts Jesus' suffering and angry protest *as God's own*. This is what the "ransom" myth and "blood covenant" known to Mark (10:45 and 14:24) imply: God's own self is affected by Jesus' death.

In "process" categories, Mark's story of Jesus' death on the cross implies that God's power is "relational" or "reciprocal" rather than "unilateral" or "one-directional."[73] Jesus' death illustrates God's capacity to *be influenced by others* as well as to *influence others*. If the power of God to be influenced by others has been largely overlooked in the interpretation of Mark's story of Jesus' death, God's power to influence others also has not always been seen through the lens of this story. The only direct action on the cross is that of Jesus, who acts in concert with God, or in God's stead. God's action can be seen in the cross of Jesus, therefore, precisely only in the actions of another, Jesus, whose actions God has influenced in a "call" (1:9-11) and through prayer (14:32-42), which are forms of divine persuasion. So the cross, as a sign of God's power, relativizes the apocalyptic visions in which God's power is understood in terms of direct, "one-directional" or "unilateral," and typically violent, action.

Although the Gospel of Mark still retains the confidence that the struggle with evil will come to a final victory (understood in apocalyptic terms), its way of telling the story of faith thrusts this vision of final victory into the background in favor of the open, unfinished, and precarious story of the present. God is at work in this present, relating to all existence and influencing it, but not determining it. Mark begins a reworking of the vision of the end—a reworking that we are called upon to complete and to actualize in our own unfinished stories.

It is possible, therefore, to understand faith as being oriented toward a God who is in this twofold sense a Companion. God's power takes the form not only of accepting angry protests but also of joining in them. It also affects the actions of others, persuading them to struggle against suffering and its many causes. Such a faith is able to help us overcome the bitterness and isolation of suffering, and so to help us be ready to enter into the struggle of others in and against suffering—in short, to embody God's own redemptive purpose within the physical, personal, and social realities of the world. The outcry of protest can then be a call to work out one's faith by striving toward eliminating as many causes of suffering as one can, reducing the amount of suffering and bringing relief when and where suffering occurs.

Even in the actual suffering world in which outcries to God arise, God can be known as more actively related to the experience of suffering than the terms *Companion* and *Co-sufferer* suggest. God is actively working in us and through us to bring about new and creative, liberating and reconciling possibilities for the fulfillment of life as God envisions it. This transformational view of suffering in no way diminishes the pain or unfairness or abhorrent dimensions of suffering to which so many are (and have been) subjugated. Nor, on the other hand, should this transformational view be interpreted as promoting or accepting suffering as such, much less as an invitation to masochism. The point is that, through the experiences of the relational power of love, God can and does use the bearing of suffering as a transformational agent to reconcile and redeem us and the world. God did so in the death of Jesus and desires to do so through us.

From the preceding discussion, four affirmations about the meaning of suffering emerge, which can be sketched in the movement from Mark's narrative to the perspective from which this book is written. First, *no one ever suffers alone,* since God participates in the suffering of the world. In the Gospel of Mark, God takes up a position of solidarity with both the afflicted whom Jesus heals and that same Jesus who becomes a victim of injustice. God is the fellow sufferer who understands, the all-inclusive and all-pervading one who quite literally feels and is affected by every creature's existence. From our perspective, God extends care to the whole of reality and feels the pain of the nonhuman world. The emphasis on human suffering in this section of our book is a reflection of Mark's own perspective, in which a concern for the human world comes through more clearly than the more inclusive concern for the whole world, of which there are only hints (for example, in the more apocalyptic motifs).

Second, *the suffering of innocent persons is never forgotten.* Innocent suffering remains indelibly a part of God's memory forever. In "process" terms, God brings to each emerging moment the deeply felt remembrance of such suffering in order to evoke its remembrance in the memory of the human community—or at least in the memory of that part of the community whose "story" is directly affected by innocent suffering. The Church's celebration of the Lord's Supper as a meal of remembrance, as well as the commitment of the proclamation of the suffering and death of Jesus to writing by Mark—and by other New Testament writers—and the subsequent preservation of that writing by the Church, exemplify this truth. And God does stimulate human memory in propitious moments of human experience—for example, when a personal tragedy prompts recognition of our oneness with the suffering of others, or when storytellers, such as Mark, passionately tell stories of suffering and in that telling make those experiences of suffering come alive for hearers or readers.

Third, *God actively seeks to eliminate all unjustifiable suffering.* In Mark, God works through Jesus to heal the sick and to deliver those who are broken. God vindicates Jesus through the resurrection, and God will in the end bring God's rule to fruition. In our own terms, God tries to persuade all creatures to realize their optimum possibilities and seeks to bring about in history those conditions most conducive to freedom, dignity, and creativity. God thus calls all human beings to enter into the pains of others and to join in the struggle against conditions that give rise to unjustifiable suffering. Seeing God's power as being relational actually sponsors human activism.

Fourth, *suffering can contribute to the meaningful future that God offers to a broken situation.* The terrible losses in history are real. But these tortured and destroyed lives are not simply lost. Their existence, including their suffering, is taken into God's memory, as we have said above. More than this, as the mystery of the cross reminds us, human suffering may, sometimes at least, contribute strategic possibilities to God's urge toward a future without unjust suffering. In Mark, this theme is expressed in apocalyptic terms. From our perspective, this point can be made in another way: God's power is capable of creating a future even where we can see no way to hope, and even out of the wreckage of our efforts.

As was said above, such a faith does not avoid or bypass protest. It does not simply resolve the problem but gives us a vantage point from which to wrestle with it, so that our position at the beginning of this section—that we can respond most fruitfully when we hold in tension the differing approaches to suffering—is valid. We must state clearly that protesting faith, or faithful protest, gives up the certainty that God's "will," understood as a definite outcome determined in advance, will win out. This does not mean that we must trust in a powerless God. On the contrary, God's power, understood in "relational" terms as *influencing* the actions of literally all others and *receiving* the actions of literally all others, is sufficient and unsurpassable even if it is not all-controlling. A divine power, limited by the contingencies of the world with respect to the *outcome* of God's acts but not with respect to God's *aims, purposes,* or *will,* stands as an alternative to the power of the traditional theist's God, whose supposed *will* to struggle against suffering is challenged by the many forms of carnage, injustice, and oppression that drench history with blood and tears and so give rise to the outcry of protest.

Mark, like our modern artists and writers who shun accepted religious "explanations" of why people suffer, is reserved in "explaining" why things happen as they do to Jesus. Yet, Mark does turn our attention to the searing question that arises from suffering: How can we grasp meaning out of the ordeal of suffering and hold on to it in life and thought? Whatever answer one gives, it will not bring the security of a door closed tightly shut against the question that suffering poses to life's meaning. We have proposed an answer by holding in creative contrast the three elements of Mark's story of Jesus' death: active endurance of suffering out of trust in God and devotion to God's purposes, working for the elimination of suffering and faith in God's deliverance from suffering, and the outcry of protest against outrageous suffering.

Human suffering threatens all networks of meaning, even Mark's and ours. No single answer satisfies. Mark's Gospel offers an unflinching look at the issue of suffering. It offers us a world in which God responds to suffering as God responded in Jesus—and in which God will never abandon anyone, even when sufferers feel that they have been abandoned. As we persistently bring our world into contrast with the world of Mark, it is hard for us to imagine an area where our world can be expanded more profoundly than in the way we face suffering, since our ordinary ways of understanding it are so inadequate. And so the message of this Gospel sets us, like the women at the empty tomb, on our way with faith—on our way into the open, unfinished story of God's continuing purpose of setting us free from everything within us and outside us that cuts us off from life.

CHAPTER SIX

"SELF-DENIAL"

A Sermon on Mark 8:34 by John B. Cobb, Jr.

> Then Jesus summoned the crowd with his disciples and
> said to them, "If any of you wish to follow me, you must deny
> yourself and take up your cross and follow me." (Mark 8:34)

Take up your cross!" That is not an attractive idea. If taken literally as a command to go get yourself crucified, it would have few takers, and those we would declare sick.

But taken at the symbolic level at which it was intended—and at which it has always been heard—this call for self-denial, for devotion to a cause that transcends one's own interest, to give one's life for the neighbor, has in fact had enormous power. Which of us has not been stirred by that ideal?

As a youth, especially in adolescence, I heard the call for self-sacrifice. The idea of giving myself wholeheartedly to something beyond myself was deeply moving and exhilarating. It mattered less just how that "something" was understood. If I had been in Germany in those years, it might well have been the Fatherland to me. Fortunately, I heard the call in a Christian context. I should give myself to God, to Jesus, to the church, to the cause of peace, to the battle against racial injustice.

There was much in my response that was obviously immature, sentimental, self-deceptive, and even hypocritical. I know that. But I remain grateful to those preachers and youth leaders who touched me with the call to take up

130

my cross and who gave Christian content to the direction of devotion that was involved. I feel deeply troubled that so many young people grow up in today's world either hearing no call to self-denial at all or hearing it only in idolatrous forms—as when they are invited to give themselves wholly to a "christ" who supports patriarchy, anti-Judaism, Christian exclusivism, or militaristic nationalism. It is my earnest hope that the mission of the church can again attain the convincing clarity that supports the call to youth to consider quite concrete ways in which they may serve God rather than themselves, in which they can find their lives by losing them.

There are many reasons for the loss of power today in the call to self-denial. We have learned that the forms that call took in earlier days—to the monastery or to the foreign mission field, for example—were far more ambiguous than the church had once supposed. To renounce all direct expression of our sexuality no longer appears to many as a healthy ideal. And we have learned that Christian missions were bound up in many ways with cultural, economic, and military imperialism.

We need not impugn the motives of those who have "taken up their crosses" in these ways. Indeed, it would be totally wrong to belittle the enormous positive accomplishments of the monastic and missionary movements to which they devoted themselves. Supercilious criticism shows much more about the critics than about what they criticize. I rejoice that monasticism continues and that there are still thousands who give their lives in service to the church in other countries. But I cannot call for wholehearted commitment to either cause. The best monks and nuns today are those who know the ambiguity of their roles. The best foreign missionaries are those who are deeply sensitive to the complex mixture of good and evil in what they are doing.

Youth need wholehearted commitment, and these older roles cannot inspire that wholeheartedness without deception. In the 1960s, young people created their own ideals, bewildering in their diversity, for which they could deny themselves. Many of us feel nostalgia for those days. It was more satisfying to try to channel those energies into constructive action, difficult as that often was, than to deal with those today who have no broader interests than their own success. But the youth of those days could not sustain their ideals because their ideals could not sustain them. From "taking up their crosses," they did not move to more sophisticated and critical forms of "cross-bearing." For the most part they sadly dropped their "crosses" altogether.

Into the vacuum came the religious cults. They have far more staying power. They can channel the need for a transcendent purpose that disciplines the inner wayward-ness. In their more eccentric forms, they may now be declining. But within our churches themselves the cult mentality is gaining momentum. One needs only to see what is happening in the largest of all Protestant denominations in our country. The ancient symbols of the prophetic struggle with idolatry are transformed into idols that command the devotion of millions. The Bible itself is transformed from the story of God's work with and through sinful people into an object of devotion. Even the cross, the supreme symbol of divine love, is turned into a weapon used against those who live by other images. There are some who cynically manipulate this situation, but there are thousands, perhaps millions, who "take up their crosses" in all sincerity for idolatrous causes in the name of Jesus. This, and worse, will continue until those who recognize this idolatry for what it is proclaim the true and, therefore, non-idolatrous meaning of "cross-bearing" in our time.

But have I spoken too positively in favor of "taking up one's cross" even in a symbolic sense? In our psychological age, skepticism of such ideals runs deep. Even in my childhood, on a mission field, before psychological sophis-tication had spread its influence, one of the more common sayings I used to hear was "It takes a saint to live with a martyr." The missionaries knew how difficult it is to deal with those who self-consciously deny themselves for the sake of others. They were aware of the self-deception that is involved in maintaining one's self-image as one who is continuously sacrificing for God and others, at least in the more blatant cases.

With the rise of psychological sophistication, there grows also the suspicion that not only the blatant cases alone but also all who are moved by the ideal of self-denial are caught up in self-deception. The ideal as such, in the view of many, is sick. We need to recognize that we are inherently self-concerned persons, and we need to stop thinking pejoratively of that fact. Instead we should affirm ourselves and devote our energies to realizing or actualizing ourselves—refusing and exposing every other ideal as repressive and as leading to dishonest and destructive modes of expressing our self-interest.

Which of us has not been deeply touched by this gospel of self-actualization? Indeed, which of us who has first been shaped by the teaching of self-denial has not found relief and help in this gospel? We have turned, within as well as outside the churches, from the call to "take up our crosses" to the offer of abundant life. We have felt that we breathed more freely in this context, that we could liberate ourselves more truly from bondage to the law.

It was only gradually that we learned from bitter experience the one-sidedness and inadequacy of our new abundance, when this was divorced from the belief that only those who lose their lives will find them. Our youth abandoned our churches in droves, many turning either to drugs or to religious cults. Our psychologists began writing about collective narcissism.

In a day when the United States is the world's greatest military and economic power, its people have lost interest in the rest of the world except as a place to take vacations, and when their young people are called to fight there. Even after a decade of attempts by the United States government to crush the Sandinista revolution in Nicaragua, the great majority of citizens can hardly locate it on the map, much less understand the remarkable struggle of its people for a social revolution without loss of civil liberties and human rights. We cannot be proud of our record as self-actualizers!

And so, I would call again for us to "take up our crosses," to find what that means in our time, to proclaim it again in our churches, to give it concrete form—especially for our youth in those crucial formative years. And yet I am held back. There is another problem, more challenging and serious than that posed by humanistic psychology in the past generation. It comes from women.

What really happens, they ask, when the church calls for people to "take up their crosses"? Perhaps for the men who hear the call it is a healthy check to their ambition and self-assertion. Perhaps it may channel their ambition and self-assertion in ways that are socially more constructive.

But what happens to the majority of the audience—the women? From infancy, they have been brought up to understand that the woman's role is to serve her menfolk—her husband and her children. She brings with her to church both this socialization and her conscious or unconscious desire to discover her own capacities and to express them, to function in the family and in society in a role equal to that of men, to find her own identity in distinction from her service role. Then in church she hears that she should "deny herself and take up her cross." Whereas for the man these words may have only the vaguest relation to the immediate decisions of life, the woman knows very well what they mean. They call her to give up her hopes for her own life and to subordinate herself to the welfare of the other members of her family.

Women are rejecting Christianity today for many reasons—because its God is masculine, because it points to a male savior, because it is part of a patriarchal culture and has indeed sanctioned and sanctified that culture, because even today it resists giving full equality to women. But for some women who have understood themselves as Christians, the deepest problem with continuing that identification is their correct understanding that the Christian message calls for self-sacrificial love. Their need, they are convinced, is for self-love and for nurturing in one another the willingness to take the risk of asserting the self and its needs. The call to "take up the cross" works directly against their liberation.

And so, where are we left? Should we preach self-denial even when we know that many who hear are oppressed by that message? Surely not. Should we forever abandon this feature and emphasis of the gospel? On the contrary, it seems that we have been too silent on this already. Should we divide the congregation between men and women, preaching self-denial to the men and self-love to the women? Perhaps, but that seems hardly practical. Alternately, we can emphasize that the only self worth sacrificing is a strong self, a realized self. In this way, we can hold the call to self-affirmation together with the call to self-denial for both women and men.

134

To the deepest questions there are no simple answers. We must struggle to find in the full richness of the scriptures the many words that severally constitute the gospel for different people in different stages and walks of life. Reinhold Niebuhr once captured this, with a different issue in mind, in his famous aphorism that held that we should "comfort the afflicted, and afflict the comfortable."

Perhaps to recognize more deeply the depths of diversity of need in the human situation, to learn to be all things to all people, to discern the rich complexity of Christ's work in the world, and to give ourselves responsibly to sharing in that work—perhaps just that is the "cross" we are now called to bear. Perhaps at times to "bear the cross" will mean to be silent about the cross. But it cannot always be so. At the deepest and final level, the way to life leads through death, even if that death be to the self-image of finding life through serving others. That self, too, we must deny as we "take up our crosses" and follow Jesus.

B.
Paul

CHAPTER SEVEN

PAUL'S INTERPRETATION OF JESUS' DEATH

1. Narrative Elements in Paul's Letters

A major reason for the use of story in preaching is the power of narrative to engage the listener in the world of the story. The primary story that is to be told in preaching is the story that gives the church its identity. This story includes both the familiar stories of Israel and of the church from its birth to the present and the less familiar stories that have been minimized in our collective memory (see p. 53). At the center is the story of the death of Jesus. Because telling this story in preaching is crucial to the formation of the hearers' Christian identity— that is, of their identity in God's love in Christ—it will repay the preacher to attend to the telling of this story by early Christian preachers, and that includes Paul.

The thinking of Paul, of course, has been preserved in the form of letters, rather than in the narrative form characteristic of early Christian gospels. This difference cannot be overlooked. Paul directly addresses the concrete concerns of early Christian communities—concerns that are relatively hidden in the narrative form of the Gospel writers. Obvious narratives and narrative elements can be found in Paul's letters, as we will show, but they stand out in Paul's more typical discursive style.

Nevertheless, the letter form itself implies a story. At the very least, Paul's letters imply "occasions" in the lives of communities of believers and in Paul's own life. In principle, providing one had access to enough clues in a letter, one could reconstruct a story implied in the letter. Moreover, often Paul's arguments about the consequences of a community's course of action and his instructions concerning the "right" action it should follow take the readers beyond the known "story" into the future, filling them with expectations clothed with fear or hope.[1]

This narrative character of Paul's letters can easily be illustrated simply by quoting a few lines of Paul's letter to the Galatians:

> I am amazed that so quickly you have turned away from the one who called you by the grace [of Christ] toward another gospel. (1:6)

> O foolish Galatians! Who has bewitched you, before whose very eyes Jesus Christ was publicly portrayed as crucified? (3:1)

> Before the coming of faith we were kept in custody under the law, while we were imprisoned [under sin], so that the law was our custodian until Christ, in order that we might be justified by faith; but, since faith came, we are no longer under a custodian. (3:23-25)

> I testify again to every man who accepts circumcision, that he is obligated to do the whole law. You are cut off from Christ, you who would be justified by the law; you have fallen away from grace. (5:3-4)

> Neither circumcision nor uncircumcision is anything, but [only] a new creation [matters]. Peace be upon all who follow this rule, and mercy be also upon the Israel of God. (6:15-16)

From these lines we could plot a "story," as Paul would tell it, of the Christian communities in Galatia. It would tell of their conversion through Paul's preaching the story of the crucified Messiah and their subsequent persuasion to comply with the ritual requirement of the Jewish law. And it would tell the ironic story of their fall from grace if they obeyed the letter of the law. If, however, they continued to live out of their God-given freedom from the human condition for which the law was given, they would be blessed with peace.

The story on which the Galatians' story hinges is that of the crucified Messiah. The hearing of this story led some in Galatia to faith. We might say that the story transformed their lives, but they believed that, through Paul's telling of it, *the Spirit* transformed their lives. Moreover, Paul believed that the Spirit grafted them onto the story of Jesus and, through it, to the story of God's promise to Israel. The persuasive power of Paul's arguments lies in the echoes that one hears in them of these interlocking stories.

Too often Paul's interpretation of Jesus' death has been thought of simply in terms of the ideas Paul had about it. Attention has focused on the relatively abstract and discursive forms of thought in Paul's letters with which theology has been familiar. But Paul's ways of speaking about the death of Jesus and about how believers relate to it also contain narrative elements that presuppose or imply a "story." By attending to these elements, the reader will be drawn into Paul's narrative world, while, at the same time, approaching the issues that theologians have discussed in more abstract form.

The longest narrative passage in Paul's letters is Galatians 1:11–2:14, an autobiographical story that Paul tells as part of "the truth of the gospel." In I Corinthians 11:23-26, Paul hands on a traditional account of the "last supper." Among the christological traditions Paul received, Galatians 4:4 presupposes or implies a story of the "sending" of God's Child "born of a woman" and "under the law"; Philippians 2:6-11 tells a story of Christ's obedience and exaltation; and Romans 1:3-5 implies a story of Jesus as one who "was descended from David according to the flesh" and was "designated Son of God in power according to the Spirit of holiness by his resurrection from the dead" (RSV). The numerous references to the Messiah who died and was raised, as for example in Romans 4:25, allude to a story told in terms of a related theme.[2] More allusive is I Corinthians 2:6-15, where the largely didactic language nevertheless is suggestive of a story about God's primordial wisdom, which enters the world in the form of a human being, whom the powers of the cosmos crucify, but who continues to be known through the Spirit of God. This is ultimately a story about God's victory over "the rulers of this age, who are doomed to pass away" (I Cor. 2:6).[3] I Corinthians 15:20-28 is an apocalyptic drama about God's victory over God's enemies (see also I Cor. 15:51-57); and Romans 11 suggests an eschatological "story" about God's dealings with Israel, which is oriented differently.

In other passages, the narrative element is less direct; yet, it is clearly implied by language suggestive of a "story." An important example is Romans 5:6-21, which "tells" two stories of Jesus' death as a saving event (vv. 6-11 and 12-21). Jesus' death is not explicitly mentioned in Romans 5:12-21, but "the act of righteousness" *(dikaiōma)* in verse 18 and "the act of obedience" *(hypakoē)* in verse 19 are easily and rightly understood as alluding to Christ's act of dying "for the ungodly," which is the focus of verses 6-11. The narrative features are clear, even if the dominant interpretive tradition has been more concerned about "doctrinal" content. One could also mention the story of God's redemptive action in Israel's history, which lies behind or in Galatians 3:6–4:7, and whose main events surround the figures of Abraham (vv. 6ff.), Moses (vv. 15ff.), and Jesus (vv. 23ff.).[4] Paul's letter to the Romans as a whole suggests a story of God's self-disclosure in the history of Israel and the transformation of this history in the story of Jesus.

To recognize this narrative pattern in Paul's message is not to say that Paul was a teller of stories. He was not himself a skilled narrator; and, as has often been pointed out, he did not have the gift of telling a tight, symbolic, brief story like the parables in the Gospels. His illustrations usually turn into allegories. Apart from the question of his narrative skill, there is a reason for his interest in allegory, which directs attention to a particular way of reading a story. The narrative pattern was already built into the Christian message that Paul shared with his churches. In his letters he was concerned with insisting on a particular interpretation—or on particular interpretations—of the message. The Gospel parables, which are often contrasted with Paul's allegories, are more ready to leave the interpretation to the hearer; for this reason allegorical explanations are sometimes provided for them.[5]

In addition to this contrast between Paul's letters and the parables in the Gospels, there is another contrast with the Gospels. The Gospel passion narratives, which are themselves closer in content to the narrative elements in Paul's message than are the parables, can be interpreted as historical "reports," and they frequently are. Paul's letters, however, rarely are. It is commonly thought that the Gospel narratives contain information about historical events, but that Paul's letters express the historic significance of events for particular occasions. The contrast between a report of an event as "historical" and its interpretation as "historic" is helpful as a way into the contrast between Paul and the Gospels; it has been an important key to much recent New Testament interpretation, especially of the existentialist type. If this contrast is made into a sharp dichotomy, however, it is misleading, since all reporting also includes interpretation.[6] Just as the passion narratives of the Gospels do not overlook the historic significance of the historical events—indeed, they are thoroughly shaped by an understanding of this significance—so also Paul does not neglect the historical events whose historic significance he presents. Nevertheless, although one could say that the Gospel writers were as interested as Paul was in the historic significance of Jesus' death, one cannot say that Paul was as interested as the Gospel writers were in the historical events surrounding the death of Jesus.

This contrast with the Gospels is evident if we ask what we can learn from Paul's letters about the historical events surrounding Jesus' death. The data are few, but we can learn something from Paul's letters. The statement that "the Jews" killed Jesus (I Thess. 2:14-15)[7] contains information about the ethnic identity of some of the participants in Jesus' death, but the particulars are left out. Also left out is the participation of Roman officials—a fact that can be inferred from the manner of Jesus' death, crucifixion, a further fact handed on by Paul.[8] Paul's letters also allude to Jesus' "betrayal" by one of his own closest followers, as would seem to be implied by I Corinthians 11:23: "On the night when he was betrayed" (RSV). But elsewhere in Paul's letters (for example, Rom. 8:32), the word here translated "betrayed" refers to *God's* act of "handing over" Jesus.[9]

This survey of what we can know about Jesus' death from Paul's letters shows that Paul's explanation of the historic significance of Jesus' death does not hand on much knowledge about its historical details. Of course, the extant letters of Paul might not include everything that Paul wrote; even if they did, it is not likely that Paul wrote in his letters everything that he knew about Jesus' death. But Paul's letters leave the impression that the belief that God chose to bring about salvation through the event of Jesus' death depends on no more than the knowledge that Jesus died by crucifixion. Paul's presentation of the historic significance of Jesus' death, however, entails two further beliefs about Jesus: first, that Jesus' death was an act of Jesus' obedience (Phil. 2:8 and Rom. 5:18-19) and love (Gal. 2:20); and second, that God "raised Jesus from the dead," a conviction found throughout Paul's letters.

But from this survey, it is also clear that Jesus' death is not told simply as a part of the story of Jesus. It forms a "subplot" within a story about God's redemptive action. To be sure, it is the *focal* "subplot," but it is told in service of a larger story. The historic significance of Jesus' death, in Paul's view, can best be seen when that event is placed within narratives about God's redemptive dealings with the world, which can be traced in the historical order back to Abraham and Moses (as in Rom. 3:21–4:25 and Gal. 3:6–4:7), and even to Adam (as in Rom. 5:12-21 and I Cor. 15:42-50).

This larger "story" extends beyond the human realm to God's victory over all the "powers of this age."[10] Jesus' death, therefore, is not only an act of Jesus' obedience and love, but it is also an act of *God's* love (Rom. 5:8 and 8:39) and faithfulness (Rom. 3:1-8).[11]

We now turn to a more detailed examination of these two "stories," the story of Jesus (pp. 142-44) and the story of God (pp. 144-51). A discussion of how they are taken up within the church as its own story follows (pp. 151-57). It is here that the story of most interest to so many modern believers will also appear—the story of the individual believer. Then we turn to the way in which Paul's interpretations of Jesus are shaped and conditioned by particular occasions in his churches (pp. 157-61), and to Paul's use of tradition (pp. 161-63).

2. *Jesus' Death as Jesus' Story*

When Paul speaks of Jesus' death as something that Jesus did, as opposed to something that God did to him,[12] Paul speaks of it as an act of love and obedience.[13] The pregnant phrase "for us" (in Gal. 2:20), moreover, points to Jesus' death as an act of *sacrificial* love.

We have become so used to the image of Jesus' death as a sacrifice that it is hard for us to realize how little background for such a faith there was at the time. In chapter 4, we observed that death as *sacrifice* or *martyrdom* was not emphasized in Judaism (pp. 82-85). It is at least possible that neither the first Christians nor Jesus himself thought in this way about Jesus' death. Isaiah 53 seems to have had little connection with messianic thinking except as it was drawn into this circle by Christians. Nevertheless, one important example of suffering and martyrdom was seen as religiously meaningful: the case of the Maccabean martyrs. In trying to understand the terrible days of the struggle between the Maccabean patriots and the dominating power of the Syrian Empire in the hellenistic age, the seemingly meaningless suffering and loss of life of patriotic, religious Jews was seen

to benefit others. Their faithful obedience to the righteousness of God became a power with which others in the
community could identify and thus find both strength to
endure and acceptance with God.[14]

Whether or not this exact historical background is
correctly identified, this pattern of faith was present in
Paul's churches and was central to him. As we shall see,
Paul's way of telling the story of Jesus is complex, for the
story is at once the story of Jesus and the story of Christ, the
pre-existent Child of God. The same love and obedience
characterize Jesus Christ, whether he is spoken of as the
Jesus about whom little is reported except his death or as the
Christ who entered into our history and died. For Paul, the
two are the same, and the story is the same.

Jesus' death is, of course, understood as more than the
martyrdom of a servant of God. The earliest tradition
handed on by Paul, which holds that this martyr "was *raised*
on the third day in accordance with the scriptures" (I Cor.
15:4 RSV; italics added), is linked to a story in which the
awaited new age has begun with Jesus' death and
resurrection (see I Cor. 15:20-28). Already in this tradition,
the story of Jesus or Christ intersects with the story of God
by the way in which the former is the focal point in the
coming of the new age God intends.

The story of Jesus, whose central event is the crucifixion,
is about a faithful servant of God who, out of obedience and
love, gives his life for others (Gal. 1:4 and 2:20). Because of
this self-sacrificial act, the crucifixion became the focal event
in God's redemptive dealings with the world: He was raised
from the dead (I Cor. 15:4 and often); he was highly exalted
(Phil. 2:9-11); and he was put forward as the expiation of
sins (Rom. 3:25). In short, he was designated God's Child in
power (Rom. 1:4), so that he "lives by the power of God" (II
Cor. 13:4 RSV).

These passages and others reflect the way Paul thinks of
Jesus Christ as the beginning of a new age. In using the bold
language of the new age to speak of the way Jesus' story
shows forth the story of God, Paul was doing what all, or
virtually all, of the early Christians did. The terms

Messiah—or Christ—resurrection, realm of God, and *the Human One* are all taken from the language of the new age. It was the strongest language available to speak of how new and different life was in the circle of faith. In fact, this language strains the story pattern almost to the breaking point, for what had been a straightforward story of how God's purpose *would* move toward its great consummation in the new future has become a story of how this purpose *has* come to its high point in Jesus Christ while it *still* waits for its final fulfillment in the future. Nowhere in early Christian literature is the tension between present and future stronger than in Paul. And it is clear that many of his hearers wished to release this tension by putting more emphasis on one side or the other, usually on the present, which they wished to believe was now free of problems for the believer.[15] Against these exponents of an oversimplified faith, Paul insisted that God's faithfulness is shown not by extracting the church from human difficulties, but by giving it the power to live fully and humanly in the difficult present (I Cor.).[16]

3. Jesus' Death as God's Story

The significance of Jesus' death, in Paul's view, comes to light in the context of the story about God's redemptive action in the world. As the focal "subplot" within this larger story, it expresses that God has destined believers not for wrath but for salvation.[17] Paul, therefore, can also say that the death of Jesus shows *God's* love (see Rom. 5:8 and 8:39). What Paul means is that it shows God's desire to save believers from the wrath that is intended for God's enemies and to do so by the sacrificial death of Jesus, whom God has "sent."[18]

An aspect of the story of God's faithfulness that has challenged successive generations of interpreters is its emphasis on the power of God and the utter confidence that God would prevail. To those who found themselves without power or direction, the gospel promised entry into a story that was not their own faltering course, but the unfolding of the divine purpose, which would not fail. Sometimes Paul speaks both of the past (Rom. 9:19-29) and of the future (Rom. 8:28-30) as if the outcome were determined in advance by God's purpose. Other ways of speaking suggest more openness, so that God's decision enters into the process as it unfolds; an example of this is the Philippians hymn (2:6-11). Romans 3:25, a key passage—usually translated, "whom God put forward as an expiation by his blood" (RSV)—could be understood as "whom God *regarded* as an expiation," a translation that would include God's participatory response to Jesus' death.[19]

The story of the fulfillment of God's purpose reaches also to the past. Paul has to argue that God's faithfulness is demonstrated in the historical order—which is to say that God keeps God's promises—since it might seem that Paul's view of the saving significance of Jesus' death would negate the Jewish law.[20] The consistency of God's story would be called into question if it appeared that God had shifted purposes along the way—shifted, that is, from the Jewish law to Christ as the means of salvation.[21] One way Paul seeks to demonstrate God's consistency is to say that God's purpose has always been that salvation should come through faith, not through the Jewish law (see Gal. 3:6-22; Rom. 3:27-4:25). The law of Moses was added only "because of transgressions" (Gal. 3:19).[22] But this does not mean that the law was given to create new life or to make individuals righteous (Gal. 3:21); that was to be the function of Jesus' death.[23] Paul saw no conflict here with the law, since the law itself promises a blessing to all who have a faith like Abraham's (Gal. 3:6-9; Rom. 4:1-25), just as the prophet Habakkuk (2:4) promises that "the righteous shall live out of faith."[24]

And Paul understands the law and faith to have different results. Far from bringing victory over sin and death, the Jewish law introduced accountability for sin and thereby increased transgressions.[25] Jesus' death, on the other hand, brings freedom from the power of sin and death (see Gal. 5:1-24; Rom. 6:1-8:39). As a result, persons formerly limited by the pervasive force of sin are now able to engage fully and gladly in life and to really live.

The picture sketched here of the place of the law in God's story is complicated by the fact that a few times Paul speaks as if those who lived under law, both the Jewish law and the "law written on their hearts" (Rom. 2:15), which was known to non-Jews, could rightly respond to God. He speaks of the possibility that the conscience of Gentiles might "perhaps excuse them on that day when, according to my gospel, God judges the secrets of human beings by Christ Jesus" (Rom. 2:15b-16).[26] By implication, the same could be true of followers of the Jewish law who followed it "through faith, [and not as if righteousness] were based on works" (Rom. 9:32).

There is thus a tension in Paul's thought about human existence under law, a tension that arises from the contrast between his insistence on human responsibility, on the one hand, and his confidence in God's sovereignty on the other. Some interpreters believe that Paul's insistence that the law was never intended to bring salvation is, therefore, implicitly qualified by the openness Paul occasionally seems to have shown to the possibility of a true response to God apart from Christ.[27] These interpreters are concerned with showing that Paul's strong statement of God's opposition to evil implies human responsibility and freedom, which could be used in right ways.

Others believe that Paul consistently placed the Jewish law in the limited framework that is sketched above.[28] They hold that in Romans 9:32 Paul was not thinking of earlier periods of response to the Jewish law but of his own time in which, he believed, faith was present only as faith in Jesus Christ. In this view there is no tension in the function of the law, which is clear and consistent, but there is a tension between human responsibility and the unavailability of freedom in the period before Jesus. We will see in the next chapter that this tension, whichever way it is interpreted, can be fruitful in bringing Paul's vision into creative contrast with our own.

Another way Paul shows the continuity in God's purpose

is to speak of Christ as Abraham's "offspring" and co-recipient of God's promise (Gal. 3:16, 19, 22). This association at the very least places Jesus within the larger story of God's dealings with Israel, but it also may indicate a direct parallel between Abraham and Jesus as exemplars of "faithfulness." Such a reading is possible if the genitive phrases in Galatians 2:15, 3:22, 26, and Romans 3:22, 26 are translated "the faith *of* Jesus," rather than "faith *in* Jesus."[29]

Besides the language of the new age and that of past faithfulness, Paul had other ways of clarifying how new life came through the death of Christ. One way is his contrast of Christ with Adam, as in Romans 5:15-21. Each is considered the representative head of a kind of humanity: Adam is seen as representing a humanity that is self-destructively disobedient toward God, and Christ as representing one that lives a new life in obedience to God.

God's story can be told in still different terms. Paul, using the language that has become so central in Christian theology, tells how it was through Christ's death that God's justice—or righteousness—was made effective (Rom. 3:21-26). This story, using language drawn from the law court, speaks of human beings who, though guilty of disobedience, are acquitted by God. Later theologians discussed the question of how far this means that they are forgiven even though they are sinful—and go on being sinful—or how far it means that they are transformed as well as forgiven.

This discussion has taken a new turn with the work of Ernst Käsemann and others who have emphasized that, for Paul, God's righteousness is not a distributive justice that responds after the fact to human deeds, but a power that creates a new situation. Drawing on Jewish usage, these scholars have recovered the dynamic, salvation-creating force of God's righteousness as Paul perceived it. They make it easier for us to understand how, for Paul, there was no question that a transformed life would follow in the life of faith.[30]

It is interesting, however, to note the interplay between Paul's statements and what readers have heard in them. Paul spoke of God's justice (or righteousness) and of a new situation for human beings. He spoke of God's taking responsibility for the human situation. He also emphasized human responsibility and its being "measured," so to speak, against God's justice (or righteousness). This emphasis, which is expressed in the forensic language of the law court, has been a primary source in our Western tradition for the intensification of individual self-consciousness, with a focus on personal responsibility and a highly individual grasp of what faith and salvation mean. The preaching of such a view of individual guilt and repentance has done much to bring about a sense of personal responsibility, not only for what one has done, but also for the kind of person one is.[31] Such attention to one's own standing before God is an inevitable feature of forms of Christian life heavily influenced by Paul's letters.

The highly individualistic way in which sin and forgiveness—and indeed human existence as a whole—have commonly been understood under the influence of Paul, however, is very different from Paul's own understanding. His emphasis is on *God's* justice (or righteousness)—on *God's* taking responsibility for the whole human condition—and on the continuity, as well as the discontinuity, between the old and the new life. This emphasis is apparent not only in what he says about the church, but also equally in his emphatic point that in offering salvation through Jesus' death, God has not abandoned Israel but is faithful to the promises made to them in their law (Rom. 9-11).

God's "story," of which Jesus' death is a part, is "told" not only as a story of dealings with the people of God, but also on a scale that includes the whole cosmos. Here it is a story—in the ontological order, the most general order of reality—about God's sovereignty among the multitude of powers that affect the condition of the world and existence in it.[32] Confidence that God is victorious in keeping these powers—which Paul regards as objectively real—from separating us from God's love (Rom. 8:31-39) is based not only on the inner testimony of the Spirit (Rom. 8:12-17) and on the faith that in prayer the Spirit intercedes for believers before God (Rom. 8:18-25), but also on the witness of Jesus' death and resurrection. In these events, the believer sees that God liberates the sufferer (Rom. 8:18-25) and that this Jesus who died for others now speaks on their behalf before God (Rom. 8:31-34). What this means is that Christians see reflected in Jesus' death and resurrection a God who "in everything works for good" (Rom. 8:28). This promise produces confidence that God will be victorious over all the enemies of God in creation, including sin and death.[33]

To conclude this section dealing with Jesus' death as the focal subplot in God's own story, special attention should be given to an intriguing feature of the hymn in Philippians 2:6-11.

> [Christ Jesus,] although having a divine form,
> did not consider equality with God something to be
>   seized;
> rather, he emptied himself
> and took the form of a slave.
> When he appeared as a human being,
> and was seen in human likeness,
> Christ humbled himself
> by becoming obedient to the point of death—
> even to death on a cross.
> Therefore, God exalted him to the highest position
> and gave as a gift the name which is greater than
>   any other name,
> that at the name of Jesus every knee should bow—
> in heaven, and on earth, and beneath the earth—
> and every tongue confess
> "Jesus Christ is Lord,"
> to the glory of God the [Creator].[34]

It is customary, and probably right, to regard the Christ figure as the primary subject of this hymn. Certainly the surface grammar suggests a plot in which the obedient one, who is crucified and exalted, is the principal figure. The hymn begins in the Greek with a relative pronoun, whose antecedent is Christ Jesus, who is the subject of the verbs in verses 6-8; and it concludes with a chorus of cosmic powers worshiping Jesus as Christ and Lord (vv. 9-11). But the surface grammar also places *God* in an active role in the dénouement of the narrative, for the tension built up by the self-emptying of a figure who gave up the divine form and "became obedient to the point of death" (vv. 6-8) finds resolution in *God's* action (v. 9). This divine action prompts the worship of Jesus as Christ and Lord, which is the purpose of God's action (vv. 10-11). Moreover, the goal of this worship is to give God "the glory" (v. 11). All this explicit attention to God makes the hymn as much a disclosure of God's being and action as it is of Christ's. It portrays the justice of God's dealings with those whose obedience is unconditional.

A feature of this hymn is the "offstage" story implied by its opening, which strikes a sinister note. The one who becomes the protagonist of the story could have become an *enemy* of God. Violent seizure of "equality with God" was a real possibility, since[35] the Christ figure already had a "divine form."[36] This sinister note implies an unstable world in which God's rule is subject to challenge. This same note also sets the stage for the drama that follows, at the conclusion of which an orderly, stable world can be seen. God's sovereignty is secure, precisely as it is shared as a gift with the one who might have seized it.[37] When all creation worships Jesus as Christ and Lord, God's rule is established. The worship of the crucified and exalted Christ within the community of faith contributes to the effectiveness of *God's* power. And when the attention that the death of Jesus draws to the redemptive activity of God in the world leads to participation in that activity, God's power increases and becomes more visible in and to the world.

So it is that the story of God's purpose, which lies behind what Paul says about the death of Jesus, sometimes embodies images that could suggest that God is in complete control and that the story is simply unfolding according to plan—that it was "predestined" (see Rom. 8:29-30; 9:19-23). At other times, the story is set forth in images that leave room for dramatic struggle and for the creative participation not only of Jesus as the Christ but also of the believing community—as in the Philippians hymn in its particular setting (Phil. 1:27–2:18). It is to this last-mentioned function of the story of Jesus' death that we now turn.

4. Jesus' Death as the Church's Story

These two stories, Jesus' and God's, are taken up within the believing community of Christians as their story. Paul's preaching of the crucified Messiah (see Gal. 3:1-5; I Cor. 1:17–2:5) presents Jesus' death and resurrection as an event in which they are invited to participate by faith. The part of the story of Jesus that is made up of the plot against him is relevant to the church because they recognize in it the same forces that were at work in themselves and now have been or are being transformed. The central point of the story, of course, is its invitation to take part in the salutary effects of Jesus' death.[38]

The act of faith, as a response to the proclamation of the crucified Messiah, can be understood as the opening of oneself to the patterns of love and obedience in the event of Jesus' death, which encourages the formation of those patterns in one's own life. Paul speaks of this effect of faith as a transformation of human existence, by means of which a person is no longer dominated by the power of the "present evil age" (Gal. 1:4) or "the world" (Gal. 6:14-15) or by "the flesh with its passions and desires" (Gal. 5:24) or even by one's own "self" (Rom. 6:1–8:17), but by "Christ who lives in me" (Gal. 2:20) or by the Spirit (Gal. 5:16, 25). This believing response to the message of the cross would not be complete, however, if it did not also lead to acts of love (Gal. 5:6; 6:9-10). One of the ways that the story of the crucifixion of Jesus is taken into the church's story, therefore, is to see in it forms of love to which the believer is called. One form of love is the bearing of another's suffering (see Gal. 6:2)—a form of love seen in Jesus' death (see Gal. 2:20).

But Jesus' death offers more than a model of sacrificial love, for in it can also be seen a form of faith that enables one to hope in the face of the fragile conditions of human existence in the world.[39] This hope has its ground in the faith that God deals justly with those who suffer "for righteousness' sake"—a faith dramatized by God's resurrection and exaltation of the crucified Messiah.[40] Ultimately, Jesus' death and resurrection offer hope before God in an *eschatological* sense.[41] That is, faith is not only a full and unreserved commitment to life in the precarious moment, but also a recognition that life under God's purpose is moving toward a future in which God will also be at work—and, Paul did not doubt, in which God will triumph over the forces that are destructive of life and of God's purposes. In short, by orienting its story to the story of Jesus' death as the focal "subplot" within God's story of a faithful and sovereign redeemer, the church sees itself and the world as known by God—not forgotten or ignored—and known not with wrath but with love (see I Thess. 1:9; Gal. 4:8-9).

The story of God's faithfulness made known and actual in the death of Jesus intersected concretely with the story of the church in the repeated occasion of the Lord's Supper.[42] The meal reactualized the death of Jesus. As Hans Conzelmann puts it, "Remembrance [I Cor. 11:24-25] is more than mere commemoration; it means a sacramental presence."[43] Here, too, the narrative element is apparent, for the Lord's Supper embodied both remembrance and presence, uniting the believers in one body (I Cor. 10:17-18); it also embodied an orientation to the future.[44] The death of Jesus was the focal point that bound the past, the present, and the future together.

The compression of the story element into its central moment, the death of Jesus, in Paul's whole vision of faith has often been noted. It is not too much to say that at the heart of the three stories we have sketched lies a vivid metaphor, which appears in two forms, more concretely as the cross, more broadly as the metaphor of death. The transformation of the abhorrent image of the cross from a symbol of ignominious death into a salvific symbol of life is at the heart of Paul's lasting legacy of faith.[45] Paul transformed the word *cross,* with its culturally repulsive and religiously scandalous associations, into a vital metaphor that serves as the interpretive key to his whole view of faith.

Christians early found the tension of life-and-death in the metaphor of the cross too difficult to maintain, and they transformed the cross into a venerated symbol of triumphant salvation. As a result, its profane and harsh elements were all but eliminated. This same contrast with Paul is evident in the churches of today, as we shall note in the next chapter (see pp. 171-73).

For Paul, death was more than a biological fact; it was a menacing force that demonically exerted power over existence. Death and sin were closely related (Rom. 5:12, 17; I Cor. 15:21). Though Paul can say that death came into the world through sin (Rom. 5:17), that does not exhaust his insight. Even though sin has been decisively overcome by the death of Jesus, death continues to exert its influence (I Cor. 15:24-26). Believers are still subject to its lingering power, though they no longer have to fear it (I Thess. 4:13-18). J. Christiaan Beker puts Paul's view this way: "As Christians we are constantly *subjected* to the reality of death and suffering, though we are only *threatened* by the possibility of sin."[46] Since death has this meaning for Paul, one would expect that the metaphor for the new age would be "life," as indeed it often is (I Cor. 15:20-23, 51-52). But in the present situation the new is present only proleptically, and believers still suffer and die and are under pressure to sin. In this perplexing situation, the death of Jesus provides the interpretive key. What looks like failure and "death," pure and simple, Paul interprets as God's offer of life through death. In this way, Paul finds positive and redemptive meaning in the perplexing tensions of life in the interim before "the End."

The metaphor of death is so complex and dense that it has to be read in more than one way. On the one hand, God's action in Jesus brings about a polar reversal, so that the negative, life-threatening effects of the old structure of existence have been transmuted through the power of the resurrection into positive, redemptive agents. For instance, baptism means incorporation into Jesus' *death* (Rom. 6:1-11), and the break with the old life is a *crucifixion* (Gal.

2:19-20; 6:14). The very language that had been used to speak of destruction is creatively turned to speak of new life.

On the other hand, the metaphor must also be read as holding two elements in creative contrast, rather than as total reversal, for death and resurrection are closely held together. Death is not simply life by total reversal. It is by holding together the seeming opposites that Paul opens the way to a deeper insight that life and fulfillment are not to be found directly, but come indirectly in the midst of their seeming opposites. In II Corinthians 4:7-12, Paul holds life and death together, both in the tension within his own existence—"perplexed, but not driven to despair" (v. 8 RSV)—and in the tension between himself and his congregation—"So death is at work in us, but life in you" (v. 12 RSV).[47]

This sketch of the story of the believing community displays two aspects of what we may call "unfinished business." On the one side, what are relations between this community and its individual members? And on the other, what about the wider world beyond the church? For Paul, the new life already at hand, as well as its future completion, is a shared life, very much the life of a *community*. The hope toward which the world is moving is a life into which all will come *together*. At the same time, the shape of Pauline faith did a great deal to throw the individual's spiritual and personal life into focus. The immense weight of responsibility that the Pauline style of faith uncovers and generates has pressed many believers toward a preoccupation with their own spiritual state and their own individual story.

To some extent, this process had already begun in Paul's own time; part of the troubles he had in making his kind of faith intelligible to the Corinthians, for instance, resulted from the way in which many of them heard him in a much more individualistic way than he intended to be heard. In later times, and into our own time, trying to hear Paul has often led to a highly individualized kind of faith, in which believers are concerned with their own personal stories to such an extent that the story of the church is eclipsed. Particularly in the last few centuries, when many other forces have been working for individualism, Paul has often been heard in this way.

It must be granted, as we noted above (see pp. 147-48), that concern for one's own spiritual state is a genuinely Pauline theme. But it is important to observe that Paul develops this theme in such a way that it is interwoven with an emphasis on the highly interpersonal and interactive dimensions of a life of faith, which call for mutual responsibility. For him, the individual's story is not to be the center but a part of the church's story.[48]

The direction of Paul's language has invited this concentration of attention on the isolated self. Many of his most powerful statements about the love of God, which overturns our expectations and breaks through our destructive and self-destructive condition to open new possibilities of life, are clearly cast in terms of the story of the church. But the kind of reflection about human existence that they invite naturally turns the reader's or hearer's attention to self-examination. Romans 5:6-11, which is perhaps Paul's most concentrated expression of the church's story, speaks of the common situation of humanity before God. Verse 6 (RSV), for example, says: "While we were still weak, at the right time Christ died for the ungodly." Similarly, in Romans 3:24 Paul says that "they"—not "I" or "you"—are justified. But both of these statements can easily stimulate a new and deeper awareness of one's inner self.

In several striking places, of course, Paul does speak about the "I." The most striking of these are Galatians 2:18-20—with its concluding reference to Jesus "who loved me and gave himself for me" (RSV)—and Romans 7:7-25, where Paul describes the struggle of the self (the "I") under the domination of sin. Both of these passages have very understandably contributed to what we may call the intensification of self-awareness. So far as Paul himself is concerned, however, both of these passages speak about the "*typical* I."[49] No doubt he brought his own story to bear on his interpretation of the general human condition and of the life of faith. But for him, these were thoroughly intertwined. The interplay of self and community is a clearer problem to us today, since the ties of a person to the communities to which he or she belongs are often so fragile.

On the other side of the Christian community, there is the larger community of humanity and, as well, the whole cosmos. For Paul, as we noted above (see pp. 148-50), God's story has a cosmic setting. In his presentation of his faith to his churches, however, he was not much concerned for this aspect of the human story.[50] He does, it is true, take the theme of cosmic redemption into his message of hope.[51] The word *ktisis* ("creation") in Romans 8:19-22 has been taken to mean the "human creation."[52] But it is more natural, especially in the light of the cosmic setting of so much apocalyptic, to take it in its usual sense as the *whole* "creation." Paul's way of relating God's story and the church's story, therefore, does open the question of the relationship between human beings and the wider cosmos, but this theme is suggested rather than developed (see also Gal. 6:14-15).

Paul's interest focuses much more on the question of the relation between the wider human circle and the church's story. Passionately concerned for this wider circle, Paul expresses the conviction that the story of the wider circle has meaning only in relationship to the church's story—a story that is open to the future and moving to the future. It is here that life and true humanness are to be found. And it was precisely the death of Jesus as the Messiah that opened the community of faith to all people. Conversely, it is in relation to the story of the believing community—in essential continuity with the story of Israel, in which the death of Jesus as the Messiah was the central event—that the story of the whole of humanity had meaning.

Paul's limitation of the human story to the story of the believing community will be problematic to many modern readers.[53] A context for further thinking about it, however, can be found in another aspect of "unfinished business" in Paul's vision of this human story. That is the relation of the church's story to God's story.

The human story of a community of faith can be told as a

story into which persons are invited—that is, as an invitation to women and men to take God's story for their own. It could also be told equally well as a story into which persons are drawn—that is, as a story in which God takes the initiative and brings them into God's story. Either way, the church's story is a continuation of God's story, in which human beings participate in the fulfillment of God's own purposes. As Paul understands it, the fundamental theme of the church's story is the justice of God. Since God's justice was primarily demonstrated in the story of God's working with Israel, Paul strives to show how this relationship between God's story and the human one has to do with God's justice, as we have suggested above (see pp. 147-48). Nevertheless, Paul also recognizes the incompleteness of what he can say about God's story. In liturgical language, Paul confesses that God's story is greater than he can comprehend (see Rom. 11:33, 36).

5. Jesus' Death in Paul's Pastoral Theology

These, then, are the themes that Paul's interpretation of Jesus' death lifts up. They have been presented in a somewhat synthetic construction of Paul's interpretation of Jesus' death in three "stories." It must also be said—and emphasized—that Paul comes to deal with these three stories as he meets a wide range of pastoral concerns. It is in the service of these practical and pastoral concerns that the question of Jesus' death usually comes up in his letters.

In I Thessalonians 1:1-10, for example, we find an emphasis on Jesus' resurrection, in anticipation of the consolation in 2:1–3:13. The latter offers comfort in the view that, although suffering is the human "lot," the God who raised Jesus from the dead, and the Jesus who brings deliverance from the coming wrath of God, will not leave anyone in suffering forever. In the same letter, 5:9-10 focuses on Jesus' sacrificial death in answer to the question of whether Christians who have *died* ("fallen asleep"), as much as *living* Christians, will be (or live) "with the Lord always"; just as they are joined with Jesus in his death "for us," so also will they be joined with him in his resurrection (4:13–5:11). By means of a double entendre, "whether we wake or sleep" (5:10 RSV), which has to do both with mortality (compare JB "alive or dead") and with morality (see 5:6-7), Paul brings together the promise and demand of hope.[54]

In the letter to the churches in Galatia, where the issue is whether the benefits of Jesus' death are only for the believers who live in obedience to Jewish law, the central concerns of Paul's interpretation of Jesus' death are ethical and soteriological rather than consolatory. Hope for the believers' resurrection, a secondary concern in the letter, is tied to the Spirit[55] and so only indirectly to Jesus' resurrection from the dead (but see 1:1). The belief that Jesus' sacrificial death brings deliverance from the "present evil age" (1:4) supports Paul's argument that the Galatians had no need for the Jewish law. The law had been given "because of transgressions" (3:19). Since the Messiah has come, however, the believer has no need of this "peda-gogue" (3:23-25),[56] for the crucified Messiah "gave himself for our sins, so that he might rescue us from the present evil age" (1:4).

Paul's emphasis on the "word of the cross" in I Corinthians 1:10–2:5 is a response to the Corinthians' one-sided emphasis on power in charismatic experience. They needed to be reminded that the power that they had came as a gift from Paul's proclamation of the crucified Messiah (2:2), who is "preached as raised from the dead" (15:12 RSV). Here the "word of the cross" (1:18) is "the foolishness . . . and the weakness of God" (1:25 RSV), because it is the proclamation of the crucified Messiah (1:23). But this same "word of the cross" is also the power and wisdom of God (1:24). The Corinthians have received the power of which they boast from Paul's preaching— which is the power of Christ to be sure, but precisely as the crucified one (2:1-15).

The dialectic of weakness and power in Paul's interpreta-tion of Jesus' death in the Corinthian correspondence (it does not occur elsewhere) shifts in II Corinthians 10–13. There he responds to "super apostles," who had contempt for Paul's weakness where the "signs of a true apostle" (12:11-13) were concerned. Paul argues that, just as Christ was "crucified in weakness, but lives by the power of God" (RSV), Paul himself is weak in respect to Christ but will deal with the "super apostles" out of the power of God (13:3-4). Here Paul draws a parallel between the events of Jesus' death and resurrection and Paul's own action. The emphasis is on what Paul promises (or threatens!) will follow upon his acknowledged "weakness." As resurrection followed the death of Jesus, so also, when Paul deals with the "super apostles" in Corinth, a demonstration of God's power will follow Paul's "weakness"!

It is important to note that Paul does not say in the Corinthian correspondence that Jesus' crucifixion is itself a model of power. He does say that God takes what is weak, "the word of the cross," and *through* it offers power to those who believe that the crucified Jesus is the Messiah. But there is no illusion about the *weakness* of crucifixion and preaching about a cross.[57] "The word of the cross" remains a "stumbling block" and "folly," not only for Jew and Greek, but also for us, since it could hardly have been anticipated—and even in retrospect it is difficult to understand—that God would choose to make the crucified one the Messiah.[58] Nevertheless, that is what Paul preached, and that is what the Corinthians believed when they received the Spirit and power from his preaching of "Jesus Christ and him crucified" (I Cor. 2:1-5 RSV).[59]

Another dimension of Paul's interpretation of Jesus' death is brought out in his letter to the Philippians when he responds to a situation in some respects similar to those of Galatians and II Corinthians 10–13. Evidently some Christians who had found their way into the church in Philippi created strife over their zeal about being Jewish (see 3:2ff.). Paul responded by declaring that he found their worldly standards of excellence, which he once shared, to be "refuse" (a polite translation!), because in the death and exaltation of the Christ he had discovered standards of a higher order (see 3:2-16)—and this in the Messiah of Israel who could also claim for himself all their criteria of noble birth and more! Central to his argument is a hymn in which God's standards of excellence are dramatically portrayed (2:6-11; see above, pp. 149-51). God highly exalts Jesus, not because of his external form, but because he became obedient to the limit—namely, to death itself—more than that, to death on a cross. The well-placed "therefore" in 2:9 makes it clear that God acted upon seeing Jesus' radical obedience. All other standards of excellence would henceforth pale in comparison no matter how noble they once appeared. As in Galatians and in the Corinthian correspondence, Paul again brings out how Jesus' death undermines conventional values. But here the connection made between Jesus' death and exaltation is logical: The former is the reason for the latter. As a result, the assurance implied by the demand "have this mind-set among yourselves which was in Christ Jesus" (2:5) is strengthened and provides a foundation for the exhortation not to be frightened in anything by their opponents (1:28) and "with fear and trembling" to make their salvation effective (2:12).

In summary, it should be clear that Paul's interpretation of the death of Jesus is relatively fluid and situation-specific. Depending on the pastoral occasion, Paul develops diverse interpretations in each letter. Even Romans is no exception; it is as dependent on a particular occasion as are the other letters.[60] The forensic language and law court imagery connected with Jesus' death[61]—far from being the absolute center of Paul's theological reflection—are actually prominent only in Romans, where they are specifically occasioned by Paul's defense of God's salvation of the gentiles through faith and of God's faithfulness to Israel, which are two sides of the same coin.[62] Therefore, as important as the juridical dimension is, and as powerful as its presentation in Romans is, it is one among the many different emphases of Paul's interpretations of Jesus' death. His letters resist the identification of one systematic "doctrine" about the saving significance of Jesus' death. Indeed, they constitute a prime example of the interplay of contrasting proposals and of suggestive imagery.

6. Jesus' Death in Paul's Tradition and Interpretation

As this chapter concludes, it is important for the preacher today to observe the way Paul reflected on the traditions he received—the way he transformed past proposals into new ones. Paul had no direct knowledge of the events of Jesus' death. Unlike the risen Jesus, with whom Paul claimed immediate experience, the events of Jesus' death were known to him only through traditions.[63] Paul's interpretation of Jesus' death, therefore, directly concerns *texts*—whether written or oral—and only indirectly the *event* itself. These texts, or traditions, as Paul represents them,[64] contain Paul's predecessors' interpretations, which he delivers to others, continuing the transmission of tradition.

Of course, Paul claimed to know directly the crucified Jesus.[65] Paul believed that his interpretation took place in the context of a living presence—in modern terms we can say, a field of force—so that both the community and the divine presence contributed to the way in which the traditions were encountered and reexpressed. Thus Paul exhibits a freedom to interpret them in his own way. In the examples that follow, there is uncertainty in the details; we do not have the exact expressions of faith that came to Paul, probably almost entirely in an oral form. All would agree, however, that Paul both received and modified tradition.[66]

Paul shifts the emphasis of I Thessalonians 1:10 and 5:10, for example, from *forgiveness* of sins—implied by the notion of deliverance from wrath and the "for us" phrase—to the *avoidance* of "immorality."[67] His primary interest, new in these texts, is the assurance they offer regarding the unity of the living and the dead in Christ (see I Thess. 4:13-18; 5:10).

The traditions behind Galatians 1:4; 2:20; and Romans 3:25 also emphasized "forgiveness of sins."[68] Paul replaces this theme with that of "deliverance"—the transformation of an age such that sin no longer has the power it once had. Apocalyptic thought, of course, plays a part in Paul's interpretation of these traditions. Paul, however, transforms Jewish apocalyptic when he employs its conceptuality to argue that the sacrificial death of the Messiah ushers in an age in which Jewish law is no longer in force. Nils A. Dahl has suggested that Paul's view of the provisional character of the Jewish law should be understood in the light of the view in Judaism that certain "prescriptions and decrees" were in principle provisional, remaining valid only until an agent of God comes.[69] Paul's innovation was to apply this view to the whole law, concluding that the coming of Jesus as the Messiah brought an end to the age of the Jewish law.[70]

Although Paul appears to have preserved the traditional meaning of I Corinthians 15:3-7, he has placed it within an apocalyptic discourse. Here the emphasis is less on "forgiveness of sins"[71] than on "resurrection of the dead" (15:12-19). Moreover, the tradition (vv. 3-7) is tied to a narrative about God's victory over all the enemies of God (15:20-28). That may also be traditional; whether it was the original meaning is doubtful. At the end of Paul's discussion, the two themes—victory over sin and victory over death—come together (15:51-57). Paul's immediate concern—namely, the charismatic Corinthians' disregard for responsibility for their bodily existence—introduces a note that the tradition may not have emphasized: Although Christ died "for our sins" (15:3), a day of judgment still lies in the future (11:26). This last passage, coming as it does at the conclusion of the traditional "words of institution" (11:23-25), represents Paul's own interpretive addition to the Lord's Supper tradition (11:27-34).

No doubt there were varied styles of Christian hope in the church prior to Paul. His own eschatological message combines a strong hope for the fulfillment of God's purpose—and soon, in all probability[72]—with an awareness of how this impending event, combined with the anticipation of the end in the death and resurrection of Jesus, transformed the present situation. In contrast to many in Corinth, Paul held that the present was indeed genuinely transformed, but transformed in such a way that the cross of Jesus Christ is the mark of present existence.[73]

Finally, the hymn in Philippians 2:6-11 probably did not originally have a hortatory function, as it does in 1:27–2:18, but simply offered praise to elicit the acclamation "Jesus Christ is Lord." Indeed, certain features resist transferring the hymn from Christ to the believer—namely, the original divine form of the Christ figure, the "likeness" of Christ's human form, and Jesus' exaltation as Lord. Paul's hortatory interpretation[74] does not attempt an item-by-item transfer from Christ to the believer. That was possible in gnostic exegesis, because gnostics believed that human beings, like Jesus, came from "above" and would return there. For Paul, the hymn points to the ground of the confidence in salvation from God that puts away all fear of one's opponents (1:28), so that Paul draws attention to a certain pattern of obedience (2:8) and divine response (2:9-11) that can and does apply to the existence of believers.

What this review of Paul's use of traditions shows is that he was both *dependent* on the traditions he received about Jesus' death and its interpretation, and at the same time *independent* of them in developing his own pastoral interpretations. Paul did not claim to be an eyewitness of the death of Jesus as a past event in history, which was mediated to him by tradition and proclamation, but he did claim an immediate experience of its salutary effects.[75] Paul preached out of what he knew—namely, the significance that Jesus' death has for the present. The preacher's situation today is analogous.

CHAPTER EIGHT

PREACHING GOD'S JUSTICE

Interpreting Jesus' Death in the Letters of Paul

1. Issues in Telling the Story

I n the previous chapter we approached what Paul said about Jesus' death in terms of several interwoven stories, in each of which the death of Jesus is the central turning point. "Story" is an imaginative form that is metaphoric rather than systematic. It tends to be more tolerant of logical inconsistencies and can leave open questions about the coherence of its premises, thereby enabling it to bring into creative contrast elements that stand in tension; in some forms, it is free from the burden of historical evidence. It draws its power from its ability to propose a meaning or value, expressed in the form of a narrative of a possible chain of events, of which we might imagine ourselves to be a part. In other words, it seeks to engage our will and action as well as our understanding by inviting us to allow our own vision of life, and the values derived from it, to be creatively transformed by that of the story.[1]

Sometimes this transformation through imaginative participation in a story takes place spontaneously. Often, however, profound obstacles hinder our being drawn into the story—as when the world of a story is too distant from the reader's own world. On such occasions, it is not enough for the preacher merely to propose to hearers that stories as Paul told (or presupposed) them are their own. What is needed is a more profound undertaking—namely, to make it possible for Paul's stories of Jesus' death to interact with the stories in which persons live today in such a way that their stories are creatively transformed by interaction with Paul's. In this way, the preacher can help others to grapple with the distance between the stories that Paul told (or presupposed) and the stories that unfold in the world as we know it.

As we said earlier (see chap. 2), our encounter with the Bible is most effective not just when we "translate" it into terms that are intelligible to us, but when we allow its different vision to challenge and enlarge our own world, as we hold in tension the contrast between its way of speaking and our own. Often that means highlighting features of the biblical text that make little sense in our world. However, this is not an approach to the Bible that requires our giving up our own world and the stories that shape it and are shaped by it to exchange them for "biblical" ones. Instead, we propose a way of reading the Bible in which our vision of reality is transformed as a result of a creative interaction with the visions of the biblical text, a transformation that also often alters the perspective of the hearer/reader in a way that opens possibilities of the biblical text that have usually been overlooked.

In our chapters on Mark, we focused attention on the question of meaning in suffering posed by the story Mark tells of Jesus' death, since the theme of suffering plays such a central role in Mark's story of Jesus' death. Although this theme also appears in Paul's letters, a great deal of what Paul has to say about the death of Jesus is said in terms and images of divine justice. The theme of "God's justice," therefore, forms the center of the present chapter.

God's justice has usually meant that God would win out in the end and that "you can't get away with it." As the proverb has it, "The mills of God grind slow, but they grind exceeding fine." Paul stands in this tradition of judgment when he says in Romans 2:6 that God will judge each one according to his or her works. But Paul has always been a disturbing voice in the tradition of divine judgment. In the first place, we see in his letters a new vision of God's justice in tension with the traditional one, for here God's justice is shown in that God "justifies the ungodly" (Rom. 4:5). God's righteousness becomes a gift instead of a standard to be met.

Further, studies of early Christian hope regarding "the End" have helped to recover an added dimension in Paul's understanding of God's righteousness—namely, that it is an act of power, the creation of a new environment into which believers are drawn. This latter emphasis corrects the thrust toward individualism that can be part of the "sheer gift" reading of God's righteousness. This emphasis is congenial to the emphasis of this book on the "story" quality of God's relation to human beings, though the end to which Paul looked forward as the full expression of God's righteousness will have to be reinterpreted in our perspective.[2] For both aspects of God's righteousness—the gift side and the power side—the death of Jesus is at the center of Paul's vision. From the beginning, Paul's readers have had to struggle with the tension between a more traditional scheme of rendering to each what is due and a subversive theme of God's rendering good even though it was not due.

It is all the more a struggle for us. Our world presents little evidence that would encourage people to believe that they will get what they deserve. The innocent suffer and righteousness seems to receive no reward, while the wicked seem to go unpunished. Insofar as American religion functions naively to assert a simple faith in people getting what they deserve, it will in the end be an escape from the harsh realities we face, and it will serve a self-righteous ideology. Difficult as it is to enter into Paul's thought, his letters can serve the disturbing function they have always had, if we listen to them with care. In the process, we shall have to discover anew what God's justice is.

The stories that contribute to the shape of the world in which we live include other features that make it difficult to enter into Paul's vision of God's justice. Among this cluster of stories, one dominant American story places such a high value on the independence of the individual that it excludes from view our real interdependence. Another lacks hope, while others provide a form of hope based on confidence in the success of such mundane resources and human activities as technology, law and order, education, psychology, and the military. Paul's vision, on the other hand, points to the extra-mundane justice of God as the basis for hope, interpreted in part in apocalyptic terms.

What is the modern Christian to think? Some turn to an apocalypticism far more extreme—and also more nega-tive—than Paul's. Some divide their minds between a modern vision and ancient apocalypticism. Others simply reject what the ancients, including Paul, have to offer.

Is there a better way than any of these? In this chapter, we propose that each of the stories by which Paul and modern Christians live has something to offer. Paul is not so committed to apocalypticism that he is not open to the real value of what is humanly achievable.[3] And the dominant views of life in our world can be genuinely enriched, challenged, and creatively transformed when they include a recognition of our real interdependence, not only in relation to other human beings and other creatures, but also in relation to God as a transmundane reality. The creative synthesis toward which preaching can move us, therefore, need neither deny our own distinctive, modern perspectives nor be disloyal to the depths of Paul's thoughts about the death of Jesus and God's justice.

Most of the time modern Christians will find that the "story" of Jesus' death as Paul "tells" it speaks from a world very distant from their own. Yet we do not always need to begin by dealing directly with this distance. Sometimes we are astonished at the way the deep symbols of our heritage can speak without being explained. This kind of speaking often takes place most readily in times of crisis, but most preaching occurs in more ordinary circumstances. Yet even in less difficult times, modern Christians are often more ready than we think to enter into the difficult world that is offered to us by Paul's letters.

In preaching from Pauline texts, it is not easy just to "tell the story." That is because the "stories" Paul had in mind are often presented in so compressed or even so indirect a fashion. Often the "story" or narrative aspect is not spelled out or told in full at all (as we saw in the previous chapter). This compressed manner of presenting the story of Jesus' death is one reason why preachers and theologians so easily move to a more abstract or doctrinal way of speaking about what Paul says about the cross. In this section of the chapter, we will look at three of the great passages on Jesus' death in Paul to uncover the "stories" that lie in or behind them, with the aim of spelling them out in preaching.

a. In *Galatians 2:19-20* (compare 6:14), three stories are intertwined: "my" story, the story of Jesus Christ, and a story of the community of faith, which brings the first two together even though it is not explicitly expressed. One can begin with any one of these stories, but it was the question of how to understand the church's story that started Paul on this whole discussion in Galatians 1 and 2.[4] If we are to do justice to Paul, we shall have to show how all three stories are connected. Here "my" story is a story of finding through giving up, of life through death, of being crucified with Christ, of being made alive by Christ. Another way of speaking of "my" story, using different terms but amounting to the same thing, is found in Paul's reference to living in the "flesh" by faith—that is, living in "the whole sphere of that which is earthly and 'natural,'"[5] which so easily appears to have nothing to do with faith and which so easily becomes the locus of destructive impulses. "My" story, in other words, is a story of the affirmation of life in the midst of a precarious existence and not a "story" of a journey to a secure place (as this passage is so often read).

The story of Jesus Christ as it appears here is cast in the same pattern, except that the ending of it is more complex. Paul scarcely mentions the resurrection in Galatians;[6] yet, he surely presupposes it in the phrase "I no longer live myself, but Christ lives in me." The circumstances called for speaking of Christ in such a way that the triumphant ending of the story was held back; it was not a time for making that point. As Paul tells the story here, Jesus Christ has drawn "me" into his story by sharing my precariousness, symbolized by "flesh" and death. It is on that basis that the (implied) narrative moves forward.

We noted in the previous chapter (see p. 155) that the "I" or "me" in this passage, which sounds so personal to us, was for Paul a very much more generalized "I." That is to say, Paul offers what he says as the typical experience of the believer, a shared experience, which is how the church's story appears indirectly in this passage. The church is the fellowship of those who share the gift that is encountered in Jesus, "who gave himself for me." This point is made more clearly by the use of the first person plural in 1:4: "[Christ Jesus] gave himself for our sins, to rescue us from the present evil age." The style of the community's life is set forth especially in the later part of Galatians, which makes actual the life of mutual and self-giving love that 2:20 expresses.[7]

b. In *Romans 5:1-11,* we see much the same interweaving of our story and that of Jesus, except that it is all cast in terms of "we" instead of "I." Here the believers' story is spelled out as a kind of ascent in the midst of difficulty, a story of the growth of character. Of course, we know that suffering does not always produce "endurance" and that having to endure suffering does not always produce "character" (v. 4).[8] It will not do for us to use what Paul says as a general explanation of why we have to go through suffering. We should beware of this use of these verses in preaching, for Paul was not speaking of a general moral discipline through which we grow. He was writing to those who (so he believed) knew that a great transformation had taken place in their lives, even though they were in the midst of the same old story. Their story had a direction that focused in hope.

The ascent of the believers' story might well be set in counterpoint to the descent of Jesus' story.[9] Here, however, Paul does not emphasize the movement of descent in Jesus' story so much as the sharp contrast between what we see in ourselves and what we see of God in Jesus. Romans 5:1-5, which traces the upward movement of the believer, is set over against 5:6-11, which pictures God's love made known in Jesus, not by stages but by successive repetitions of the amazing love that Jesus' death represents. This love overturns and forgets the kind of calculation of degrees of virtue that is presupposed in the growth of character in verse 4. The strongest possible contrast is drawn between what we deserved and what we got: Christ died for the "weak . . . ungodly . . . [unrighteous] . . . sinners . . . enemies [of God]." Thus movement in our story is set over against the finality of Jesus' story.

Many modern Christians will balk at the dark picture of "us" that Paul draws. It is not necessarily our part to force this down their throats! Paul's point lies somewhere else—on the unexpected good news of the freedom and release that could not have been calculated or predicted. That is something we can speak of without insisting on Paul's particular profile of human bondage. This picture, of course, Paul had already set forth in detail in Romans 1–3.

At the same time, Paul's negative view of the present human condition, which is presupposed here (and more directly expressed in a passage like Rom. 3:21-26), needs to be confronted in preaching. It can be liberating, paradoxically, even for those who resist it, as readers of Paul have experienced through the centuries. Paul's story of human failure—a failure all too evident to us today (though we cast it in terms of education, psychology, sociology, economics, and politics, which are different from Paul's own terms)—is also a story of unexpected deliverance. That—not the negative view of the human condition—is what really makes it hard to accept. Time and again the encounter with this message has opened unwilling eyes to the web of destructiveness in which we find ourselves enmeshed, which Paul in his own way so graphically describes in the early part of Romans. The actual destructiveness of the world is so unavoidably evident in all our recent history, but Paul's strong affirmation of the possibility of a new world into which we enter by faith is not so evident. Moreover, it would seem that Jesus' death has contributed so little to the "progress" of history that it has made little difference to the actual world in which we live.

It is important, therefore, to emphasize that in Romans

5:1-11 Paul tells "our" story as an *unfinished* one. It is a story of hope, that mysterious affirmation of life and of the future in the midst of *incompleteness*. Interpretations of hope range from those that locate hope on a trajectory or path that can be seen to head toward its conclusion, to those that stress that hope is "hoping against hope" (Rom. 4:18), affirming life in spite of its apparent hopelessness (Rom. 8:18-25). Paul can be read in both ways. In I Corinthians 15 and Romans 11 he situates hope in the clear context of the final victory of God's purposes. In Romans 8:18-39 he presents hope in the situation of conflict, with the ground for hope expressed as the love of God, from which nothing can separate us (v. 39).[10] In our present passage, hope is joined to the gift of God in Jesus to affirm the confidence that the journey of faith has a direction, which is expressed in the series of qualities of character in Romans 5:3-4. As in Galatians 2:20, the stress is on continuing faith and hope in the midst of the precariousness of life.

c. In *II Corinthians 4:7-12*, the metaphoric tension of death and life comes to powerful expression. Paul begins by asserting that the suffering that he (as well as other believers) experiences—"afflicted in every way . . . perplexed . . . persecuted . . . struck down"—does not have the devastating effect of leaving him "crushed . . . driven to despair . . . forsaken . . . destroyed" (vv. 8-9 RSV), effects that are characteristic of suffering in our ordinary experience or, in Paul's framework, in the passing aeon. The reason for the difference is that within our "earthen vessels," which are under assault by death and its agent, suffering, the transcendent power of God is now at work (v. 7).

God's power is at work, on the one hand, neutralizing the old aeon's devastating effects of suffering and death and, on the other hand, transmuting suffering and death into the constituent features of the redemptive life—the cruciform life, the life that is the representation of the life of Jesus. Consequently, in the paradoxical world of present existence in the interim, that which was once life-defeating—namely, death (specifically, death by crucifixion, and the many other forms of suffering that come from persecution)—now has become the means for giving life, particularly as it is manifest in the life of believers, in the cruciform life. The afflictions suffered by preachers of the gospel of Jesus Christ, precisely because of their preaching, are signs of "death at work"—not just "death," but *Jesus'* death, through which life is born in others. That is what Paul means in the pithy maxim concluding this passage: "So death is at work in us, but life in you" (4:12).

This passage suggests that a central path to recovering a theology of the cross can be found by taking seriously the term *death* as the metaphor that today best conveys the original meaning that "the cross" had in the communication between Paul and his hearers. Like the cross in Paul's day, death—not only physical death, but also death experienced as psychological and spiritual meaninglessness—is a feared and sometimes terrifying reality that haunts the contemporary psyche.

Paul's message opens the possibility of transforming this harsh metaphor into the polar tension of life and death that we see in this passage from II Corinthians. The metaphor of death, assisted by the hermeneutical agency of "the cross," can bring new meaning to the phenomenon of dying, particularly if in preaching we allow the two Pauline metaphors, "cross" and "death," to be heard in concert, with the metaphorical reach of each resonating with the other. The "word of the cross" can open us to freedom from perceiving death as a life-threatening power, so that death can be seen as a life-enabling power, even a redemptive and liberating power essential to the creative advance of life.

An encounter with this passage can be an important corrective to the temptation of Christian masochism, which interprets the way of the cross as in some way dying for the self, a path of seeking to be worthy of salvation because of one's sufferings. If we can affirm life-in-death in the tensive, metaphorical way that we find in Paul's metaphor, we may find ourselves surprisingly sustained by the Spirit and in a transformed, reconciled relationship with others. As Paul put it, "While we live we are always being given up to death for Jesus' sake, so that the life of Jesus may be manifested in our mortal flesh. So death is at work in us, but life in you" (II Cor. 4:11-12 RSV).

d. These remarks about "telling the story" on the basis of Paul's stories about the death of Jesus have reminded us that the story approach is both perennially powerful and at the same time full of questions. In the recent discussion of story and theology, no consensus has been reached. On the one hand, the story approach has been liberating because of its concreteness and because it often enables us to enter quite directly into the biblical message.[11] On the other hand, we have been reminded that stories have a "constructed" character—that is, they are put together by our imaginations and are not necessarily representations of how things are.[12] As we said above, at certain times it is enough simply to "tell the story." Preaching influenced by Karl Barth (see pp. 18-19), for example, would tell how God has already changed the human situation, in order to free persons from their preoccupation with themselves and to free them for the life that is there for them as they open themselves to what God has done. Preaching, however, also has to go behind the story, so to speak, to engage aspects of the encounter between faith and life that do not come to expression simply by "telling the story."

2. Rediscovering Our Interrelatedness: The Death of Jesus in Jesus' Story

The previous chapter has shown us that in Paul's letters the meaning of Jesus' death within *Jesus' story* is proclaimed in a cluster of statements about Jesus' love and obedience, which were "for us." Jesus' death thus points toward both *God*, through Jesus' faith in and obedience to God's righteousness, and *us*, through Jesus' act of sacrificial love for us (see pp. 142-44). Classic passages that suggest these themes for preaching are Romans 3:21-26 and 5:6-11, with the metaphors of expiation (Rom. 3:25) and death "for us" (Rom. 5:8).

The language that was so central for Paul is difficult for many today. Behind the strangeness of Paul's images, there lies a deeper strangeness that arises from the present, pervasive loss of the sense of the interconnectedness of life. Many wonder how one life, or death, especially one so distant, can have an influence on us. The language of sacrifice is left hanging, with little or no reference point in experience. This is true when we think of sacrifice in our modern, generalized sense of sacrificial giving, but it is even more true of sacrifice in the ancient sense of cultic expiation. In Paul's time many people could unreflectively project a sense of human and organic relatedness upon the cosmos and upon their social world. We are still just as interdependent on one another and on the cosmos as human beings have always been, but the ideology of individual freedom and action has masked that interdependence.[13]

We are as interdependent in the joyful and creative experiences of life as we are in our anguish, but anguish often has a unique power to open our eyes to the unnoticed connectedness of life. Charles Dickens, in *Bleak House,* found an illustration of our relatedness in the way disease and its tragic consequences spread from the slums to the homes of the aristocrats.[14] With the threat of the end of human life, or even of all life on earth—even the death of this planet itself—in a nuclear holocaust, the period of the ideology of "rugged individualism" could be closing, in spite of the efforts of politicians and the media to promote it.

The interconnectedness of all people, and of all people with the rest of the planet, as with the whole universe, is driven home to us in the modern age by such events as the depletion of tillable soil and proximate sources of firewood for subsistence farmers in Brazil as a result of the "development" of Brazil's urban centers; the tragic destruction created by earthquakes and swarms of tornadoes; the new life made possible for others by the decision of a young person dying of a brain tumor to donate vital organs for transplantation; the effect of the mismanagement of industrial wastes on the world's forests and wetlands; and the outpouring of compassion around the world, inadequate as it is, in response to famine in Ethiopia, itself the result of the interconnectedness of weather patterns, land use and mismanagement, and patterns of life deeply ingrained in very old cultures. In the face of such developments, some people, Christians included, become despairing of hopeful solutions. Others find hope in some form of (often negative) apocalyptic vision of "the End." Still others, including Christians, look to political, economic, and technological solutions for confidence about the future. Whatever our response might be, the inescapable interconnectedness of all things is being brought home with graphic images once again.

A principal way to explore the meaning of the death of Jesus lies at just this point. In the Christian tradition, Jesus' death decisively brings into view the inescapable confrontation with our interconnectedness, both with one another and with God. All of the theologies of atonement presuppose this dimension of the church's memory of Jesus' death.[15] We agree with Daniel Day Williams that what we see in the death of Jesus is best understood from the point of view of our experiences of reconciliation between persons, which can be described as having four phases or elements: disclosure and recognition of the rift, loyalty in spite of it and suffering as its consequence, the speaking of the healing word, and the emergence of a new community in which the actuality of the reconciliation is carried forward.[16]

From this point of view the death of Jesus opens our experience both to the sheer interconnectedness of human beings with one another and to the connections between our existence and God's. Neither set of connections is complete without the other. We need to have our eyes opened to the depth and extent of the human connections, as noted just above, in order to think honestly about what we shall do with our lives. We also need to be reminded of our interaction with God in order to be open to the possibilities of forgiveness and of new life, for at the heart of the story of Jesus' death is the image of God receiving the brokenness of the world into God's own self, suffering with the world and transforming the consequences of the world's brokenness so that new possibilities emerge.

Artists and poets have often shown how suffering and death, particularly of the innocent, can in fact have the effect of "redemption." In William Inge's play *The Dark at the Top of the Stairs,* the suicide of Sammy Golden, a sensitive young student at a military academy in a small town in the Southwest, is the hinge of the action. Sammy took his own life after an experience of anti-Jewish bigotry at a high school dance at the local country club. This act shocks the other lead characters into self-awareness and releases the healing powers inherent in human interaction. Reenie Flood, Sammy's date for the evening, must face her tendency to let her own self-consciousness blind her to the hurts and needs of others. She had been in the women's lounge (mortified because no one but Sammy wanted to dance with her), when Sammy had looked for her after the insult and finally left, dejected. "He asked for me," she says in a flash of introspection, "for *me.* The only time anyone ever *wanted* me, or *needed* me, in my entire life. And I wasn't there. I didn't once think of . . . Sammy. I've always thought I was the only person in the world who had any feelings at all."[17]

Reenie's mother, Cora, is also deeply affected. In dealing with Reenie's despair, she has to face her own role in the establishment of her children's neurotic patterns. Her overprotectiveness has encouraged her son's fears of "the dark at the top of the stairs," and her tendency to seek vicarious fulfillment through her daughter has prevented Reenie's fulfillment and has kept her in self-pitying seclusion. "I've always felt that I could give [the children] life like a present, all wrapped in white, with every promise of happiness inside." "That ain't the way it works," replies Rubin, her husband. "No," she concludes. "All I can promise them is life itself."[18]

The redemption displayed here is very much a this-worldly phenomenon, even though Inge acknowledged that he was "drawing a little on Christian theology to show something of the uniting effect human suffering can bring into our lives."[19] Apparently Inge saw in the Christian proclamation of the redemptive significance of Jesus' death a way of explicating the dynamics of human interaction. Inge was not thinking of a cipher for "religious" redemption but of a testimony to the potentialities inherent in the human situation. The play shocks the audience into awareness of the human denial of human values and the human potential for recovering them.

This illustration deserves attention because it shows so well how one of the things we must do to make Paul intelligible is to bring to light again something that we already partly know about the depths of our lives.[20] A play like *The Dark at the Top of the Stairs* would mean nothing to us unless we already somehow knew that our lives were distorted and unless we could also recognize the chance for freedom and a new start, through the rediscovery of our interconnectedness, which is also one of our human potentialities. We also recognize in this play the harsh reality that people suffer, often tragically, from the mistakes of others; and in those times we can see our interconnectedness in a new light.

It is just because the play is so secular in orientation that it is able to illumine Paul's proclamation of the death of Jesus in an important way, for it shows how the theme of human transformation through another's death can be intelligible. On the other hand, the play raises questions it cannot answer. Do the values that human beings express have any *ultimacy*? Is there an often hidden, but pervasive, pull or lure toward the actualization of these values?

It is a shortcut to move simplistically—as is often done in sermons—from the "Christ" figure in modern literature directly to the New Testament, saying in effect, "and in just this way God has redeemed us through Christ." If we are able to draw this parallel, it must be based on two steps that the playwright did not, and for Inge's own purposes did not need to, take. First, we must be able to stretch what Inge calls the unifying effect of shared suffering to affirm that our sharing of life is infinite in its range, is indeed cosmic in scope as Paul himself believed in his own way: "The whole creation has been groaning in travail together until now" (Rom. 8:22 RSV). Second, we must be able to see the concrete story of Jesus' death as specially revealing the liberating presence of God in our interconnectedness.

As Inge's play illustrates so well, guilt itself is a mark of interrelatedness, even though we cannot always easily recognize it as such. But unless we can rebuild our awareness of our mutual belonging together, our preaching about the death of Jesus will fall back into the framework of God's judgment upon the individual's guilt. That is why it is important to recover a sense of how our interrelatedness can become a source of transformation.

A fresh approach to the meaning of our interconnectedness places our deep and often painful awareness of our human unity in the framework of a vision of all reality as internally related—that is, the world seen as a web of relations in which each part is affected and changed by its relations.[21] This means that there can be a measure of freedom on every level of being, and not just in human existence. In such a universe, the past influences the coming-to-be of every present but does not absolutely determine it. Within such a framework, it is possible to speak of God's ongoing activity in the world precisely in terms of providing coherent possibilities for every future and luring the world toward the achievement of the highest possible values. Such action is persuasive, as opposed to coercive, and does not require us to think of God's action as disrupting the natural order, precisely because God is understood as working within it. This is one way to understand the work of the Spirit in creation itself (see Gen. 1:2) as well as in Christian communities and individuals.

To say that God in every moment lures us toward an ideal future is to say that God liberates us from the negative futures that have been made for us by others and by ourselves. Bondage is real because our present moments are heavily influenced by negative elements in the past, by social pressure, and by limiting habits. Yet, liberation is real, too, since God in love and forgiveness grants creatures the power to move beyond what the influences of the past, even the best of them, in themselves would allow. Furthermore, there are elements in the past that sustain and strengthen us in the present. Our common past is the ground of our unity, and past events can work to open us to God's love and forgiveness.

If we can move in a universe such as this, we can affirm that the rediscovery of our interconnectedness, which Inge has portrayed in dramatic terms, actually opens our eyes to the deeper realities of all of life. From such a perspective, it will be natural to relate preaching about the death of Jesus to the painful self-discovery that Inge portrays and which, cast in Christian form, is rightly a central emphasis in preaching. But it is also important to stretch our hearers' visions to see that the self-discovery that Jesus' death can awaken is equally fundamental to the liberated life to which God is calling us, to confront and respond to suffering that arises from social structures (as in liberation theology) and to respond to the threats to the earth (as in ecological theology)—and to help them recognize in all of this the indivisible salvation of the world.[22]

The second step in relating Paul's story of Jesus' death to themes in modern literature and modern experience (as we said above) is to clarify how *the liberating presence of God,* which makes us aware of our interconnectedness, is specially manifested in the death of Jesus. Paul's story of Jesus' death, as we shall see in the next section of this chapter, shows God always and everywhere engaged in persuading people away from the influence of the web of destructive forces in their past (sin, death, the flesh, the world) toward the highest possibilities in their future—the "things" or "fruit" of the Spirit.[23] To proclaim Jesus' death as God's redeeming act is to anchor to a specific point our knowledge of the grace and hope that God offers, to acknowledge that we as Christians look to this event for the definitive sign of God's redeeming love.

We acknowledge this event as the locus and central point of the actual emergence into human history and human consciousness of what is for us the explicit and thematic representation of that love. From this point, the Christian community of faith, in which the experience of redemption is nurtured, comes forth. This one element in our past works with peculiar power to open us to God's present call and gift. It is this event that the church proclaims.[24] Yet, it is possible to acknowledge this event as containing the power of salvation only because the proclamation points us to a grace and power that, unrecognized, have been at work in the world "from the beginning." This is what the Christian tradition means when it speaks of God's "prevenient" grace.

Before we leave the subject of Jesus' death in Jesus' story, we should recognize that the images of self-giving and expiation are ambiguous and must be used with care in preaching. The images of "expiation"—though Paul used them at key places (e.g., Rom. 3:25), they are not frequent in his letters—and of sacrifice are indispensable. However, they can express our destructive impulses as readily as our healing ones. Both images presuppose or imply a world so deeply caught in a web of evil that its salvation could come only by a great, dramatic act of God. The images of this act seem to appeal to sadistic and escapist motives, which offend higher moral sensibilities.

This insight has been recognized since ancient times,[25] and it is one of the principal reasons why these images need to be reworked if they are to be appropriated in any fully reflective sense today.[26] These images often persist at a partly unconscious level. But when preaching about Jesus' death accepts as a good thing—and as part of God's "will"—the fact that the innocent suffer because of the sins of others, or when preaching about death, suffering, and self-sacrifice conveys a love of death (as an end to life and the self) more than the love of *life,* then the interrelatedness that these images convey and empower can be a destructive one. Many of us have heard preachers who were really expressing their own fears and unresolved negative feelings about life and about themselves when they spoke about the death of Jesus and about the conflict that brought it about. It is only when one has allowed the healing that is beyond our inner conflict—the sense that life is a blessing, that there is hope, and that life and hope are constant gifts from God[27]—to speak through the message of the death of Jesus that one is free to speak about its positive meaning.

3. Discerning God's Justice: Jesus' Death in God's Story

For Paul, Jesus' death is the key event in a story in which God "sets things right." This story looked back especially to the Torah, which, until Jesus' death, had been the primary gift of God that disclosed the justice of God.[28] Paul could also look back to Abraham and to Adam.[29] Just as important, this story about God's justice looked forward to the final triumph of God (see Rom. 11 and I Cor. 15). It also included victory over more-than-human cosmic powers, a victory that had already begun with the death of Jesus.[30] The whole of the reality that affects human beings was thus included in the scope of God's victory (see Rom. 8:18-39; Gal. 6:14-15).

This story of God's interaction with the world—including the nonhuman world, although the latter was of secondary concern to Paul—appeared to Paul to be the only overarching story that drew together the stories of individual people and set them free to live together. A basic choice in our preaching on any theme concerned with "God's story" is the choice of how to relate this unifying Christian story to the diverse "stories" in which we find ourselves and our lives situated today. There are two rather simple options: (1) Are we going to present the story that Paul tells as the only story that links human beings together at the fundamental level of their lives? (2) Or shall we show how the Christian story presents a pattern that can also be seen, at least in part, in stories (like Inge's play) that have no explicit connection with it? There are also more complex options. Paul, through the image of Jesus Christ, reached beyond and transformed the story of God's justice that he received from Jewish scripture and tradition. Does this suggest (3) that we ourselves are invited in a similar way to reach beyond the established form of the "revisionary" story that Paul expresses or implies—to express more fully its own intention?[31] Or (4) should we perhaps open it to creative transformation by letting it interact with different perspectives?[32] If preaching follows this final path, its task will also be to engage the questions of the relation between this story and others (for example, the Jewish Torah-story; see pp. 184-86), and of how the expressed or implied Pauline story (or those of other New Testament writers) exercises controls on the direction that any given sermon might take.[33] Today's preachers encounter these difficult questions, which are inescapably raised by the tension between God's story that we find expressed or implied in Paul's letters and the other stories in which we live and which compete for our loyalties.

A passage like II Corinthians 5:19 ("in Christ God was reconciling the world to God's self, not holding their transgressions against them, and entrusting to us the message of reconciliation") does not explicitly refer to the death of Jesus, but the reference to *"through Christ* God was reconciling the world to God's self, *not holding their transgressions against them"* (see also II Cor. 5:18) clearly makes the connection. To preach on this text according to the first option suggested above would be to emphasize the new life offered exclusively to believers and the new community through and in which the message of reconciliation is exclusively expressed. The second approach would show how the pattern of reconciliation through Christ touches a universal, or at least extremely widespread, human potentiality, illustrated by "secular" stories like Inge's play.[34] A third way to preach on a text like II Corinthians 5:19 would be to take as clues to Paul's true intention his opening of the message of reconciliation to the whole world and his linking of what took place in the particular historical figure, Jesus, to the Messiah and (in other passages) Abraham, figures who have universal significance in Judaism. One would then offer a way of hearing the text's own pointing beyond what happened in Jesus to God's reconciling activity always and everywhere.

Finally, one could go beyond the story that this passage presupposes or implies as the only unifying, meaningful story for all, opening the hearer to a creative synthesis that embraces the particularities of this story and those of other stories about God's reconciling activity in the world. One might, for example, propose how the Christ-story, with its affirmation of the "new creation" that God's reconciling activity signifies (see II Cor. 5:17; Gal. 6:15), and the women-story, with its emphasis on the emancipation of women and men from patriarchal attitudes, institutions, and social structures, can mutually enrich one another.[35] This last approach would not mean ignoring differences, nor would it mean trying to find a universal standpoint or trying to see other stories as "crypto-Christian" (a danger to which the second approach is prone). Rather, it would mean standing in one's own Christian story and affirming it, while allowing it to be transformed by the interaction with others. Of course, one could claim that the "women-story" is a "revisionary" Christ-story that already embodies the kind of creative transformation we are proposing. These brief suggestions show that different preaching emphases need not be as mutually exclusive as they are often taken to be (see pp. 23-24).

All of these approaches to preaching on this passage have in common an encounter with the text's own transformed vision of God's justice. Nowhere does Paul deny that our deeds have consequences that are often destructive of ourselves and others and that God continues to pass judgment on what we do and how we live our lives. The preacher ought not to deny these truths about human existence in the world and before God. To claim expressly, or by the implication of silence, that God has no concern for the personal, social, economic, and ecological evil that human actions can create—and do create to such a massive extent—would be to offer hearers a god whose morality fails to rise to our own sensibilities and who could not be trusted to lead us creatively into the future. But that is just what we do when our preaching has nothing to say about judgment as a dimension of God's justice.

The justice of God that we encounter in Jesus' death, as part of the story Paul transmits about God's activity, includes this element of judgment.[36] But it reaches beyond the consequences of human actions in God's judgment, for Paul also sees in Jesus' death God's "not holding their transgressions against them" (II Cor. 5:19).[37] We, like Paul, may still speak of justice in terms of judgment, which is very much a part of the truth of the Christian message and of experience. Now, however, a more profound justice appears in the death of Jesus, which represents our acceptance by God "although we were still sinners" (Rom. 5:8). In that acceptance is offered the possibility of new life, toward which God is forever seeking to persuade us.[38]

Paul himself grappled with this new vision of justice primarily in relation to the Jewish law. What he saw in Jesus' death was so different from what he saw in the Jewish law that the question was raised for him of whether God's purpose had shifted (see Rom. 9:6). Yet, unlike many (if not most) later Christians, Paul still included the Jews within the scope of God's purpose (see Rom. 9–11). The effort to profile the new event, nevertheless, led to sharp negative judgments on the way of the Jewish law,[39] even though Paul never thought of himself as separated from Judaism.

From such passages as Galatians 1:13-14 (in which Paul speaks of his "*former* life in Judaism" [RSV]) and Philippians 3:6-8 (where Paul speaks of those Jewish things of which he might boast as "loss"), one might get the impression that the Christian Paul no longer thought of himself in terms of the "Jewish" story. But especially in the two letters (Romans and Galatians) that focus on the tensions between Judaism and emergent Christianity, however, Paul continues to identify himself as a Jew[40] and to identify "the churches of Jesus Christ" with "the church of God" (Gal. 1:13-14, 22-24), with "the Jerusalem above" (Gal. 4:26), with "the Israel of God" (Gal. 6:16), and with Abraham's legitimate offspring (Gal. 3:6–4:7; 4:21-31; Rom. 4). The issue that Paul addresses in these letters is that the belief in the crucified Jesus as the promised Messiah has transformed the understanding of what it means to be "Jewish" and the vision of Israel's future in the world. For Paul, and for his predecessors in the faith, the cross of Jesus Christ offers salvation to Gentiles and Jews *alike,* so that faith, as trust in and obedience to God, is no longer worked out in terms defined by the Jewish law. Now it is worked out in terms of the Christ-event, as obedience to Jesus Christ and to the love of God of which Jesus' sacrificial death is a witness—not as two separate acts but as one and the same.

With this shift in the center of faith as trust in and loyalty to God—from the Jewish law to Jesus Christ—comes a new emphasis on "freedom." In life before and apart from faith in Jesus Christ, the Jewish law *restrained* a person's "evil impulses."[41] But in the life of faith centered in the crucified Jesus as the Messiah, the believer is *set free* from the forces that compromise one's trust in and loyalty to God.[42] Although Paul speaks of this new life "in Christ" as the end of life "under the law" (see Gal. 3:23-25; Rom. 10:4), he also speaks of it as the actualization of the promise made to Abraham (see Gal. 3–4; Rom. 4) and as the fulfillment of the law.[43]

The tension in understanding how these two stories—those of Jews and Christians, the Torah-story and the Christ-story, as we could call them today—relate to each other is still a central challenge to the self-understanding of Christians and a sign that we must rethink the single-story pattern in which we have usually modelled God's story. Surely Paul was right in rejecting the notion that God's fundamental purpose would change. Surely he was also right in affirming that, for him and for his communities of faith, the death of Jesus was at the heart of the revelation of God's justice and that this faith was to be proclaimed as an invitation to all. But Christians have so continually drawn out the distinctiveness of their own story by making negative judgments about the Jewish story—an act of Christian self-definition that has had enormously disastrous consequences—that we can see it now as a principal point where our preaching needs to be recast. We need to remember that Paul, in his effort to proclaim the Christ-story—which was for "the Jews first, then for the gentiles" (Rom. 1:16)—equally resisted the attempt to reject the Torah-story entirely, as in I Corinthians, and the attempt to subordinate the Christ-story to the Torah-story, as in Romans (which expresses both sides of Paul's views) and Galatians.

If we are to retain the story-form of thought, we are called upon to take seriously the insight that some passages in Paul's letters move in the direction of affirming the implication that the two stories—with the one focused on the law and the other on Christ—both have validity.[44] We live in a web of stories (see pp. 166-67), and we can affirm that God is at work in all of them. At the same time, we live in a particular history, a history for Christians in which the death of Jesus is foundational. Here is a clear case for exploring the possibility that the whole of God's purpose can only be expressed as the many stories interact with one another and move toward becoming one in a creative synthesis.

A similar stretching of our thinking takes place when we turn from the story's past to its future. The hope for the final triumph of God, most fully expressed by Paul in I Corinthians 15, served to express the trustworthiness of God—an issue that was at stake here just as in the connection between Jesus and the law (see Rom. 9–11 as well as Rom. 3). We expect a story to reach a resolution in which everything is, so to speak, in its place. This natural human way of constructing stories played a part in the development of apocalyptic stories of God's triumph, stories that Paul, like other early Christians, took over from a strand of Jewish tradition. They also transformed these stories by putting the death of Jesus at their center.[45] The insecure position in society of Paul's congregations made the victorious resolution of the apocalyptic story all the more important to them.

For centuries it seemed that God's complete triumph in the end was simply to be presupposed, even though at many times, when people felt secure in the world, this confidence was not a central issue. In our own time, the evident loss of security leaves us deeply divided over how to look toward the future. We know that we live "in between the times," that the world as we know it is changing radically, and that it is not clear what the outcome will be. It seems that ours is a time in which only the apocalyptic symbols of *destruction* capture the imagination and find expression in the arts.

This is not surprising, in view of the clear threats of total, or at least extremely devastating, destruction that we have witnessed or that appear imminent. How can the ancient apocalyptic symbols of promise be brought to bear in a relevant and credible way today? It is hard to think of a more pressing question for Christian preaching in our day.

A passage that speaks quite directly to this question is Romans 8:35 (RSV): "Who shall separate us from the love of Christ?"[46] For Paul, it was precisely the moment that seemed to derail the purpose of God from its direction of liberation that was used by God to uncover and disclose that purpose. It is noteworthy that in this climactic section of Romans 8, Paul moved away from the language of a divinely predetermined outcome, which he had used just before,[47] to the language of struggle.[48] In the struggle, the love of God is stronger than the forces arrayed against it, so that "nothing in all creation" can separate us from it.

Our preaching on these themes can thus emphasize that side of the future as Paul presents it, which offers a predetermined outcome, or it can emphasize the image of God made known in the death of Jesus, present in a genuine struggle for the liberation of life, to which Paul also bears witness. The two images are in real tension, for the predetermined outcome ultimately tends to override or blur the reality of the genuine struggle that we experience in history and in life. At the same time, the image of a predetermined final triumph is a powerful way of speaking of God's trustworthiness. It appears in recent Christian thought, for instance, in Pierre Teilhard de Chardin's "omega point," which is a unifying final goal of the cosmic process.[49] Another, quite different vision of God's purpose as genuinely open, with no predetermined end, is more consonant with the freedom that we experience and with the genuine openness of the outcome of the lives that we live.

We recognize the strength of the image of the predetermined final end. Nevertheless, we believe that the gap between this religious language and the actual daily struggles of men and women, both in their individual lives and in their efforts to cope with and to alter the social structures within which all live, can best be bridged by understanding God as being constantly at work, in a spirit revealed in the death of Jesus, in a cosmic process that is itself everlasting. Because this process includes the freedom, in varying measures, of all God's creatures, no specific results within any given historical stream are ever assured. What is assured, however, is that God will never abandon the world but will always be actively engaged in it, both luring it toward the greater good and retaining eternally such good as is in fact realized.[50] If there is in this vision no *final* triumph, there is nonetheless an *ongoing* triumph that, precisely because it involves no point of absolute resolution, points ever to new futures and new modes of realization. Such a vision provides both assurance and challenge. Human history and the entire cosmic process are in one sense in God's hands. In another sense, however, they are in the *world's* hands, so that in a perhaps unexpected way, we are encouraged to the *praxis* that is so central to liberation theology.

It is also possible to envision "the End" as occurring through political, economic, and technological advances that serve just and sustainable societies around the world. Such visions of "the End" were beyond the possibilities open to Paul and his contemporaries, but they are vivid and available to us. Still another vision is that history leads nowhere and holds no meaning—in short, that "history," in the pregnant sense of the term, is an illusion and nonsense. While each of these views contains something true about reality, our faith will be empowered and made more real if we can move toward the "open" story vision, in which real achievements and genuine meaning occur, but in which we do not expect everything to be wrapped up in a final resolution on the plane of observable history.

4. Called to Liberation: Jesus' Death in the Church's Story

Paul has so long been read as a theologian of the depths of the individual soul that it may seem quixotic to turn to his letters for the theme of liberation. The theologies of liberation, a recent phenomenon whose roots reach back to the social gospel movement that began around the turn of this century, are usually far more interested in the Exodus story, the Hebrew prophets, and Jesus. Yet, in the whole of the Bible, it is Paul who has so much to say about "freedom." Part of the reason for the neglect of Paul as an ally to liberation theologies is that Paul's interpreters traditionally have been preoccupied with what Paul has to say about the inner struggles of individuals with sin and death.[51] There is no denying that these interpreters have provided profound insights into human existence that can still speak powerfully to us.[52] It would be a great loss to the church's mission if their witness were to be ignored as other perspectives are taken up. But Paul does say things that an "introspective" perspective misses, for Paul also addresses some of the social issues of his day, which continue to be vexing problems. And he draws our attention to features of the larger world to which everything belongs—forces that hold everything in bondage, forces from which God alone makes liberty possible.

These dimensions of Paul's thought move us beyond a simple "introspective" view to consider social and cosmic concerns, and thus are grounds for regarding Paul as a valuable resource for liberation theologies. Nevertheless, just these dimensions are precisely the second major reason why Paul has not been regarded as helpful for this purpose. This is because what Paul has to say about the role of women in a patriarchal society[53] and about the institution of slavery,[54] the two primary social issues to which Paul addresses himself in his extant letters, has worked against an alliance with liberation. Furthermore, what Paul says about the bondage of everything under "cosmic forces" is phrased in such mythological language[55] as to make it hardly intelligible and credible in our day,[56] let alone readily serviceable to liberation theologies.

Our concern here is not to defend Paul against his critics. But his vision is taking on new relevance. The appalling oppression of so many people around the globe and the threat to the earth's capacity to support life enable us to understand afresh what Paul meant when he wrote about the creation itself "groaning" for the day when it will be "set free from its bondage to decay and obtain the glorious liberty of the children of God" (Rom. 8:21 RSV). What we need now is a vision that leads to actions that promote the liberation of life. If Paul is of some help here, we should listen with critical attention.

As we have suggested throughout this discussion, Paul is deeply committed to an interactional view of the person. For Paul, to be fully human is to live in community with others. Also for him, it was in the church, the new community of faith called into being by the crucified Messiah and sustained by the Spirit, that the transformation to an essentially communal human existence was taking place. Paul's understanding of human existence was never as individualistic and personal in a private sense as it became in some later forms of Christian faith and life. When Paul spoke of "cosmic powers" in whose sway everything is held, of course, he meant mysterious and (to us) mythical forces, but these powers were also embodied as palpable personal, social, and political realities.[57] There is an objectivity to the power of destructive possibilities we inherit from past actions, persons, and other creatures that make plausible Paul's depiction of "sin" as a cosmic power that is able to hold everything in bondage (Gal. 3:22). The consequence of our actualization of these possibilities is always death, sometimes—too often—the cruel, physical death of others as well as (or instead) of ourselves, but always the death of better possibilities that cannot be retrieved. In this sense, Paul's claim that "the wages of sin is death" (Rom. 6:23 RSV) has a ring of truth.

Furthermore, just before Paul's list of cosmic powers in Romans 8:37-39 is another list—"tribulation, or distress, or persecution, or famine, or nakedness, or peril, or sword" (v. 35 RSV)—which includes the actions, or inaction, of persons and governments among the forces that threaten to "separate us from the love of God [seen] in Christ Jesus our Lord." The "rulers of this age" (I Cor. 2:6-8) can be seen in Jesus' own compatriots who played a role in Jesus' crucifixion and who hindered evangelistic efforts among the gentiles (I Thess. 2:14-16).[58] And the "elementary forces of the universe" (Gal. 4:3)[59] are represented by the Jewish law and by pagan religions and have their counterparts in the social institutions of "pedagogues" and other overseers of minors within the household (Gal. 3:23-25; 4:1-2).

In short, those things from which Paul promises that Christ brings freedom are as much social and political in character and in reality as they are personal and cosmic. Liberation was not for Paul a purely "spiritual" matter, which could be divorced from historical realities. Luther presents a one-sided picture of Paul when he denies that the liberty Christ brings is in the political sphere (for example, "human slavery" or "tyrannical authority") and locates it only in the "conscience."[60] Paul was not what we would call a social activist, but he was engaged in the creation of a new community, in which the accustomed, patriarchal, social world was transformed in thought and reality within Christian communities.[61] The great contrast between Paul and the contemporary church is that for him the transforming power of God within human society and its forms was to be seen in one particular "society": the church. We, however, have a different social location, in which the lines between the church and the society are not as sharp as they were for Paul.

On the one side the gospel itself has contributed to increasing the sense of responsibility of citizens for the institutions and structure of the dominant society as well as to the actual possibilities for effecting changes in them. The common person during the period of the early Roman Empire, in which Christianity arose, had little power to effect large social changes, so that responsibility was limited to one's own personal needs and those of one's family and closest associates, who comprised the smaller societies in which individuals lived. Today, however, especially in constitutional democracies, it is possible to address directly the public institutions and social structures of one's world, so that the work of creating a new community entails possibilities today that were not open to Paul and the earliest Christian communities.

On the other side, the church has largely been reshaped by values, practices, and beliefs arising from the culture. The social situation of the ancient church changed from a threatened and sometimes persecuted community to being supported and often guided by the Roman Empire. Inevitably, imperial interests altered its character. Even where there is no legal establishment of religion, as in the United States, social acceptance means that many join the church for its sanction of general cultural values rather than primarily to be conformed to Christ.

Where freedom is at stake in our world—the world economies, ecology, and nuclear arms—Paul cannot provide specific solutions. What his letters can do is remind us of the power of the Spirit to move us to reshape our questions and to lead us beyond merely repeating the answers that we have received from our past. That is what II Corinthians 5:17 ("the old has passed away, behold, the new has come," RSV) implies, at least in part. The attempt to look to Paul for direct guidance would lead to such rigidities as those that were once current about women's clothing in church (I Cor. 11:2-16), or women's speaking in the worship service (I Cor. 14:33b-36), or about slavery (I Cor. 7:21 and Philemon).[62]

If we look more closely, we can see that, in questions of social structure and freedom, Paul's churches were indeed different from most of the "societies" of the time. The picture of the role of women and slaves, for example, in the Pauline churches, much discussed today, was uneven, but women and slaves enjoyed freedom as leaders and participants to a far greater degree than in most analogous groups at the time.[63] Christian women and slaves, as well as Paul, ascribed this freedom to Christ and to the Spirit whose power was made available through the proclamation of the gospel of the crucified Messiah.[64] A liberating force was at work in them, a power to enable new patterns of human interrelationships to emerge—what Paul called a "new creation" (see Gal. 6:15; II Cor. 5:17).

We should not romanticize this freedom. In many ways, the Pauline churches were very much like other "societies" of their time. The forces that enabled them to assert their distinctive identity converged from various aspects of their wider world.[65] Nevertheless for Paul the dynamic center of the power of transformation was the Spirit that was made effective through the preaching of Jesus' death and resurrection.[66]

For our purposes, the most important thing about this vital center of the power of transformation is the light that it casts on the difficult problem of power. Paul himself was well aware of the tension between different kinds of power. His statement in I Corinthians 2:2, 4-5 is classic:

> For I decided not to know anything among you except Jesus Christ, and him crucified. . . . My speech and my message were made effective, not by persuasive words of wisdom, but by a demonstration of Spirit and of power, lest your faith rest in human wisdom rather than in the power of God. (Compare II Cor. 10–13.)

Here Paul was striving to identify two kinds of power. The power that he was rejecting was not physical compulsion, but the kind of "hidden persuasion" or psychological pressure that comes from the use of expert skills of speaking. He regarded these skills (public relations techniques, we might say) as forms of human pressure or self-assertiveness. This is clear from the connection between this passage and the section that immediately precedes it (I Cor. 1:10-31), which deals with the self-assertiveness of factions within the church in Corinth.

Over against the kind of power that exerted pressure from the outside, Paul set the power associated with the cross and with the Spirit, which were seen as conveying God's power. As we noted above (see pp. 158-59), Paul claims not that the cross was itself a form of power[67] but that, taken with the resurrection,[68] it was the way through which God's surprising power was introduced in a new and effective way.

God's surprising power was stronger than the "powers," the mysterious forces of destructiveness that held creation in their grip, even though these continued to exert their force in Paul's world—and still do so today. It was only by "the eyes of faith" that they were seen to be powerless. But freedom from sin and the readiness to accept and to find freedom in the web of actually given and partially transformed relationships were firmly grounded in the *experience* of faith.

For Paul the presence of the new power was known only in the church, where it was manifest in a wide range of spirit-guided experiences and activities.[69] Paul was by no means as anti-charismatic as he has been portrayed by many modern theologians. What he objected to was the kind of spiritual life in which people tended to be shut up within their own Spirit experiences and closed off from other members of the household of faith. Over against this distortion of true Spirit-centeredness, Paul proclaimed a presence of the Spirit that opened people to their mutual interdependence (I Cor. 12–14).

While it was far from Paul's intention to work out a general theory of power,[70] we may rightly claim that his struggle to understand the power of the Spirit made available through the word of the cross (I Cor. 2:1-5; Gal. 3:1-5) is congenial with our earlier proposal about two different kinds of power (see pp. 110-14 and 124-29). "Unilateral" power simply exerts pressure on others and seeks to achieve its results by limiting their power. Persuasive power, on the other hand, opens up new possibilities for others, thus enhancing their power. It is relational in that it not only influences others but is open to being influenced by them—that is, it interacts with others in such a way as to affirm, and even to increase, their own power.

Paul struggles with the polarity of these two kinds of power when, for instance, in II Corinthians 10:1-2, he says "I . . . entreat you, by the *meekness and gentleness* of Christ" (v. 1 RSV, italics added), and then immediately adds that if necessary he will "show boldness with such confidence as I count on showing against some who suspect us of acting in a worldly fashion" (v. 2 RSV). Likewise, Paul wrestles with this polarity when, in Galatians 5:24, he says, "Those who belong to Christ Jesus have crucified the flesh with its passions and desires" (RSV). Earlier he says, "You must walk by the Spirit and not fulfill the desires of the flesh" (Gal. 5:16), implying that the "flesh" and its "desires" are not dead and that the Christian must choose between responding to those desires or to the Spirit. In Paul's letters, the kind of power that we see revealed in Jesus' death and resurrection, however, is the "relational" kind. To proclaim that the powers of evil are overcome by the surprising power of God in the cross and the resurrection of Jesus, then, means to affirm the profound effectiveness of the reciprocal power of love.

To preach this gospel involves us, as Paul clearly saw, not only in telling the story of Jesus but also in creating an environment in which the freedom it proclaims can become a reality for those who hear the story. We tell the story of Jesus to point to the decisive source of this freedom in our history, which is vital if we are to keep alive the vision of God's Spirit carried by this story and the community of faith centered around it. But to tell this story fully, we need to tell the other stories with which it is essentially linked. These are especially the stories of Israel and the ancient Hebrew people, who also knew of the liberating and life-bearing Spirit of God, and the story of the church up to the present day, in which the same Spirit of God brings life and freedom. In such a way, our preaching could express the truth of the church's doctrine of the Trinity, that the Spirit of God, which moved across the primeval waters bringing order out of chaos, is the same Spirit that spoke through the prophets of Israel and Jesus of Nazareth and in the church—and that each moment in these stories embodies the reality of God.

The freedom that is at the center of the gospel, and which all these stories proclaim in their own ways, has been expressed in traditional religious language as the awakening of faith to the gracious reality of God as the source of liberation from sin and death. But this truth is only a part of the full freedom that comes from God. As Paul also glimpsed, the "new creation" signified by the death and resurrection of Jesus includes emancipation from the social realities, including religious thought and institutions, that limit, rather than expand, freedom—social realities that manifest and have their origin in the power of sin and, therefore, produce death instead of life.

At many times in the history of the church, freedom from sin and death has been taken to mean only an awakening to the reality of our "being in the world with other beings" and to the truth that everything in the world is forever embraced by God's unbounded love. This awakening has been understood as changing life because it enables us to meet life differently (as in the Inge play). To put it in the language of Bultmann's existentialist theology, Jesus' death presents the possibility of a new understanding of human existence as an understanding of the self, the world, and God. But deeply rooted in the Christian heritage is a larger grasp of this freedom as involving the kind of awakening to the indivisible truth of the world in God's everlasting love that arouses planned action to change the structures of societies that destroy individuals and divide them from others—and appear to separate them from the supreme love of God.[71]

These two aspects of the freedom of faith are interlocking for Paul. Certainly for Paul the aspect of this freedom that may be called "redemption"—what God alone does for the whole, indivisible world, and which Paul describes with various images, but especially with the term *reconciliation* (II Cor. 5:18-19)—has consequences for the other aspect, which we could call "emancipation," the liberating actions of persons, communities, and nations in response to God's redemptive purpose and action.[72] But Paul could only dimly glimpse the full extent of the implications of the latter aspect of the freedom of faith. Also, Paul's letters could be read as indicating a ranking of the former (redemption) before the latter (emancipation).[73] For us, however, it seems better to hold both as equal aspects of the indivisible salvation of the world.[74]

One important type of Christianity has for centuries insisted that the freedom of faith be worked out in the transformation of social structures. "Sectarian" Christianity focused this transformation within the community of the church. The Pauline churches were of this kind, insofar as Paul himself limited this type of structure-transforming faith and action to the "household of faith" (see our discussion on pp. 191-92). We owe an immense debt to these "sectarian" Christians, like the Mennonites and (especially the early) Quakers, for holding before us the insistent claim that all the patterns of life were to be transformed by faith, even at the cost of withdrawing from much of the common life of society because it seemed refractory to such transformation.

Today it is easy to follow the path of assuming that the structures of the wider society are indeed resistant to transformation, or (as some hold) that they are self-regulating in some impersonal way (for example, to the extent that they are guided by certain "values"—technological, political, or economic—that function more or less like sociological "laws") so that we do not have to take direct responsibility for them. With these so-called "realists" (they are really escapists!), we agree that it is both difficult and risky to try to reshape the patterns of our social world and of our relation to the whole earth—difficult because of the drag of custom and risky because the results are usually uncertain. Paul's image of principalities and powers distinct from individuals is all too apt!

But we completely reject the inference that we should, therefore, let things take their course. Such a view can make sense only when one thinks of social relations as mechanical or as interchanges that are external to an individual's essential identity. Few, however, would hold that social relations were external to the essential identities of communities and nations. Once we see that social relations are internal, mutually influencing the identities of participants, we cannot but see that this wider reach of our interconnectedness extends our world of responsibility to the social (and "natural") relations that are part of the indivisible truth of the world in God.

A more creative reading of Paul, therefore, sees that the world in which transformation is expected, and to which our responsiveness is committed, must be enlarged. Whereas for Paul the locus of liberated life was the church, we propose that we are called to move outward from this focus to view all experience in the light of Paul's vision of the indivisible transformation of the whole world.[75]

5. Conclusion

The move from the New Testament world, with its struggle to understand God's justice within the community of faith, to our contemporary world also involves the continuing, difficult and painful struggle to deal, through faith, with two aspects of power, as can be seen from the following statement by John C. Bennett about the threat of nuclear destruction:

> These effects [the possible "nuclear winter" that is thought to be a consequence of widespread use of nuclear weapons] point to what I have called "Judgment." There is debate about how God acts in relation to each event which judgment includes. That God acts directly in persuading consciences we know from experience; we think of persuasion in terms of God's grace and in terms of the presence of the Holy Spirit. The processes that lead to judgment as human catastrophe are immanental processes that signify divine righteousness in relation to the sinful arrogance and callousness of humanity. Alfred North Whitehead's statement, "The fact of the instability of evil is the moral order of the world" (*Religion in the Making,* chap. 3), gives us hope; but the other side of the coin is that this instability of evil destroys so much good and has so many victims. We have always known it, on a much smaller scale than that of a nuclear holocaust.[76]

The encounter with the deeper kind of power as the expression of God's "setting things right" does not separate us from the older focusing of justice on consequences. But now we see that, although God is directly present in this justice, as God is in all events, God's purpose is only dimly revealed in such consequences because they are so heavily determined by the past that they inherit. Thus we may speak with Bennett of "immanental processes that signify divine righteousness." As he clearly sees, there is no guarantee that these processes will render "to each one what is due"; they may be widely and even totally destructive. Against this world of destructive consequences, we place the justice that is disclosed in Paul's interpretation of Jesus' death. We see in this justice a God whose power is greater because it is truly responsive to us and takes into itself the life that we give to it and to the world. This is the justice that "makes righteous" and that never gives up in the face of human or cosmic destructiveness.

We have been rereading Paul to find in his letters some contacts and contrasts with our cultural presuppositions that will open us to the presence of God. If some of these reflections seem distant from preaching, perhaps that may be because we have not yet become used to preaching in this way.[77] We find that the cultural context of our day calls us to renew our preaching in the spirit of the kind of rereading of the New Testament we have set forth here. We saw earlier that Mark calls us, against all simplistically triumphalist ideologies, to a theology of following Jesus in which suffering may be an expected part. A fresh reading of Paul calls us both to a new recognition of our interrelatedness and to a new openness to the God who is the God of all life and creativity. It is central to Paul's proclamation that God's victory in Jesus is precisely the victory won on the cross, that the Lord of all creation is still "Christ crucified." In that proclamation of the death and resurrection of Jesus, we hear God calling us to increase the reality of this triumph over evil in our world—in ourselves; in social, economic, and political relations; and in the natural environment.

CHAPTER NINE

"DELIVERANCE FROM
AN EVIL AGE"

A Sermon on Galatians 1:1-5 by David J. Lull

When I was in junior high school, I had a pen pal in Oslo, Norway. We would exchange letters, family photographs, and pictures of our countries. Then we lost interest, and the letters stopped.

My wife, Karen, also had a junior high pen pal. Hers was in New Zealand. Although Karen writes more letters than anyone I know—and probably more than anyone knows—I am still amazed that she has kept up correspondence with her pen pal to this day, nearly thirty years later. A whole network of persons who have never met, except through Karen's and Judy's letters and photographs, have been brought together through their correspondence.

This morning we read the opening of Paul's letter to the churches of Galatia. Through this liturgical practice, we are drawn more deeply into the stories of Paul and the Christians in Galatia. At the center of their stories is the story of Jesus' self-sacrificial death, which is also the central feature of the opening lines of Paul's letter:

> Grace to you and peace from God our Father [and Mother] and our Lord Jesus Christ, who gave himself for our sins, that he might deliver us from the present evil age, according to the will of God our Father [and Mother], to whom be the glory for ever and ever. Amen.

In addition to the liturgical form of this wish, expressed as a prayer, linguistic evidence points to a pre-Pauline, Jewish-Christian tradition as the source of these lines. It is likely, therefore, that we have here one of the earliest expressions of Christian faith centered in the event of the cross of Jesus. By reading these lines this morning, we strengthen our connections with the central story that gives us our identity as Christians.

Although some of this prayer sounds familiar to us—"grace and peace" and the self-sacrificial death of Jesus "for our sins"—parts of it sound quaint, especially the part about "deliverance from the present evil age." Even the most optimistic observer of our present age will have to admit that there is little evidence of "deliverance from evil." We can all find some triumph over evil in our age to celebrate—the end of black slavery in America, for example—but who can doubt that the sway of evil is as strong today as it was in Paul's day? Black slavery as it once was is gone, but slavery through the denial of economic opportunity continues, and racism still breaks out in ugly violence.

In the face of the undeniable reality of evil, the question forces itself upon us: Can God's word still speak to us through the faith of the first Christians who believed that the cross of Jesus brought "deliverance from the present evil age"? One common way to resolve this question is to "spiritualize" the prayer in the opening lines of Paul's letter to the Galatians. This solution is at least as old as Martin Luther, the great German reformer, who believed that this prayer has to do with a grace that brings peace to our conscience with assurance of the forgiveness of our sins. Important as this assurance is, it is only part of this early Christian witness of faith.

These early Christians believed that people were both responsible to God for their actions and captive to the sway of the forces of evil. The forgiveness of sins would ease the conscience burdened with guilt, but it leaves the person—indeed, the world—captive to the power of evil. What is needed is deliverance from captivity to evil, freedom from the power of its influence. This deliverance, too, was sought in the cross of Jesus.

A contemporary story illustrates the significance of the difference between forgiveness and freedom. In a small urban church, the pastor discovered that there had been incidents of sexual abuse in the church-run day care center. After identifying the person responsible, the pastor called on the individual. During the visit, the pastor emphasized the loving forgiveness of God seen in Jesus' self-sacrificial death for sinners. The child molester interrupted the pastor and said: "I know I am forgiven, at least by you, Jesus, and God—I might even be able to forgive myself—but I am still a child molester! How can I stop behavior that is destroying myself and others?" The pastor then had the good sense to find a treatment program for this individual. What was needed was the offer of real possibilities of change in patterns of behavior and of relationships with others. These possibilities for change would complete the only partial "deliverance" that had come more easily with words of forgiveness.

So also for the Christians in Galatia, forgiveness wasn't the problem for which the cross of Jesus was the solution. The problem was captivity to powers of evil. Popular moral philosophers and the laws of Greece and Rome had taught them the difference between virtue and vice. They knew stories of figures like Heracles, Socrates, and Diogenes, whose lives triumphed over evil. But the people themselves did not live lives of virtue, and they had not known true freedom from evil for themselves.

In Paul's story of Jesus' self-sacrificial obedience to God, even to his death on a cross, they might have seen another "hero" who had embodied their ideal of freedom from the power of evil. But Paul's preaching offered them more: a God who had made Jesus free and who, through God's Spirit, would also make them free. As they turned in faith to this God, they found that God's Spirit brought them personal freedom from the power of sin.

Their story—the story of the power of the cross and the Spirit to set people free from the destructive patterns and cycles of the past—was not, however, a story of unbroken freedom. In spite of their newfound freedom, or perhaps because of it, they listened to new missionaries who sought to persuade them, though Gentiles, to live in obedience to Jewish customs—in particular, to observe the law of Moses—as a condition of their full inheritance of God's promise to bless all the nations in Abraham. Paul wrote to the Galatians to dissuade them from submitting to this form of cultural captivity.

When Paul wrote to them that "there is neither Jew nor Greek, slave nor free, and no male and female, for all are one in Christ" (Gal 3:28), he testified that the cross of Jesus also brings deliverance from *oppressive social structures.* In contrast to a traditional Jewish social order in which Jews withdrew from contact with Gentiles, and in contrast with the then dominant, patriarchal society in which both Jews and Gentiles lived, Paul presents them with a vision of a new social order for the churches of Galatia in which there would be no distinctions between Jews and Greeks, slaves and free, men and women. The Spirit, with which they had been filled after hearing Paul's preaching of the crucified Messiah, had already testified to them that this new social order was part of God's new creation. Although they were Gentiles, and therefore did not live according to traditional Jewish customs, the Spirit had witnessed to them that they, too, were children of God, when the Spirit in their hearts inspired them to call upon God, in the language of the Jews, as *Abba* (Gal. 4:6).

Paul's struggle to preserve the freedom that the cross and the Spirit offer was and continues to be hard fought. The next generation of Pauline churches saw the reestablishment of patriarchal social patterns as normative for Christians, as the letters to the Colossians and Ephesians testify when they instruct wives to be subject to their husbands and slaves to obey their masters. This retreat from the new order of the household of faith continued in the third generation of Pauline churches, as can be seen in the Pastoral Epistles. There women are told to learn "in silence with all submissiveness" and are prohibited from having "authority over men" (I Tim. 2:11-12). These letters unwittingly bear witness to the women and men who, after the first wave of enthusiasm about the freedom that the cross and the Spirit had given them, continued the struggle to maintain and expand that freedom, even in the face of resistance from their brothers and sisters in the household of faith. These letter writers wouldn't have instructed Christian women and slaves to conform to patriarchal patterns of submission unless some of them had rejected those patterns in the name of Jesus, who had given his life that they might be delivered from the power of evil—even the evil embodied and created by oppressive social structures.

Their struggle still goes on, and we still look for evidence that the Spirit and the cross of Jesus bring freedom from the present evil age, which remains with us. The recent, and still unfolding, "Nicaraguan experience" illustrates how the Spirit and the cross can liberate people from "an evil age."

The Nicaraguan world, deeply shaped by colonial oppression, to which both Soviet and American involvement continue to contribute, offers few opportunities for the liberation of women from poverty; from grief at the loss of husbands, sons, and fathers; and from the abuse and violence of their own men.[1] But a group of men belonging to one of the many "Christian base communities" in Nicaragua gathered one day to study the Bible, as had become their custom. Only, this day they were looking for guidance on how, as Christians, to relate to women, treating them with more respect and dignity.

The church had given them the scriptures to search, and the church's ministries of Word and Sacrament must have contributed something to the start of their surprising new search of those scriptures. It is also true that much can be found in the Bible—and much in the life of the church, especially in its sacramental ministries—that could be (and is) used to justify patterns of abuse of women. Nevertheless, these men testify to the power of the story of the cross of Jesus to set at liberty men and women captive to destructive patterns deeply rooted in societies today.

And so we return to our text:

> Grace to you and peace from God our Father [and Mother] and our Lord Jesus Christ, who gave himself for our sins, that he might deliver us from the present evil age, according to the will of God our Father [and Mother], to whom be the glory for ever and ever.

The word of God for the people of God? Because of the testimony of women and men in the churches of New Testament times and of men and women in the churches of Nicaragua today, we can say Amen!

POSTSCRIPT

A text or two or three, a vision of life and of God's activity in the world, stories of individual lives and of the life of a community of faith—these are the basic resources for preaching. Effective preaching engages each seriously and creatively, and it allows each of these dimensions to interact with the others. The biblical interpretation and theological reflection in the preceding chapters on the Gospel of Mark and the letters of Paul demonstrate how that task can be carried out from a clearly defined perspective—in our case, a "process" perspective.

We have proposed that the aim of preaching is the freedom that comes from serving the Spirit: freedom from ignorance and freedom for the Truth that embraces all truths, freedom from a sense of worthlessness and freedom for a sense of worth, freedom from oppressive attitudes and actions and freedom for freeing perspectives and behavior, freedom from isolation and freedom for interrelatedness, freedom from destructive suffering and injustice and freedom for abundant life and justice, freedom from all forms of bondage and freedom for genuine liberty. This freedom that comes from the Spirit takes concrete forms. For some it will be a freeing relationship within a family. For others it will be freedom for the basic necessities of life: food, shelter, education, and medical care. For others it will be freedom from war and for sustainable peace. For others it will be freedom of political expression, movement, and association. For others it will be freedom for meaningful work—and the list goes on. The Spirit creates forms of freedom for each occasion. The preachers' task is to discern what form(s) of freedom the Spirit is calling forth.

A paradoxical danger of biblical preaching is that reverence for the biblical text will stifle discernment of the form(s) of freedom toward which the Spirit is leading. An equal danger is that preaching will bypass scripture and offer only those forms of freedom that listeners find familiar, comfortable, and congenial with accustomed patterns of life. We have offered a way to cope with these real dangers: Take biblical proposals seriously but not as absolute authority, and do the same thing, at the same time, with proposals from contemporary sources (including this book). That is what we have done in the preceding chapters on Mark and Paul.

We have moved from exegesis to theology to sermon, first with the Gospel of Mark and then with the letters of Paul. The focus was on how we might preach about Jesus' death. With Mark, we chose the theme of God and suffering; with Paul, God and justice.

Of course, other preachers should not feel limited to, or by, what we have done. If they find our path to preaching for freedom a creative path, they are invited to take it up. If not, we hope they will have been stirred to find their own way to preach in the service of the Spirit.

Similarly, our intention is to open up the possibilities of preaching on the death of Jesus today. Such possibilities must be discovered for each generation of the church if the word of the cross is to be the word of life it really is. Here, too, other preachers are free to take up our proposals or to find their own. But no task of Christian preaching is more important than enabling hearers to encounter "the passion of Jesus, the passion of God" in today's world.

Our chapters on Mark and Paul are one attempt to carry out this task. It remains for other occasions to take up other New Testament resources for preaching on the death of

Jesus (for example, the Fourth Gospel and the book of Revelation). Of course, preachers need not be limited to this theme. Preaching for freedom in the service of the Spirit ought to be the aim of every sermon, whether the theme is the ways that make for peace, the reign of God, adoration for the Creator, or thanksgiving for God's beneficence. We have begun with the themes of suffering and justice in Jesus' death because these are central to the death of Jesus, and the death of Jesus is central to the gospel, as Mark and Paul attest—indeed, as the whole New Testament attests. When Christian preachers today learn what Paul meant when he said, "I decided to know nothing among you but Jesus Christ, and him crucified" (I Cor. 2:2 RSV), they can preach sermons on any theme, and their sermons will convey "the passion of Jesus, the passion of God" in today's world.

NOTES

Chapter 1. The Aim of Preaching

1. For a review of the literature, see the journal *Homiletic*.

2. Karl Barth, *Evangelical Theology: An Introduction*, trans. Grover Foley (New York: Holt, Rinehart and Winston, 1963).

3. Rudolf Bultmann, "Epilogue," in *Theology of the New Testament*, vol. 2, trans. Kendrick Grobel (New York: Scribner's, 1951/55), pp. 237-51.

4. Gerhard Ebeling, *Theology and Proclamation: Dialogue with Bultmann*, trans. John Riches (Philadelphia: Fortress Press, 1966).

5. Wolfhart Pannenberg, *The Apostles' Creed in the Light of Today's Questions*, trans. Margaret Kohl (Philadelphia: The Westminster Press, 1972).

6. See Johann B. Metz, *Faith in History and Society*, trans. David Smith (New York: Seabury Press, 1980), and Jürgen Moltmann, *The Gospel of Liberation*, trans. H. Wayne Pipkin (Waco: Word Books, 1973).

7. Dorothee Sölle, *Political Theology*, trans. John Shelley (Philadelphia: Fortress Press, 1974).

8. Ian Pit-Watson draws significantly from Heinrich Ott (see *Preaching: A Kind of Folly* [Philadelphia: The Westminster Press, 1976]). David J. Randolph takes Ebeling's approach seriously (see *The Renewal of Preaching—A New Homiletic Based on the New Hermeneutic* [Philadelphia: Fortress Press, 1969]). And Fred Craddock develops a Kierkegaardian theology of preaching (see *As One Without Authority: Essays on Inductive Preaching* [Enid: Phillips University Press, 1971]; *Overhearing the Gospel* [Nashville: Abingdon Press, 1978]; and *Preaching* [Nashville: Abingdon Press, 1985]).

9. Compare I Corinthians 15:45; Galatians 3:1-5 and 6:15.

10. See David J. Lull, *The Spirit in Galatia: Paul's Interpretation of Pneuma as Divine Power* (Society of Biblical Literature Dissertation Series, 49 (Chico: Scholars Press, 1980); idem, "The Spirit and the Creative Transformation of Human Existence," *Journal of the American Academy of Religion* 47 (1979): 39-55.

11. Phillips Brooks, *Lectures on Preaching* (New York: E. P. Dutton, 1877), p. 6.

12. Compare John 1:8 (John the Baptist "was not the light, but came to bear witness to the light" [RSV]).

Chapter 2. Preaching and Freedom

1. See especially *Romans 8:1-15; II Corinthians 3:17; and Galatians 4:21–5:25.*

2. J. Dominic Crossan, *Cliffs of Fall: Paradox and Polyvalence in the Parables of Jesus* (New York: Seabury Press, 1980).

3. Elizabeth Achtemeier, *Creative Preaching: Finding the Words* (Nashville: Abingdon Press, 1980), p. 35.

4. Alfred North Whitehead, *Process and Reality*, corrected edition, eds. David Ray Griffin and Donald W. Sherburne (New York: Free Press, 1978), p. 259.

5. Karl Barth, "The Strange New World Within the Bible," in *The Word of God and the Word of Man*, trans. Douglas Horton (Grand Rapids: Zondervan, 1935), pp. 28-50.

6. Rudolf Bultmann, *Jesus Christ and Mythology* (New York: Scribner's, 1958).

7. Gerhard Ebeling, *God and Word*, trans. James W. Leitch (Philadelphia: Fortress Press, 1967).

8. Wolfhart Pannenberg, *Jesus—God and Man*, trans. Lewis L. Wilkins and Duane A. Priebe (Philadelphia: The Westminster Press, 1968).

9. Dorothee Sölle, *Christ the Representative: An Essay in Theology After the Death of God*, trans. David Lewis (Philadelphia: Fortress Press, 1967).

10. This "deistic" view is still represented in modern theology by the existentialists and others indebted to a nature/history dualism.

11. We discuss this question of the end in relation to Paul's letters on pp. 186-88.

12. Throughout we have replaced the male-biased translation "kingdom of God" with "realm of God."

13. Matthew 19:23-26; Mark 10:23-27; and Luke 18:24-27.

14. Albert Schweitzer, *The Quest of the Historical Jesus: A Critical Study of Its Progress from Reimarus to Wrede*, trans. W. Montgomery (New York: Macmillan, 1957).

15. Compare II Timothy 3:16; II Peter 1:20-21; and Jude 3.

16. Matthew 19:24; Mark 10:25; and Luke 18:25.

17. Matthew 19:23, 25-26; Mark 10:23-24, 26-27; and Luke 18:24, 26-27.

18. Compare Matthew's "softer" interpretation with its "exceptive clause" (5:32 and 19:9) and the "harder" teaching in Mark 10:10-12 and Luke 16:18 (also compare I Cor. 7:10-11, followed by a more permissive rule in 7:12-16).

19. Compare I John 4:1; I Corinthians 12:3; and Galatians 5:22-23.

Chapter 3. The Ends of Preaching

1. Paul Tillich, "Being, Individualization, and Participation," in *The Courage to Be* (New Haven: Yale University Press, 1952), pp. 86-90.

2. See Acts 1:5, 8; 2:1-41 (and often).

3. John 16:13 (compare 14:16-17, 25-26; 15:26-27; and 16:4b-15).

4. See the biblical portrayals of David and Peter, just to name two of the most central figures.

5. H. Richard Niebuhr, *The Meaning of Revelation* (New York: Macmillan, 1941), pp. 87-88.

6. For the relationship of Jesus' identity to that of Christians, see John 1:12-13 (also compare Gal. 3:26–4:7).

7. Reinhold Niebuhr, *Moral Man and Immoral Society: A Study in Ethics and Politics* (New York: Scribner's, 1932).

8. See Galatians 3:1-5; Acts 1:1-11; and John 14:16-17, 25-26; 15:26; 16:1-15, respectively.

9. I Thessalonians 1:9 (compare Gal. 4:8-9).

10. See Galatians 3:5 (compare I Cor. 2:9-11).

11. See Galatians 4:5-7 and Romans 8:12-23.

12. See Acts 2:11 (compare 2:22).

13. For illustrations, see pp. 34-35 and 68-70.

14. James W. Fowler, *Stages of Faith: The Psychology of Human Development and the Quest for Meaning* (New York: Harper & Row, 1981).

15. We return to this question in more detail in chapter 5. For a critique of "self-denial" as "the" solution to "the" human predicament, see Valerie Saiving, "The Human Situation: A Feminine View," in *Womanspirit Rising: A Feminist Reader in Religion,* eds. Carol P. Christ and Judith Plaskow (San Francisco: Harper & Row, 1979 [orig. pub. 1960]), pp. 25-42, and Susan Nelson Dunfee, "The Sin of Hiding: A Feminist Critique of Reinhold Niebuhr's Account of the Sin of Pride," *Soundings* 65 (1982): 316-27. Compare Daniel Day Williams, *The Spirit and the Forms of Love* (Washington, D.C.: University Press of America, 1981 [orig. pub. 1967]), esp. pp. 84-88 and 192-213; Bernard M. Loomer, "Two Conceptions of Power," *Process Studies* 6 (1976): 30-31; and the literature cited by Elisabeth Schüssler Fiorenza, *In Memory of Her: A Feminist Theological Reconstruction of Christian Origins* (New York: Crossroad, 1983), p. 95 n. 56.

16. Fowler, *Stages of Faith,* p. 299.

17. For the rendering of the christological titles "Son of Man," "Son," and "King" as "Human One," "Child," and "Ruler" respectively, we have followed the proposals of *An Inclusive-Language Lectionary (Readings for Years A, B, and C),* Prepared by the Inclusive-Language Lectionary Committee of the National Council of the Churches of Christ in the U.S.A. (Atlanta: John Knox Press, 1986). The quotation of Mark 8:31 is from *Readings for Year B,* p. 75.

18. We have touched on a range of ethical questions that we cannot pursue here. For a discussion of the human situation in its wider setting—that is, in relation to the Spirit—see Charles Birch and John B. Cobb, Jr., *The Liberation of Life: From the Cell to the Community* (Cambridge: Cambridge University Press, 1981).

Chapter 4. Mark's Story of Jesus' Death

1. Frank Kermode, *The Genesis of Secrecy: On the Interpretation of Narrative* (Cambridge: Harvard University Press, 1979).

211

2. For a discussion of ambiguity in terms different from the "process" categories we have employed, see Bernard Brandon Scott, *The Word in Words: Reading and Preaching* (Philadelphia: Fortress Press, 1985), pp. 19-25, 45-53, and (in specific reference to Mark) 53-56.

3. Martin Hengel, *Crucifixion in the Ancient World and the Folly of the Message of the Cross*, trans. John Bowden (Philadelphia: Fortress Press, 1977), p. 25.

4. Ibid., p. 42.

5. Plato, *Republic*, 361e-362a.

6. Hengel, *Crucifixion*, p. 27.

7. Ibid., pp. 81-83. Examples are Xenophon, *Ephesiaca* 2.6, 4.2.1ff., 4.6.2; Chariton, *The Adventures of Chaereas and Callirhoe*, 4.6.2ff., 4.3.3ff. (compare 5.10.6).

8. See Samuel Sandmel, *Anti-Semitism in the New Testament?* (Philadelphia: Fortress Press, 1978), and Charlotte Klein, *Anti-Judaism in Christian Theology*, trans. E. Quinn (Philadelphia: Fortress Press, 1978).

9. Martin Hengel, *The Atonement: Origins of the Doctrine in the New Testament*, trans. John Bowden (Philadelphia: Fortress Press, 1981), p. 31. On the separation of styles in presenting heroic or common people, see Erich Auerbach, *Mimesis: The Representation of Reality in Western Literature* (Princeton: Princeton University Press, 1953), pp. 20-43.

10. Origen, *Against Celsus* 2.33-37.

11. Martin Kähler, *The So-Called Historical Jesus and the Historic, Biblical Christ*, trans. C. E. Braaten (Philadelphia: Fortress Press, 1964), p. 80 n. 11. Kähler specifically cites Mark as illustrating his definition.

12. The following is a list of passages in Mark that point directly to Jesus' death: 3:6; 8:31; 9:12, 31; 10:33-34, 45; 11:18; 12:7-8; 14:1, 31, 64; 15:13-15. Others that refer to Jesus' death are 2:20; 8:34; 10:38; 14:8, 10, 17, 21, 27, 35, 36, 41.

13. Mark 15:20, 21, 24, 25, 30, 32 (twice).

14. John R. Donahue, "A Neglected Factor in the Theology of Mark," *Journal of Biblical Literature* 101 (1982): 586.

15. Mark 14:10-11, 27-30, 43-46, 66-72.

16. Mark 14:53-65 and 15:31-32.

17. The cry, "Why did you abandon me?" (GNB)—the opening of Psalm 22, one of the psalms of lament—is taken by some interpreters as portraying Jesus' abandonment by God (see Werner H. Kelber, *The Kingdom in Mark: A New Place in a New Time* [Philadelphia: Fortress Press, 1974], p. 80). Others point out that the psalm as a whole is a prayer of trust in time of difficulty (see D. E. Nineham, *Saint Mark* [Philadelphia: The Westminster Press, 1963], pp. 427-29, with a summary of divergent views). For further discussion of this passage, see pp. 115-20.

18. John Knox, *The Death of Christ: The Cross in New Testament History and Faith* (New York: Abingdon Press, 1958), p. 153. We explore this theme more fully below in chapters 7 and 8.

19. Rudolf Pesch, *Das Markusevangelium*, vol. 2, Herder Theologischer Kommentar zum Neuen Testament (Freiburg: Herder, 1977), pp. 358-59.

20. The voluminous and complex literature on the origin of the sacrament deals in part with a question that we do not here consider —namely, the extent to which Mark 14:24 and the other Eucharistic texts can be ascribed to Jesus himself. For discussion of this issue, see the quite

different views of Joachim Jeremias, *The Eucharistic Words of Jesus*, 3rd. ed., trans. Norman Perrin (New York: Scribner's, 1967), chap. 5; Sam K. Williams, *Jesus' Death as Saving Event: The Background and Origin of a Concept*, Harvard Dissertations in Religion, 2 (Missoula: Scholars Press, 1975), pp. 221-22 and 224-25; and John R. Donahue, "The Passion in Preaching and Worship," in Werner E. Kelber, ed., *The Passion in Mark: Studies on Mark 14–16* (Philadelphia: Fortress Press, 1976), p. 3 n. 7. Donahue summarizes discussion of the relation between Isaiah 53 and the Markan covenant passage.

21. Pesch, *Das Markusevangelium* 2.363.

22. René Girard, *Violence and the Sacred*, trans. Patrick Gregory (Baltimore: Johns Hopkins University Press, 1977).

23. For a discussion of slavery imagery in the Graeco-Roman world, see Adolf Deissmann, *Light from the Ancient East: The New Testament Illustrated by Recently Discovered Texts of the Graeco-Roman World*, trans. L. R. M. Strachan (Grand Rapids: Baker Books, 1978), pp. 318-38. For ransom imagery, see Deissmann, *Light,* pages 10 and 327ff.

24. See the discussion in Williams, *Jesus' Death,* pp. 165-202 (the translation of IV Macc. 6:29 is taken from p. 176).

25. Williams (*Jesus' Death,* pp. 230-54) holds that the concepts expressed in IV Maccabees were taken from that book by an early Christian congregation. Hengel (*Atonement,* pp. 71-75) believes that the image of vicarious sacrifice, though non-Jewish in origin, had become so disseminated throughout Palestinian culture that it was taken from this environment and used by Jesus himself.

26. Elisabeth Schüssler Fiorenza, *In Memory of Her: A Feminist Theological Reconstruction of Christian Origins* (New York: Crossroad, 1983), p. 318.

27. For a possible pre-Markan apocalyptic crucifixion tradition, see J. Schreiber, *Theologie des Vertrauens* (Hamburg: Furche, 1967), pp. 24-40 and 66-82.

28. James M. Robinson, *The Problem of History in Mark and other Marcan Studies* (Philadelphia: Fortress Press, 1982), p. 101.

29. Ibid., p. 63.

30. Eduard Schweizer, *The Good News According to Mark,* trans. Donald H. Madvig (Atlanta: John Knox Press, 1977), p. 277.

31. For our discussion of the relation between two forms of divine power implied by this apocalyptic vision and its Markan version, see pp. 110-14 and 124-29.

32. For the relationship between "the disciples," "the twelve," and "following" Jesus in Mark, see Ernest Best, *Following Jesus: Discipleship in the Gospel of Mark,* Journal for the Study of the New Testament, Supplement Series 4 (Sheffield: JSOT, 1981); Donahue, "A Neglected Factor," pp. 585-86; and Robert C. Tannehill, "The Disciples in Mark: The Function of a Narrative Role," *Journal of Religion* 57 (1977): 386-405.

33. See Theodore J. Weeden, Sr., *Mark: Traditions in Conflict* (Philadelphia: Fortress Press, 1971).

34. Donahue, "A Neglected Factor," pp. 585-86. The key text is 3:35: "Whoever does the will of God is my brother, and sister, and mother" (RSV).

35. See, for example, the woman who anointed Jesus (14:3-9), children (10:14-15), and Simon of Cyrene, who carried Jesus' cross (15:21). For

recent studies presenting different views of the important role of women disciples in Mark, see Schüssler Fiorenza, *In Memory of Her*, p. 320; and Elizabeth Struthers Malbon, "Fallible Followers: Women and Men in the Gospel of Mark," *Semeia* 28 (1983): 29-48.

36. Malbon, "Fallible Followers."

37. Vernon K. Robbins, *Jesus the Teacher: A Socio-Rhetorical Interpretation of Mark* (Philadelphia: Fortress Press, 1984), pp. 167-68.

38. Rudolf Bultmann, *History of the Synoptic Tradition*, trans. John Marsh (New York: Harper & Row, 1963), p. 436; and Phillip Vielhauer, *Einleitung in das Neue Testament, die Apokryphen und die apostolischen Väter* (Berlin: de Gruyter, 1975), p. 348.

39. Philip Stevick, *The Theory of the Novel* (New York: Free Press, 1967), p. 140.

40. For this distinction between "story time," the time one needs to imagine to understand the story, and "plotted time," the time that is organized into the actual narrative as it is told, see Norman O. Petersen, *Literary Criticism of the New Testament* (Philadelphia: Fortress Press, 1978), chap. 3. Compare also David M. Rhoads and Donald Michie, *Mark as Story: An Introduction to the Narrative of a Gospel* (Philadelphia: Fortress Press, 1982), who interpret Mark on principles drawn from the criticism of novels.

41. See, for example, the different views of Kelber, *The Kingdom*, pp. 132-47; and Weeden, *Mark*, pp. 50-51, 159-68.

42. See especially Mark 13:9-13, 32-37; and 4:10-12.

43. Norman R. Petersen, "When Is the End Not the End? Literary Reflections on the Ending of Mark's Narrative," *Interpretation* 34 (1980): 151-66.

44. Compare the command given by Jesus to the person healed of leprosy: "Say nothing to anyone; but go, show yourself to the priest" (1:44 RSV).

45. Schüssler Fiorenza, *In Memory of Her*, p. 322. Compare Robert H. Smith, *Easter Gospels: The Message of the Resurrection According to the Four Evangelists* (Minneapolis: Augsburg, 1983), pp. 40-45; and Donald Senior, C.P., *The Passion of Jesus in the Gospel of Mark* (Wilmington: Michael Glazier, 1984), pp. 135-37. Both agree that the women are to be understood as responding positively to the Easter message.

46. Schüssler Fiorenza, *In Memory of Her*, p. 323.

47. Thomas E. Boomershine, "Mark 16:8 and the Apostolic Commission," *Journal of Biblical Literature* 100 (1981): 225-39.

48. Dan O. Via, Jr., *The Ethics of Mark's Gospel: In the Middle of Time* (Philadelphia: Fortress Press, 1985), pp. 50-57 (see also pp. 171-92).

49. John Dominic Crossan makes this feature of the Markan narrative the center of his interpretation of the Gospel (see "A Form for Absence: The Markan Creation of Gospel," *Semeia* 12 [1978]: 41-55).

50. Rhoads and Michie, *Mark as Story*, p. 96.

51. Eduard Schweizer, "The Portrayal of the Life of Faith in the Gospel of Mark," *Interpretation* 32 (1978): 385-86. Compare Crossan, who contends that absence "may well be but the deepest and most permanent form of presence" ("A Form for Absence," p. 53).

52. John R. Donahue, "Jesus as the Parable of God in the Gospel of Mark," *Interpretation* 32 (1978): 385-86.

53. Rhoads and Michie, *Mark as Story*, p. 75. See our discussion of God's power on pp. 110-14.

54. The relationship between these two forms of divine power is more fully discussed on pp. 110-14 and 124-29.

55. Dan O. Via, Jr. (*Kerygma and Comedy in the New Testament: A Structuralist Approach to Hermeneutic* [Philadelphia: Fortress Press, 1975]) has explored, though with a different set of questions, the relation between Mark and Greek tragedy.

56. Donahue ("A Neglected Factor") has explored the important, but often neglected, presentation of God in Mark.

57. See page 214 n. 40.

Chapter 5. Toward a Theology of Suffering: Interpreting Mark's Story of Jesus' Death

1. Martin Hengel, *Crucifixion*, trans. J. Bowden (Philadelphia: Fortress Press, 1977).

2. See Mark 8:31; 9:31; and 10:33-34.

3. For the disappointment of messianic hopes with the death of Jesus, see the post-resurrection narrative of the two disciples on the road to Emmaus in Luke 24:13-35.

4. See Nils A. Dahl, *The Crucified Messiah and Other Essays* (Minneapolis: Augsburg, 1974), pp. 10-36, and Ellis Rivkin, *What Crucified Jesus? The Political Execution of a Charismatic* (Nashville: Abingdon Press, 1984).

5. Harold S. Kushner, *When Bad Things Happen to Good People* (New York: Simon and Schuster, 1981).

6. See pp. 88-92.

7. See Peter's rebuke in Mark 8:32-33, Jesus' own prayer in Mark 14:32-42, and the taunts in Mark 15:29-32. It is curious, however, that among the Gospels only Mark (14:47) lacks Jesus' rebuke of the disciple's armed resistance at Jesus' arrest (see Matt. 26:52-54; Luke 22:51; and John 18:10-11).

8. See George W. E. Nickelsburg, Jr., "The Genre and Function of the Markan Passion Narrative," *Harvard Theological Review* 73 (1980): 153-84.

9. See pp. 67 and 211 n. 15 above.

10. For the most recent discussions of Job, see Gustavo Gutiérrez, *God-Talk and the Suffering of the Innocent* (Maryknoll: Orbis, 1987), and J. Gerald Janzen, *Job*, Interpretation: A Bible Commentary for Teaching and Preaching (Atlanta: John Knox Press, 1985).

11. Here Isaiah 53 is an important parallel, although its actual influence on Mark's Gospel is difficult to establish (see pp. 82-85 and 212-13 n. 20 above).

12. See also recent studies on Paul (especially J. Christiaan Beker, *Paul's Apocalyptic Gospel: The Coming Triumph of God* [Philadelphia: Fortress Press, 1982]), and the book of Revelation (especially Adela Yarbro Collins, *Crisis and Catharsis: The Power of the Apocalypse* [Philadelphia: The Westminster Press, 1984]; and Elisabeth Schüssler Fiorenza, *The Book of Revelation— Justice and Judgment* [Philadelphia: Fortress Press, 1984]). For recent studies on apocalypticism, see especially John J. Collins, *Daniel, with an Introduction to Apocalyptic Literature*, The Forms of the OT Literature, 20 (Grand Rapids: Eerdmans, 1985); idem, *The Apocalyptic Imagination: An Introduction to the Jewish Matrix of Christianity* (New York: Crossroad, 1984); and David

Notes to Pages 100-109

Hellholm, ed., *Apocalypticism in the Mediterranean World and the Near East* (Tübingen: Mohr/Siebeck, 1983).

13. See Stephen T. Davis, ed., *Encountering Evil: Live Options in Theodicy* (Atlanta: John Knox Press, 1981).

14. See II Timothy 2:2: "Take your share of suffering, as a good soldier of Christ Jesus."

15. The Greek term is *proairesis*. For a discussion of this term in Stoic anthropology, see J. M. Rist, *Stoic Philosophy* (Cambridge: Cambridge University Press, 1969), pp. 228-32.

16. See also Dorothee Sölle, *Suffering*, trans. E. R. Kalin (Philadelphia: Fortress Press, 1975), p. 100.

17. Ibid., p. 100.

18. Ibid., p. 99.

19. See Richard Rubenstein, *The Age of Triage: Fear and Hope in an Overcrowded World* (Boston: Beacon Press, 1983).

20. See Paul Tillich, *The Courage to Be* (New Haven: Yale University Press, 1952), pp. 9 and 101. Tillich has written that Stoicism is the great alternative to Christianity for modern Western people.

21. See Revelation 21:1-4; also compare 7:17.

22. See John 17:6-24 and 14:1-7. The classic discussion of gnosticism is still Hans Jonas, *The Gnostic Religion: The Message of the Alien God and the Beginnings of Christianity*, 2nd ed. (Boston: Beacon Press, 1963).

23. The Gospel of John, which approximates a gnostic solution (not the same as a "stoic" one), offers a message of promise that suffering can be endured if one knows that God and the victim are united, as can be seen in the Johannine presentation of Jesus as one with God (see Sölle, *Suffering*, pp. 140-41). For an apocalyptic solution, see the book of Revelation.

24. It is worth noting that while Luke 22:40-46 intensifies Jesus' struggle with this question, Matthew 26:36-46 reduces it, and John 18:11 preserves only a remnant of the theme of Jesus' struggle (see 12:27) and replaces it with a prayer for the church given by a Jesus whose mission has reached its hour of "glory" (John 17).

25. See the verb "must" *(dei)* in Mark 8:31, which is replaced by future tenses in 9:31 and 10:33-34. The future tenses, which can be read in a simple temporal sense, are less freighted with a sense of "divine necessity" than *dei* is.

26. Mark 14:35 is peculiar to Mark. Instead of "all things are possible to you" (Mark 14:36), Matthew 26:39 reads, "If it is possible," and Luke 22:42 has, "If you are willing."

27. See Mark 10:28, 39; 14:29-31. Compare the portrayal of the disciples' loyalty throughout Jesus' sufferings in Luke 22:28.

28. See Mark 14:37-41, 50-52, and 66-72.

29. For a discussion of Jesus' response to violence in relation to the preaching task, see John Blackwell, *The Passion as Story: The Plot of Mark* (Philadelphia: Fortress Press, 1986), pp. 38-47, 61-68, and especially 73-80; and Bernard Brandon Scott, *The Word in Words: Reading and Preaching* (Philadelphia: Fortress Press, 1985), pp. 53-56.

30. Although these stoic and cynic elements are stronger in the "code of household duties" in I Peter 2:11–3:7 (compare Col. 3:18–4:6; Eph. 5:21–6:9; I Tim. 5:1–6:2a), such sayings as Luke 6:20-49; 9:57-62, and pars. bear comparing with "the life of a Cynic."

31. See Epictetus, *Dissertations* 3.22.

32. Sölle, *Suffering*, pp. 11-22.

33. See Elisabeth Schüssler Fiorenza, *In Memory of Her: A Feminist Theological Reconstruction of Christian Origins* (New York: Crossroad, 1983), esp. pp. 118-30 and 316-23.

34. See Mark 8:34-35; 9:31; and 14:32-42, which express the cost of devotion to God's purposes in a world in which powers exist that can oppose God.

35. See also the foretelling of the resurrection in Mark 8:31; 9:31; and 10:34.

36. For the theme of divine power after Mark 8:26, see the sayings about the *Parousia* of the "Human One" (9:1; 13:26-27; and 14:62).

37. See Mark 10:27 par. Matthew 19:26 (Luke 18:27 omits this phrase) and Mark 14:36 (for the variants of this saying in Matt. 26:39 and Luke 22:42, see n. 26 above).

38. For a discussion of the incoherence of the strict, traditional idea of "omnipotence," see Schubert M. Ogden, "Evil and Belief in God: The Distinctive Relevance of a 'Process Theology,'" *Perkins School of Theology Journal* 31 (1978): 29-34; and David R. Griffin, *God, Power, and Evil: A Process Theodicy* (Philadelphia: The Westminster Press, 1976). The view of God proposed here is more fully discussed by John B. Cobb, Jr., in *God and the World* (Philadelphia: The Westminster Press, 1969).

39. For discussions of the role of women in Mark, see Schüssler Fiorenza, *In Memory of Her,* pp. 320 and 323; Thomas E. Boomershine, "Mark 16:8 and the Apostolic Commission," *Journal of Biblical Literature* 100 (1981): 225-39; and Elizabeth Struthers Malbon, "Fallible Followers: Women and Men in the Gospel of Mark," *Semeia* 28 (1983): 29-48. See also our discussion on pp. 86-88 and 213-14, n. 35 above.

40. Matthew's parallels to Mark 15:29-32 (compare Luke 23:35-43) bring this view even more sharply into view: "If you are a Child of God . . ." and "He trusts in God; let God deliver him now, if God desires him; for he said, 'I am a Child of God'" (27:40, 43).

41. Compare the concept of "conquering" in Revelation 2:7, 11, 17, 26; 3:5, 12, 21; and 21:7.

42. Compare Schüssler Fiorenza, *In Memory of Her,* p. 135: "Jesus' death is not willed by God but is the result of his all-inclusive praxis as Sophia's prophet. . . . The suffering and death of Jesus, like that of John [the Baptist] and all the other prophets sent to Israel before him, are not required in order to atone for the sins of the people in the face of an absolute God, but are the result of violence against the envoys of Sophia who proclaim God's unlimited goodness and the equality and election of all her children in Israel."

Jürgen Moltmann, however, attempts to develop a theology of God's suffering, while at the same time maintaining the view that God is the cause of Christ's suffering (*The Crucified God: The Cross of Christ as the Foundation and Criticism of Christian Theology,* trans. R. A. Wilson and J. Bowden [New York: Harper & Row, 1974]). See Sölle's criticism of Moltmann, whom she commends for allowing for "the pain of God," but whose theology, she holds, retains "the sado-masochistic streak" in traditional Christian theism (*Suffering,* pp. 26-28).

43. See the similar interpretations of Jesus' passion in Mark by Theodore J. Weeden, Sr., "The Cross as Power in Weakness (Mark 15:20b-41)," in *The Passion in Mark: Studies on Mark 14–16,* ed. Werner H. Kelber (Philadelphia: Fortress Press, 1976), pp. 115-34; and Donald Senior, C.P., *The Passion of*

Jesus in the Gospel of Mark (Wilmington: Michael Glazier, 1984), esp. pp. 144-48.

44. Mark 9:12 and 31; 10:33-34, 45; 14:22-25; and 15:33-39.

45. John 13:2, 27; and compare 6:70-71 and 8:44.

46. See, however, Mark 8:33 (RSV): "Get behind me, Satan!"

47. Mark 14:10-11, 17-21, 30, 32-45, 50-52, 54, and 66-72.

48. Mark 3:6; 8:31; 10:33; 11:18; 12:12 (which refers to 12:27); 12:13; 14:1, 43, 53, 55-65; 15:1, 3, 10-12, 31.

49. For the treatment of this issue in John, see David Rensberger, "The Politics of John: The Trial of Jesus in the Fourth Gospel," *Journal of Biblical Literature* 103 (1984): 395-411.

50. See, for example, the role of religious authorities, God's representatives, in Jesus' trial (14:53-72) and the betrayal of Jesus by his own closest associates, Judas (14:10-11, 17-21) and Peter (14:53-54, 66-72).

51. See L. Ruppert, *Jesus als der leidende Gerechte? Der Weg Jesu im Lichte eines alt- und zwischen-testamentlichen Motivs,* Stuttgarter Bibelstudien, 59 (Stuttgart: KWB, 1972); and Rudolf Pesch, *Das Markusevangelium,* Herder Theologischer Kommentar zum Neuen Testament, 2 vols. (Freiburg: Herder, 1977). They interpret Mark in the light of the Old Testament and intertestamental motif of the suffering of the "righteous one," who is abandoned by both friend and foe. See also George W. E. Nickelsburg, Jr., *Resurrection, Immortality, and Eternal Life in Intertestamental Judaism,* Harvard Theological Studies, 26 (Cambridge: Harvard University Press, 1972), who points out that prophets, "righteous ones," the "poor," and martyrs can die at the hands of their own "good," religious people as well as at the hands of the wicked among their own people and among the Gentiles.

52. See T. J. Weeden, Sr., "Recovering the Parabolic Intent in the Parable of the Sower," *Journal of Biblical Literature* 47 (1979): 97-120.

53. For the history of the interpretation of this passage, see Samuel L. Terrien, "Job," in *The Interpreter's Bible,* ed. George A. Buttrick (Nashville: Abingdon Press, 1954), pp. 1051-53; and Marvin Pope, *Job,* 3rd ed., Anchor Bible (New York: Doubleday, 1973), p. 146.

54. See, for example, Psalms 6, 7, 13, 22, 44, 90 and Jeremiah 20:7-13.

55. See Sölle, *Suffering,* p. 79, who points to God's "silence" in Gethsemane.

56. J. Dominic Crossan, "A Form for Absence: The Markan Creation of Gospel," *Semeia* 12 (1978): 41-55; and idem, "Empty Tomb and Absent Lord (Mark 16:1-8)," in Kelber, *The Passion in Mark,* pp. 135-52.

57. See Mark 9:1; 13:13 and 26-31.

58. See II Peter 3:1-10 and Revelation 6:10.

59. *Affirmation of Faith,* used by permission of The United Church of Canada, in *The Sacrament of the Lord's Supper: An Alternate Text,* prepared by the Commission on Worship of The United Methodist Church (Nashville: The United Methodist Publishing House, 1972).

60. See also T. E. Fretheim, *The Suffering God: An Old Testament Perspective,* Overtures to Biblical Theology, 14 (Philadelphia: Fortress Press, 1984). Sölle *(Suffering,* pp. 41-43) observes that the Stoic god is victorious over the Christian God whenever divine "apathy" is defended at the expense of the image of God in the suffering of Christ—that is, whenever no room is allowed for "the pain of God" (see pp. 99-103, in which Sölle discusses stoicism and mysticism in the period from the fourteenth century to the German Reformation).

61. Compare Sölle's interpretation of Jesus' resurrection as holding hope for everyone, for in it we see that others (represented by the disciples) will go on to "suffer in accord with justice" on behalf of those who suffer senselessly *(Suffering,* p. 150).

62. Compare Sölle's treatment of stages of suffering, in which lament leads to the struggle against suffering and its causes *(Suffering,* pp. 70-74).

63. See Daniel, which is the most dramatic example of this kind of faith in the Hebrew scriptures. In the New Testament, see II Thessalonians, II Peter, and Revelation.

64. See n. 57 above.

65. The perfect participle *(ton estaurōmenon)* in Mark 16:6 emphasizes the continued result of the past event of the crucifixion.

66. Compare the resurrection narratives in Matthew 28:1-20; Luke 24:1-53; John 20–21.

67. See the attempts by the early church to supply Mark with what was deemed a more "proper" ending (compare 16:9-20, and the "shorter ending," which can be found in the marginal notes of the RSV).

68. For a full discussion of this debate, see T. J. Weeden, Sr., *Mark: Traditions in Conflict* (Philadelphia: Fortress Press, 1971), pp. 111-17. Weeden defends the "Parousia" thesis. For further bibliography, see ibid., p. 111 n. 13.

69. See Crossan, "A Form for Absence"; idem, "Empty Tomb and Absent Lord"; and Weeden, *Mark,* pp. 81-90.

70. See n. 67 above.

71. See Brevard S. Childs, *The New Testament as Canon: An Introduction* (Philadelphia: Fortress Press, 1985), pp. 92-95.

72. See Daniel Day Williams, *The Spirit and the Forms of Love* (reprint, Washington, D.C.: University Press of America, 1981; orig. pub. 1967), p. 188. Williams writes: "The resurrection was the sign that the separation from God which has been exposed in the death of the man of God at the hands of sinful men is overcome now and forever." See also Sölle's interpretation of the resurrection cited in n. 61 above.

73. For this distinction, see Bernard Loomer, "Two Concepts of Power," *Process Studies* 6 (1976): 5-32.

Chapter 7. Paul's Interpretation of Jesus' Death

1. See the distinction between story and plotted time in note 40, p. 214.

2. See Charles Talbert, *What Is a Gospel? The Genre of the Gospels* (Philadelphia: Fortress Press, 1977), pp. 72-73. Talbert distinguishes between the mythic patterns of the "immortals" and the "descending/ ascending" gods.

3. See I Corinthians 2:8; 15:20-28, 51-57; Romans 7:25a and 8:38-39. Robert W. Funk *(Language, Hermeneutic, and Word of God* [New York: Harper, 1966], pp. 275-305) sees here an allusion to the "gnostic myth of the redeemer."

4. See Richard B. Hays, *The Faith of Jesus Christ: An Investigation of the Narrative Substructure of Galatians 3:1–4:11,* Society of Biblical Literature Dissertation Series, 56 (Chico: Scholars Press, 1983), chapter 2.

5. See J. Christiaan Beker, *Paul the Apostle: The Triumph of God in Life and Thought* (Philadelphia: Fortress Press, 1980), p. 353.

6. For this distinction, see Rudolf Bultmann, *The Presence of Eternity* (New York: Harper, 1957).

7. Some scholars regard this passage as an interpolation. For an argument on behalf of its authenticity, see Karl P. Donfried, "Paul and Judaism: 1 Thessalonians 2:13-16 as a Test Case," *Interpretation* 38 (1984): 242-53, where all the relevant literature is given.

8. See especially I Corinthians 2:2; Galatians 3:1, 13; and Philippians 2:8.

9. The Greek verb *paradidōmi* can translated either way. The NEB translates I Corinthians 11:23 as "on the night of his arrest."

10. See Galatians 1:4; Philippians 2:6-11; I Corinthians 2:6-13; 15:20-28, 51-57; Romans 7:24-25 and 8:31-39.

11. See also Romans 1:17; 3:21-26; 9:6, 14-18; and 11:1.

12. See, for example, Romans 3:25 ("God put him forward") and Romans 8:32 ("God handed him over"); and compare 4:25 and I Corinthians 11:24.

13. In the Greek New Testament, another group of passages speaks of the "faith of Jesus Christ." Some have raised the question of whether this genitive ("of") should be taken as subjective—that is, as referring to *Jesus'* faith. In almost all English translations, however, this phrase is rendered "faith in Jesus Christ" (Rom. 3:22, 26; Gal. 3:22, 26). For discussion of this issue and other relevant literature, see Hays, *The Faith of Jesus Christ*, chapter 4; Luke T. Johnson, "Romans 3:21-26 and the Faith of Jesus," *Catholic Biblical Quarterly* 44 (1982): 77-90; George Howard, *Paul: Crisis in Galatia: A Study in Early Christian Theology*, Society of New Testament Studies Monograph Series, 35 (Cambridge: Cambridge University Press, 1979), pp. 46-65.

14. See Sam K. Williams, *Jesus' Death as Saving Event: The Background and Origin of a Concept*, Harvard Dissertations in Religion, 2 (Missoula: Scholars Press, 1975).

15. Among the reasons for doubting direct Pauline authorship for Colossians and Ephesians is the way the eschatological tension shifts to an emphasis on the realization of the promised future in the present in such passages as Colossians 1:13; 2:12, 15; 3:1; and Ephesians 2:5-6.

16. Interpreters of Paul all recognize both sides of the tension between the present and the future. The present is far more fully developed in the interpretation of Rudolf Bultmann (see, for example, his *Theology of the New Testament*, trans. K. Grobel [New York: Scribner's, 1955], 1.187-352). The future, apocalyptic theme in Paul has been emphasized by Ernst Käsemann (see, for example, "The Beginnings of Christian Theology" and "Primitive Christian Apocalyptic," in *New Testament Questions of Today*, trans. W. J. Montague [Philadelphia: Fortress Press, 1969], pp. 82-107 and 108-37), and by J. Christiaan Beker (see, for example, *Paul the Apostle*, and *Paul's Apocalyptic Gospel: The Coming Triumph of God* [Philadelphia: Fortress Press, 1982]). See the discussion of the interpretation of the temporal aspect of Paul's eschatology by Leander E. Keck, "Paul and Apocalyptic Theology," *Interpretation* 38 (1984): 232-33 and 240.

17. See I Thessalonians 5:9 and compare I Thessalonians 1:20 and Galatians 1:4.

18. See Galatians 4:4; also compare the reference to God's "will" in 1:4 and the phrase "in accordance with the scriptures" in I Corinthians 15:3-4.

19. Williams, *Jesus' Death*, p. 54. We shall have to return to this issue of predestination in the next chapter.

20. See Romans 1:17; 3:1-8; 3:21–26; 9:6, 14-18; 11:1.

21. See Galatians 3:15-25; Romans 3:1-8; 3:21–4:25; 9:6, 14-18; 11:1.

22. Many recent commentaries prefer reading the Greek prepositional phrase as purposive ("for the sake of"), rather than as causal ("because of"). For an interpretation of this phrase in the light of the metaphor of the "pedagogue" in Galatians 3:23-25, see David J. Lull, "'The Law Was Our Pedagogue': A Study in Galatians 3:19-25," *Journal of Biblical Literature* 105 (1986): 481-98. See also nn. 25 and 56 below.

23. See Galatians 2:19-20; 4:4-5; 5:24; and 6:14-15. See also 3:1-5, where Paul argues that the Christians in Galatia had received the Spirit, not from "works of the law," but from the proclamation of faith.

24. Galatians 3:11 and Romans 1:17, which could also be translated "the one who is righteous through faith shall live" (see the RSV).

25. Romans 4:15 and 5:12-14, 20. Galatians 3:19 is often cited with the Romans passages, a move some consider required to illumine a difficult passage in Galatians (see, for example, most recently C. K. Barrett, *Freedom and Obligation: A Study of the Epistle to the Galatians* [Philadelphia: The Westminster Press, 1985], p. 33). We prefer, however, to view Galatians 3:19 from the light shed on it by the more immediate metaphor of the "pedagogue" and other household slaves responsible for supervision of minors in Galatians 3:23–4:7 (see Lull, "The Law Was Our Pedagogue").

26. See Russell Pregeant, "Grace and Recompense: Reflections on a Pauline Paradox," *Journal of the American Academy of Religion* 47 (1979): 73-96; and C. K. Barrett, *The Epistle to the Romans* (New York: Harper and Row, 1957), pp. 48-54.

27. Hendrikus W. Boers, *Theology Out of the Ghetto: A New Exegetical Study Concerning Religious Exclusiveness* (Leiden: Brill, 1971), presses a related point in urging that the faith of Abraham provides a model of faith paralleled to faith in Christ.

28. Lull, "The Law Was Our Pedagogue"; E. P. Sanders, *Paul, the Law, and the Jewish People* (Philadelphia: Fortress Press, 1983). See also Heikki Räisänen, *Paul and the Law*, Wissenschaftliche Untersuchungen zum Neuen Testament, 29 (Tübingen: Mohr/Siebeck, 1983); and H. Hübner, *Law in Paul's Thought*, trans. J. C. G. Grieg, Studies of the NT and Its World (Edinburgh: T. & T. Clark, 1984). Options in the interpretation of Romans 2 are sketched by Pregeant, "Grace and Recompense," pp. 74-78.

29. See n. 13 above.

30. See Paul's surprise that his gospel of grace could be misunderstood as not including response (Rom. 6:1-2). The recent discussion of God's righteousness in Paul is well summarized by Manfred T. Brauch, "Perspectives on 'God's righteousness' in recent German discussion," in E. P. Sanders, *Paul and Palestinian Judaism* (Philadelphia: Fortress Press, 1977), pp. 523-42. Brauch discusses the work of Ernst Käsemann and others who have made the emphasis described above, and he notes the dissent of Rudolf Bultmann, who spoke for an interpretation of righteousness simply as "gift."

31. See John B. Cobb, Jr., *The Structure of Christian Existence* (Philadelphia: The Westminster Press, 1967), chap. 10 (esp. pp. 120-24).

32. See Galatians 4:3, 8-9; I Corinthians 2:6-13; 15:20-28.

33. See also Romans 7:24-25; I Corinthians 15:20-28 and 51-57.

34. Greek, "Father."

35. Or "although," according to another rendering of the Greek participle *hyparchōn*.

36. The key term, *harpagmon*—"a thing to be grasped" (RSV)—may refer either to violent seizure or to holding to something one already has (see W. Bauer et al., *A Greek-English Lexicon of the New Testament and Other Early Christian Literature*, 2nd ed. [Chicago: University of Chicago Press, 1979], p. 108). Though the former meaning more obviously suggests being an enemy of God, either one points to a path opposite to the one actually taken according to the hymn (see R. P. Martin, *Carmen Christi: Philippians ii, 5-11 in Recent Interpretation and in the Setting of Early Christian Worship*, Society for New Testament Studies Monograph Series, 4 (Cambridge: Cambridge University Press, 1967).

It is usually assumed that the "story" of the Philippians hymn is that of a pre-existent figure who descended to human form. This view has been challenged by such scholars as Charles H. Talbert, "The Problem of Pre-Existence in Philippians 2:6-11," *Journal of Biblical Literature* 86 (1967): 141-53; Jerome Murphy-O'Connor, "Christological Anthropology in Phil., ii, 6-11," *Revue Biblique* 83 (1976): 25-50; and James D. G. Dunn, *Christology in the Making: A New Testament Inquiry into the Doctrine of the Incarnation* (Philadelphia: The Westminster Press, 1980), esp. pp. 114-21. For a criticism of Dunn's view, see Carl R. Holladay, "New Testament Christology: A Consideration of Dunn's Christology in the Making," *Semeia* 30 (1984): 65-82 (p. 74 is especially pertinent to this point). In any case, our interpretation does not hinge on this debate, since we are only interested here in the threefold pattern of divine form, humiliation, and exaltation, which is not in dispute. Whether or not the Christ figure is presented as "pre-existent," we may, however, speak of an "original" or "primordial" situation prior to the humiliation. For a thorough study of the interpretation of the hymn, see Martin, *Carmen Christi*.

37. Note the contrast between Philippians 2:6 and 9.

38. See Galatians 2:19-20; 5:24; 6:14-15; II Corinthians 4:7-12; and Romans 6:1-11; 8:1-17.

39. See I Thessalonians 2:17–3:10; II Corinthians 4:1-12; 11:23-29; and Romans 8:18-25.

40. See Philippians 2:6-11 and the numerous references to Jesus' resurrection.

41. See I Thessalonians 1:10; 5:9; Romans 3:21-26 and 5:1-21.

42. Paul mentions the Supper only in I Corinthians 10:14-22 and 11:17-34, both of which are tantalizingly indirect about its place in the churches and about Paul's interpretation of it. The extensive literature is well reviewed by Hans Conzelmann, *I Corinthians*, trans. James W. Leitch, Hermeneia (Philadelphia: Fortress Press, 1975), ad loc.

43. Ibid., p. 198.

44. I Corinthians 11:26 (RSV): "You proclaim the Lord's death until he comes."

45. We have already noted a similar transformation in Mark, which, of course, is later than Paul and probably represents a separate line of wrestling with this transformation.

46. Beker, *Paul the Apostle*, p. 225.

47. Interpretations of Paul's view of suffering will lead into most of the issues already presented in our discussion of suffering in Mark (see chap. 5).

48. On the distance between Paul and the subjective and inward interpretation of him, see Krister Stendahl, "The Apostle Paul and the Introspective Conscience of the West," in *Paul Among Jews and Gentiles and Other Essays* (Philadelphia: Fortress Press, 1976), pp. 78-96.

49. A consensus has developed among interpreters of Paul today. On the "I" in Galatians 2:18-20, see H. Dieter Betz, *Galatians*, Hermeneia (Philadelphia: Fortress Press, 1979), p. 122. On Romans 7:7-25, see Paul Achtemeier, *Romans*, Interpretation: A Bible Commentary for Teaching and Preaching (Atlanta: John Knox Press, 1985), pp. 118-26.

50. See I Corinthians 9:9 (RSV): "Is it for oxen that God is concerned?"

51. See Romans 8:19-23, especially verse 22: "The whole creation has been groaning in travail together until now" (RSV).

52. For a discussion of the history of interpretation of the term *creation (ktisis)*, see C. E. B. Cranfield, *A Critical and Exegetical Commentary on the Epistle to the Romans*, ICC, 2 vols. (Edinburgh: T. & T. Clark, 1975–79), 1.411-12.

53. We shall return to this question in the next chapter.

54. I Thessalonians 4:13-18 and 5:1-8; and compare 4:1-12 and 5:12-22.

55. See Galatians 6:8, which speaks of the future "eternal life."

56. For a description of the social function of the "pedagogue" in antiquity—that of the disciplinarian, a slave attendant for minors—see Lull, "The Law Was Our Pedagogue."

57. See also Wayne A. Meeks, *The First Urban Christians: The Social World of the Apostle Paul* (New Haven: Yale University Press, 1983), pp. 182-83, and other literature cited there.

58. The enigma of Jesus' death is seen from another angle in Romans 5, where the tension is not between weakness and power, but between sin and justice (or righteousness).

59. Compare Galatians 3:1-5 and I Thessalonians 1:2-10.

60. See Karl P. Donfried, ed., *The Romans Debate* (Minneapolis: Augsburg, 1977).

61. See especially Romans 5:1-11 and 8:1-8. In 3:21-26 legal and cultic terms are mixed. See also the image of the prosecutor and advocate in 8:26-27, 31-39.

62. See Romans 1:17; 3:1-8, 21-26; 9:6, 14-18; and 11:1.

63. See Galatians 1:15-16; I Corinthians 9:1; 15:8; and the legendary narratives in Acts 9:1-19; 22:2-16; 26:9-18.

64. For example, I Thessalonians 1:10 and 5:21; Galatians 1:4 and 2:20 (and 3:13?); I Corinthians 11:23-26 and 15:3-7; II Corinthians 5:21; Philippians 2:6-11; Romans 3:25 and 4:25.

65. See Galatians 2:19-20; 5:24; 6:14, 17; II Corinthians 4:10; Romans 6:1-11; 8:17; Philippians 3:10.

66. There is a consensus among scholars about the examples we have chosen.

67. See I Thessalonians 4:1-12 and 5:1-8, 12-22. The term *sin* appears in this letter only in 2:16.

68. Note the predominance of the phrase "for our sins" or "for us."

69. N. A. Dahl, *Studies in Paul: Theology for the Early Christian Mission* (Minneapolis: Augsburg, 1977), pp. 172-73.

70. W. D. Davies's suggestion (*Torah in the Messianic Age and/or the Age to Come*, Society of Biblical Literature Monograph Series, 7 [Philadelphia: Society of Biblical Literature, 1952]), that it was possible in Judaism to think

of a messianic age without the Jewish law, lacks documentary support in Jewish literature before 70 c.e.

71. Note the phrase "for our sins" again.

72. See Romans 13:11-12*a* and I Thessalonians 4:13-18.

73. See our earlier discussion of II Corinthians 4:7-12 (p. 154 above).

74. Philippians 1:27–2:5, 12-18; and 3:2–4:1.

75. See p. 223, n. 65 above.

Chapter 8. Preaching God's Justice: Interpreting Jesus' Death in the Letters of Paul

1. Compare Alfred North Whitehead's comments on the relationship between "logic" and "aesthetic delight" in *Process and Reality,* corrected edition, David R. Griffin and Donald W. Sherburne, eds. (New York: Free Press, 1978), pp. 184-86. See also Robert C. Tannehill's comments on the relationship between "poetry" and "rhetoric" in *The Sword of His Mouth,* Semeia Supplements, 1 (Philadelphia: Fortress Press, 1975), pp. 15-19.

2. The "gift" aspect of God's righteousness is well interpreted by Rudolf Bultmann in *New Testament Theology,* 2 vols., trans. K. Grobel (New York: Scribner's, 1951–55), 1.274-85. Ernst Käsemann emphasized God's righteousness as eschatological power in "God's Righteousness in Paul" in *The Bultmannian School of Biblical Interpretation: New Directions?* ed. R. W. Funk (New York: Harper & Row, 1965), pp. 100-10, and in other writings. For a review of the discussion of God's righteousness in Paul, see Manfred T. Brauch, "Perspectives on 'God's Righteousness' in Recent German Discussion," in E. P. Sanders, *Paul and Palestinian Judaism: A Comparison of Patterns of Religion* (Philadelphia: Fortress Press, 1977), pp. 523-42. See p. 221 n. 30 above.

3. See William A. Beardslee, *Human Achievement and Divine Vocation in the Message of Paul,* Studies in Biblical Theology, 31 (Naperville: Allenson, 1961).

4. Note the second person plural ("you") in Galatians 1:6-9 and 2:5.

5. Bultmann, *Theology,* 1.234 (italicized in the original).

6. In Galatians, only 1:1 (and, indirectly, 6:8 and 15).

7. See especially Galatians 5:6, 13; 6:2, 9-10. Also compare 3:26–4:7, which draws out the significance of 2:1-14 for the churches in Galatia.

8. Compare Dorothee Sölle's remark that "the training value of suffering is negligible," in *Suffering,* trans. E. R. Kalin (Philadelphia: Fortress Press, 1975), p. 21.

9. Compare II Corinthians 5:21 and 8:9, which articulate the movement of descent in Jesus' story. Also compare II Corinthians 13:4 and Philippians 2:5-11, in which we see the movement of ascent as well as descent in Jesus' story.

10. Compare Romans 8:35, which speaks of the love of Christ.

11. See, for example, Hans Frei, *The Identity of Jesus Christ* (New Haven: Yale University Press, 1974).

12. See, for example, Nathan A. Scott, Jr., "The Rediscovery of Story in Recent Theology and the Refusal of Story in Recent Literature," *Journal of the American Academy of Religion* 49 (1983): 139-55. For a more complete analysis of this complex problem, see William A. Beardslee, "Recent Hermeneutics and Process Thought," *Process Studies* 12 (1982): 65-76.

13. For a treatment of "suffering" from a perspective of the basic unity, solidarity, and interrelatedness of persons, see Sölle, *Suffering*.

14. For a treatment of this theme by a historian, see William H. McNeill, *The Human Condition: An Ecological and Historical View* (Princeton: Princeton University Press, 1980).

15. For a sketch of the most important of these, see Daniel Day Williams, *The Spirit and Forms of Love* (Washington, D. C.: University Press of America, 1981), pp. 174-76.

16. Ibid., pp. 176-91.

17. William Inge, *The Dark at the Top of the Stairs: A New Play* (New York: Random House, 1958), p. 96.

18. Ibid., p. 103.

19. William Inge, *Four Plays* (New York: Grove, 1958), p. ix.

20. This observation forms one of the central hermeneutical principles of Rudolf Bultmann's "existentialist interpretation" of the New Testament (see his essays, newly translated and collected by Schubert M. Ogden, in *The New Testament and Mythology and Other Basic Writings* [Philadelphia: Fortress Press, 1984]).

21. This perspective has been identified, especially in the last two decades, with "process theology." See the different approaches of Schubert M. Ogden, "Present Prospects for Empirical Theology," in *The Future of Empirical Theology*, ed. B. Meland, Essays on Divinity, 2 (Chicago: University of Chicago Press, 1969), pp. 65-88 (esp. pp. 76-88); and Bernard M. Loomer, "Two Conceptions of Power," *Process Studies* 6 (1976): 5-32. For earlier representatives of this "process" perspective, see the writings of Alfred North Whitehead and Charles Hartshorne, with whom Josiah Royce (esp. his *The Problem of Christianity*, 2 vols. [New York: Macmillan, 1914]) should be compared and to whom "process theology" is also indebted (see Williams, *The Spirit*, pp. 180-82).

22. See John B. Cobb, Jr., *Process Theology as Political Theology* (Philadelphia: The Westminster Press, 1982); and Charles Birch and John B. Cobb, Jr., *The Liberation of Life: From the Cell to the Community* (Cambridge: Cambridge University Press, 1981).

23. See John B. Cobb, Jr., *Christ in a Pluralistic Age* (Philadelphia: The Westminster Press, 1975); David J. Lull, *The Spirit in Galatia: Paul's Interpretation of Pneuma as Divine Power*, Society of Biblical Literature Dissertation Series, 49 (Chico: Scholars Press, 1980); and idem, "The Spirit and the Creative Transformation of Human Existence," *Journal of the American Academy of Religion* 47 (1979): 39-55.

24. At the beginning of this century, Josiah Royce, a philosopher, saw that the Christian community of faith lives by the remembrance of Jesus' atoning death, which is constitutive of the church (see Williams, *The Spirit*, pp. 180-82).

25. See Martin Hengel, *The Atonement: The Origins of the Doctrine in the New Testament*, trans. J. Bowden (Philadelphia: Fortress Press, 1981), pp. 19-32. Hengel surveys ancient Greek sacrificial practices, their ancient interpretations, and their critics. Already in the Hebrew scriptures, sacrificial practices and imagery came under criticism (among the prophets, for example, see Isa. 1:12-17; Amos 4:4-5; 5:21-24).

26. See Bultmann's comments on the atonement, especially his observation that traditional interpretations of the atonement do not make it clear just how Jesus' death, or any other event of past history, could affect someone else's existence ("The New Testament and Mythology: The

Problem of Demythologyzing the New Testament Proclamation," in *The New Testament and Mythology,* pp. 1-43).

27. See John B. Cobb, Jr., "The Problem of Evil and the Task of Ministry," in *Encountering Evil: Live Options in Theodicy,* ed. Stephen T. Davis (Atlanta: John Knox Press, 1981), pp. 167-76.

28. For Jesus' death in relation to the Jewish law, see Romans and Galatians. See also pp. 145-46 above.

29. For Abraham, see Romans 4 and Galatians 3:6-14; for Adam, see Romans 5:12-21 and I Corinthians 15:20-28, 35-39.

30. See Romans 8:37-39; I Corinthians 2:6-8; 15:20-28; and Galatians 4:3.

31. That would be the approach of preaching based on Bultmann's "existentialist interpretation" of the New Testament (see Bultmann, *The New Testament and Mythology*).

32. That would be the approach of preaching based on what we have called "process hermeneutics" (see chap. 2). For further discussion and bibliography, see David J. Lull, "What Is 'Process Hermeneutics'?" *Process Studies* 13 (1983): 189-201. For essays that bear comparing with Bultmann's perspective, following different philosophical principles, see William A. Beardslee and David J. Lull, eds., *New Testament Interpretation from a Process Perspective,* Journal of the American Academy of Religion Thematic Studies, 47/1 (Chico: Scholars Press, 1979); and idem, eds., *Old Testament Interpretation from a Process Perspective,* Semeia, 24 (Chico: Scholars Press, 1982).

33. For a discussion of a related topic, the "authority" of scripture in theology, see Lull, "What Is 'Process Hermeneutics'?" and the literature cited there.

34. Compare Karl Rahner's notion of the "anonymous Christian" (*Theological Investigations,* vol. 6 [New York: Seabury Press, 1974], pp. 390-95).

35. Elisabeth Schüssler Fiorenza, *In Memory of Her: A Feminist Theological Reconstruction of Christian Origins* (New York: Crossroad, 1983); and idem, "Women-Church," in *Bread Not Stone: The Challenge of Feminist Biblical Interpretation* (Boston: Beacon Press, 1985), pp. 1-22.

36. See Russell Pregeant, "Grace and Recompense: Reflections on a Pauline Paradox," *Journal of the American Academy of Religion* 47 (1979): 73-96. For further discussion and bibliography, see E. P. Sanders, *Paul, the Law, and the Jewish People* (Philadelphia: Fortress Press, 1983), pp. 93-135.

37. For this dimension of God's justice, which includes a consideration of the consequences of human actions but moves beyond such consideration, see also Williams, *The Spirit,* pp. 182-83.

38. Leander E. Keck ("Paul and Apocalyptic Theology," *Interpretation* 38 [1984]: 235) makes a similar point when he observes that, for Paul, Jesus' cross/resurrection "dissolves" the theodicy issue and overturns the canons of "distributive justice." "A God who acts on behalf of sinners must be acting according to canons of righteousness utterly different from those which generate the theodicy problem."

39. See Romans 7; II Corinthians; Galatians 3–4; and Philippians 3.

40. See Galatians 2:15-16 (note the first person plural) and, less explicitly, Romans 9:1-5.

41. Paul's own term in Galatians 5:13-24 is "the flesh"; in Romans 7, it is "sin in the flesh."

42. See Galatians 3:19-25; 5:13-24; and Romans 5–8.

43. See Galatians 5:14 (compare 6:2); Romans 3:31 and 13:8-10. For a more complete discussion of Paul's views on the law and further bibliography, see pp. 145-46.

44. For example, Romans 3:31; 13:8-10; and Galatians 5:14 (compare 6:2).

45. This point, and what it entails, is the focus of Keck's essay, "Paul and Apocalyptic Theology."

46. Note that in the whole passage (Rom. 8:31-39), "the love of Christ" (v. 35) reappears as "the love of God in Jesus Christ our Lord" (v. 39).

47. See "foreknew . . . predestined" in Romans 8:28-30.

48. See "more than conquerors" in Romans 8:37.

49. See Pierre Teilhard de Chardin, *The Phenomenon of Man,* trans. Bernard Wall (New York: Harper, 1959), especially book 4, chapter 2. A different but related perspective on "the end point" of history is represented by Wolfhart Pannenberg (see, for example, his *Theology and the Kingdom of God,* ed. R. J. Neuhaus [Philadelphia: The Westminster Press, 1969]). Except for this feature of Teilhard's and Pannenberg's views of history, Whiteheadian "process thought" shares much in common with their perspectives.

50. The concept of hope in process theology is more fully treated, in quite different ways, by Schubert M. Ogden (*The Reality of God and Other Essays* [New York: Harper, 1966], pp. 206-30) and William A. Beardslee (*A House for Hope: A Study in Process and Biblical Thought* [Philadelphia: The Westminster Press, 1972]).

51. For a critique of this preoccupation, see Krister Stendahl, "The Apostle Paul and the Introspective Conscience of the West," in *Paul Among Jews and Gentiles and Other Essays* (Philadelphia: Fortress Press, 1976), pp. 78-96.

52. Chief among these interpreters of Paul in the ancient church is Augustine, who is followed by the reformers Martin Luther and John Wesley. In our own time, Rudolf Bultmann is the leading representative of this interpretive tradition.

53. Galatians 3:28 is usually read in the light of other, less emancipating passages (if not also less clear in their intentions!), such as I Corinthians 7:17-24; 11:2-16; 14:34-36; as well as the "codes of household duties" in Colossians, Ephesians, I Timothy, and Titus, which are now regarded as deutero- or pseudo-Pauline. For a discussion of these passages within the context of a reconstruction of the experience of women in early Christianity and reflection upon it, see Schüssler Fiorenza, *In Memory of Her.*

54. See Philemon and I Corinthians 7:21-23, both of which present the interpreter with complex problems at every turn.

55. See the image of sin and death as temporal powers introduced into the world by "Adam's transgression" (Rom. 5:12-21), the list of cosmic forces in Romans 8:37-39, the reference to the "rulers of this age" in I Corinthians 2:6-8, and the "elementary forces of the universe" in Galatians 4:3.

56. Bultmann's essays in *The New Testament and Mythology; Jesus Christ and Mythology* (New York: Scribner's, 1958); and *New Testament Theology* have made an influential contribution to the analysis of mythological language in the New Testament.

57. This is what Amos N. Wilder meant by his remark that, though we do not think mythologically, we do recognize a "metaphysical character" in perversions of social power and can, therefore, recognize a common element between Paul's language and ours *(Kerygma, Eschatology, and Social Ethics* [Philadelphia: Fortress Press, 1966], p. 25).

58. As we noted in the previous chapter, unfortunately Paul is silent about the role of the Roman governing officials and soldiers in the killing of Jesus. But he does make a point here of mentioning the role of nonchristian Gentiles in the persecution of their Christian compatriots. We also noted that there is some debate about the authenticity of this passage (see p. 220, n. 7).

59. For a recent interpretation (from a "Jungian" perspective) of this passage and others in the New Testament that have to do with "the powers," see Walter Wink's two volumes of a projected trilogy, *Naming the Powers: The Language of Power in the New Testament* and *Unmasking the Powers: The Invisible Forces That Determine Human Existence,* vols. 1 and 2 of *The Powers* (Philadelphia: Fortress Press, 1984/86).

60. See the quotation from Luther's 1535 commentary on Galatians in H. Dieter Betz, *Galatians,* Hermeneia (Philadelphia: Fortress Press, 1979), p. v.

61. Examples of his efforts can be seen in the problematic passages already mentioned (Gal. 3:28; I Cor. 7 and 11–14). See also I Thessalonians 4.

62. Compare Colossians 3:18–4:6; Ephesians 5:21–6:9; I Timothy 6:1-2; Titus 2:5; and I Peter 2:11–3:7.

63. See Schüssler Fiorenza, *In Memory of Her* and the literature cited there. This openness was not exclusive to the early church. In some "societies" (for example, the Epicurean "garden") women were allowed as much freedom as in Christian churches; in others (for example, the Cynics), women and slaves enjoyed at least as much, if not more, freedom than in Christian churches.

64. Galatians 3:1-5; 3:26–4:7; I Corinthians 2:1-5; 7:23; and 12:13 (compare Col. 3:11).

65. See Wayne A. Meeks, *The First Urban Christians: The Social World of the Apostle Paul* (New Haven: Yale University Press, 1983).

66. See Lull, *The Spirit.*

67. Even in I Corinthians 1:25, which comes closest to speaking of the cross as a form of power, Paul says that "the weakness of God," a reference to the (word of the) cross, is "stronger" than human power.

68. See Archibald Robertson and Alfred Plummer, *A Critical and Exegetical Commentary on the First Epistle of Paul to the Corinthians* (New York: Scribner's, 1911), p. 31. They comment on I Corinthians 2:2 that, for Paul, the crucifixion involves the resurrection.

69. See Galatians 3:1-5 and I Corinthians 12–14. For a more complete discussion, see Lull, *The Spirit.*

70. For a treatment of power in Paul's letters, with different questions in mind, see Bengt Holmberg, *Paul and Power: The Structure of Authority in the Primitive Church as Reflected in the Pauline Epistles,* Coniectanea biblica, NT series, 11 (Lund: Gleerup, 1978).

71. By the term *individual,* we mean to include persons as one kind—perhaps even the most important kind, at least to human beings—of individual in the world without excluding all other kinds of individuals

(other animals as well as plants and nonliving things); in short, we would include literally everything in all creation.

72. A case for distinguishing between these two aspects of salvation has been made by Schubert M. Ogden in *Faith and Freedom: Toward a Theology of Liberation* (Nashville: Abingdon Press, 1979), pp. 82-95.

73. Compare Ogden's richly suggestive programmatic essay (*Faith and Freedom*), in which he maintains the indivisibility of salvation and proposes that "redemption" and "emancipation" be ranked in a first and second order.

74. See Cobb, *Process Theology as Political Theology* (Philadelphia: The Westminster Press, 1982).

75. This vision of the enlarged scope of faith and of the task of theology is more fully developed in Cobb, *Process Theology as Political Theology*.

76. John C. Bennett, "Divine Persuasion and Divine Judgment," *The Christian Century* 102 (1985): 557.

77. Without presuming to compare the results of our effort to those of Karl Barth and Rudolf Bultmann, their quite different efforts to transform preaching, so that it is both faithful to biblical faith and critically responsive to their own cultural context, were no less revolutionary in their own day.

Chapter 9. "Deliverance from an Evil Age":
A Sermon on Galatians 1:1-5 by David J. Lull

1. What follows is based on a story told by Carl Lundborg, pastor of First and Summerfield United Methodist Church, New Haven, Connecticut, who visited Nicaragua in April 1986 through Witness for Peace as a member of a delegation from the New York Conference of The United Methodist Church.

INDEXES

Index of Modern Authors

231

Index of Passages

Bible

Index

Index

Other Ancient Sources